D1528626

CHICAGO QUARTERLY REVIEW

Volume 35
Summer 2022

The Chicago Quarterly Review is published by The Chicago Quarterly Review 501(c)3 in Evanston, Illinois. Unsolicited submissions are welcome through our submissions manager at Submittable. To find out more about us, please visit www.chicagoquarterlyreview.com.

Proud Member

[clmp]

COMMUNITY OF LITERARY MAGAZINES & PRESSES
W W W . C L M P . O R G

TABLE OF CONTENTS

NONFICTION

POETRY

ART

EDITORS' NOTE

I n February, the *Chicago Quarterly Review* lost one of its beloved editors, James Stacey.

As he lay dying in his Chicago condo, Jim had a parting request for his daughter Michelle. Would she write his obituary so he could read it before his imminent passing, at the age of 86? "He never explicitly said why," said Michelle, who was at his bedside along with Stacey's wife Carol. "I think in part it was simply because he felt I was a good writer, and he could take advantage of some in-house talent!"

A veteran journalist and author of four books, Jim Stacey had reason for confidence and pride in his daughter's talents. Her writing credits were as solid and versatile as his, among them stories in *The New Yorker*, *Cosmopolitan*, and other national magazines, as well as several nonfiction books, including *The Fasting Girl*.

Went gently, heeding the words of Tennyson

While Michelle Stacey found the assignment "unbearably sad," she delivered the words to her father's satisfaction. "Hearing the obit let him be a part of the whole process, I think, and even be able to control it a bit."

After taking inventory of her father's professional accomplishments, including his stints as a correspondent for *Businessweek* and the American Medical Association, Michelle ventured into more closeup territory:

"A raconteur who was fond of Noel Coward's plays and music and the great American songbook," she wrote, "Stacey also treasured Shakespeare (whose oeuvre he once read through in chronological order); English and Irish poetry; American writers such as Fitzgerald, Hemingway, and Henry James; opera and musical theater; bowties; and a good dry martini."

That capsule description was a recognizable but necessarily abridged version of the Jim Stacey we knew personally at *CQR*, where he was a contributing editor, a retirement gig after a half-century on the front lines of the media complex. In his *CQR* role, Jim was highly valued for his stories and for the expertise, dry wit and wisdom he brought to editorial meetings, staff lunches, and other collective occasions.

Usually one of the quieter, more measured voices in the room, Stacey would occasionally treat fellow editors to free-wheeling recollections of his early years in Chicago's Ravenswood neighborhood, recalling streetcar rides to ball parks, museums, movie palaces, and other boyhood haunts. He particularly rejoiced in theatrical memories, of having seen celebrated actors in road-company versions of Broadway plays—Anthony Quinn in "Streetcar" and Uta Hagen in "Virginia Woolf."

His love of theater also asserted itself in more demonstrative ways, to the surprise and delight of his *CQR* colleagues. He volunteered to introduce authors at *CQR* readings, performing the part with such authoritative and histrionic gusto that he became the designated master of ceremonies, whose infectious enthusiasm and high energy frequently surpassed that of the writers he introduced to audiences.

Writing about her father's reverence for poets and poetry in a longer appreciation, awaiting publication, Michelle Stacey noted that among the poems he most admired was Dylan Thomas' celebrated rant against death, "Do Not Go Gentle Into That Good Night." But instead of raging against the "dying of the light," as Thomas implored, Stacey took the opposite path, choosing Keats' "'easeful death," according to his daughter in her eulogy, the aptly titled, "A Death, With Poetry."

"He approached his own death in a very conscious way," she wrote, further speculating on his wish to preview his own obituary, "and expressed it even as a kind of 'adventure' -- to go to a place that is for all of us a mystery, because no one ever reports back. He was somehow able, even eager, to stand back from his own journey and look on it with curiosity, without fear, and even with a little pride."

Curious, fearless, proud, adventurous -- those are just a few of the many exemplary ways that Jim Stacey will be remembered, not only by his loving family and admiring comrades at *CQR* but by all those who had the good fortune to know him, personally or professionally.

* * *

This year will see more live events as well as a commitment to our next special issue, *The Ukrainian Issue*, guest edited by Halyna Hryn, editor of *Harvard Ukrainian Studies* at Harvard University. ■

WAVEFORMS
Michael Mattes

Morning Traffic Report

Two boys dart though through a field surrounding a radio tower. They scrabble over its wire fence and pick up a rising dirt path beaten to hardpan by thousands of prior shortcutters. Quieted by their nerves, they eye a brick hub-and-spoke building situated at the top of the incline. Virtue will soon accrue to this day, their first of fourth grade, but they can't see their way clear to that yet.

Short of their destination, one of the two youths, Jeffrey Alexander, senses an approach from behind and to his right. He reacts in time to plant a leg behind his assailant's lead foot and leverages him to the ground. It's Ricky Reese, a classmate he fell out with the year before, welcoming him back to the fray. Reese bucks him off, and they wrestle on the grass until a shout from an adult breaks them apart.

Alexander snatches up his pack and backs away toward his friend, Jaime—a new kid who, to his credit, didn't bolt at the sign of trouble. Reese, after a moment of indecision, peels off, spitting invective as he goes. This won't be the end of it.

The boys resume their climb, and as they approach the narrow drive leading to the staff parking lot, a yellow T-top Corvette eases by, its heartbeat drumming through the soles of their sneakers. The two have bonded over cool cars, and they gaze in admiration at the low slink of the throaty, gleaming machine.

In no hurry to take their final few steps toward institutional confinement, they track the Corvette as it throttles to a stop, then drop their packs in wonder as a lissome blonde in a red leather skirt unfolds from behind the wheel and strolls toward the faculty entrance. She pauses yards away from them and fixes her lively eyes upon the stunned Alexander boy.

"School hasn't even started yet and look at you," she says with a smile and a wave before disappearing through the door. The grass in his hair, the dirt pasted to his shirt, the freshly opened patch in his jeans—none of it, for the boy, connects to her words, only the heat that rockets through him when she speaks them. Like a freak pulse from the giant signal tower behind him.

It is a premonitory feeling. One he'll recognize and make sense of in the decade to come, but which, for a nine-year old, is unnaturally ahead of schedule.

Presently the boys enter their new classroom. There they encounter the same unearthly vision, one Caroline Trice, their teacher and inamorata for the fall and spring terms. Thus begins their most attentive year of school at any level and, for Alexander, the enshrining of a memory from a childhood in Delaware he'll mostly wish he could forget.

By day's end, others have staked a claim to the new kid, and Alexander is left to walk home alone. Lost inside himself, his defenses down, he is once again ambushed by Ricky Reese, and this time he eats his ration of sod. The taste is somehow less sour, the subjugation less complete, than it might otherwise have been.

He gathers himself up from the ground and continues on his way: over the perimeter fence, under the guy wires, across the gated road leading to the tower base and station building. As he slips into the woods toward his house, he snaps off a punk from a dead sapling and gnaws on it, thinking.

Daytime Listening

A Coke, two hard-boiled eggs, a dozen or so pretzel rods, and what else? His appetite, a kinetic force inside him as he enters his middle teens. A conveyor for beanpole growth and unchained juvenility.

He ponders the open refrigerator, then fetches a can of spaghetti from the pantry. He fits it against the electric opener and scores off the lid.

Leaning against the counter, eating straight from the can, he hears a voice. But his brother is up the street and his parents are at work. He wanders toward the hallway and the voice dissipates. Retracing his steps, he hears it anew. No. He hears music. Singing.

He repeats this a second and third time. Same result. He glances up at the heat register and wonders if it is carrying the sound, but, again, he is the only one home. Raising the window over the sink, he notices movement along the far creek bank: Jaime Livingston and two other boys skirting the wooded property line. Jaime holds a Daisy air rifle—he would recognize it at any distance. But the voice he hears—it is once again a voice, a speaking voice, not a song—is not Jaime's; not either of the boys' with him.

Jaime flicks his gaze toward the house. They were pals once, he and Jaime. One summer, years ago. They are not necessarily at odds now, just in different circles. Jaime with the farm boys, he with the outcasts. Their parents are friends still.

He shuts the window and closes his eyes, concentrates. Attempts to trace the disembodied sound. When he peers out, he sees—he is inches away from—the can opener. He distinctly hears the call letters announced for the AM station behind the woods. Then another song, a softie, which is all they ever play. Turning again toward the window, he rests his eyes upon the lattice tower, its upper section rising above the treetops. A few hundred yards away at most. The glint from its lantern nearly erased by the slanting sunlight. A moment later, the noise cuts out.

When his father returns home, he violates his own code, learned at great cost: keep your head down; never initiate; one-word answers; mockery is your defense if you need it. It has spared him untold grief and consoled him when it hasn't. But his father is an electrician, was a shipboard radio tech in the Navy. He'll know.

"I heard WDEL through the can opener."

His father stares at him. Stares as if to say, *Everything else over these last fourteen years and now this.*

"It played a song," he tells him. "I heard it. How does that happen?"

And then there is a shift. One he wouldn't understand. That throws him off-center. His father's brow unstitches, his jaw relaxes. A tenuous light arcs in his eyes; behind his eyes; deep, yet visible. A father reminded of a fleeting time before he raised his hand against his child. When some quaint notion of a son seeking wisdom and a father passing it along hadn't been so thoroughly disabused.

Disoriented, this boy, Jeffrey Alexander, he takes in but cannot fully assemble, in the aftermath, what his father has said: the Blaw-Knox tower design; the five-kilowatt signal; modulated waveforms; an oscillating metal vibrating the air; the presence of a magnet and a diode. He has the pieces but not the comprehension . . . other than that it is possible. It may have happened. His is in his right mind, inasmuch as he ever has been.

Which will have to be enough. He won't dare ask again.

That Ball is Outta Here

It is October of 1993. An early twentieth-century Jewish émigré from the eastern Pale is asleep on a recliner inside his apartment off

Foulk Road in North Wilmington. The kitchen radio is on, a vintage tabletop Silvertone he has had restored on more than a few occasions. On the sofa next to him, his adult grandson, Jeffrey, visiting from California, has just opened his eyes. The younger man yawns, checks his watch, then refocuses his attention on the broadcast. The game, he realizes, is now in the ninth inning, and the Phillies have somehow taken the lead. There are two men on base, one out, and the reliever nicknamed Wild Thing is on the mound. Retire this batter and one more and the series goes to game seven. Allow the base runners to score and the season is over.

Staring at the old AM-only receiver, a tube model with an umber, Bakelite shell, the grandson surmises he is among the very few people in the Delaware Valley experiencing this moment purely through audio . . . though, perhaps, some who are watching have turned away. Those with a refined appreciation of local lore, certainly.

On a 2–2 count, and with the play-by-play man narrating over the roar of crowd, the Phillies' daredevil closer offers up a gopher ball to the opposing team's big bat, promptly ending the game and the series. History, once again, is served.

Jeffrey looks over at his grandfather, whose head is canted to one shoulder. He stands and stretches, then steps over to a gateleg table pushed against a wall in the kitchenette. He lingers by the radio as the announcer, in his slow, baritone drawl, deftly compresses the five stages of grief into a few moments of postmortem reverie.

After the handoff to the local station, he turns off the radio, then leans over the sink and splashes his face with water. He takes an afghan from the back of the sofa and lays it gently across his zeyde's chest and legs. He often sleeps on the recliner, and it is approaching midnight, so he wouldn't think to wake him.

Before leaving, he unplugs the space heater, dims the floor lamp, then kisses his grandfather lightly on the forehead. He pauses on the front stoop and reflects on whether he'll see him again. He is still strong, still sharp, but it is far from a sure thing. On the drive to the airport to catch his red-eye, he can't find anything on the dial he wants to listen to, so he lets his mind wander.

From pogroms as a child to baseball as a nonagenarian, what wind takes you there . . .

Night Caller

Jeffrey Alexander, no longer a youth nor a young man, yet with conflict still to resolve, steps outside for air and decides to make a circuit of the building he has just exited. His brother hadn't bothered to tell him, only provided the facility name and street address: their primary school, now a convalescent home. All but one of its wings, that is. The last is a hospice. Inside, his father parachutes through the final stages of his descent. Tomorrow or the next day, at the latest.

He lingers near a bench on the east side of the grounds and gazes over the empty space toward the tower array. Not one but three now . . . *or has it always been so?* An aureole glows at the top of each mast, an aviation lamp at its center. It is a damp, chilly night, but he is held still by the vision. The same he was rarely out of sight of through nearly all his early life.

A woman emerges from a service door and asks if he is all right. Taking him for a grieving relative, he supposes. Is that what he is? It will take some time to know.

They begin to chat, and it arises that she volunteers at the hospice once a month and has done so since her aunt died there a year ago. Also that she is employed at the station, which, unexplainably, delights him.

"I am wholly unprepared for this conversation," he tells her, unable to suppress a laugh.

"Why so?"

"You have to understand, that tower . . . the main tower . . . it was the homing beacon of my childhood. I could see it while lying in bed. I cut through that field a million times, often while being chased. I climbed every tree in the woods behind it. There are . . . there are so many questions, and I can't think of a single one right now."

"You might know more than I do," she says, laughing right along. "I have only worked there a few years."

"Once—once, I heard a song through our can opener. 'Take a Letter Maria.' Then it kept happening. The phone, a box fan. I can't remember what else."

"Ah, yes. Music. There is such a thing, isn't there? Those were the old, old days for AM, before 24-7 outrage programming. And religion on Sundays, of course, though the distinction isn't always obvious. But not to complain, I have a job in broadcasting, right?"

He throws back his head and says, "I am ready to bust up again, but this isn't the place for it, is it?"

"This is exactly the place for it," she says, and he can already recite the rest: that everyone needs a release at such times, the swings in emotion are natural, and so on. He kicks himself for giving her the opening and instantly feels the need to stamp out any vague notions she might have about his fragile state of mind. His father dying, it's not like that for him. Though he can't say precisely what it is like.

"It makes you wonder, with all the ancients here," he says. "The pacemakers. The hearing aids. The steel hip joints. The dental implants. They're walking antennae. If they weren't hearing voices before they got here, they must be now."

"You forgot the dipole metal walkers."

"That's right! A perfect design."

She says she needs to be on her way and offers him her sympathies, a hair premature and unwanted besides. He thanks her for her kindness. As she strolls toward her car, something about the way she carries herself, and her irreverent charm, along with this piercing sense of where he is standing . . .

She's what, twenty years younger than he is? Time, flipped on its axis, somehow. She could be Caroline Trice, she is that arresting, though with a unity of form all her own. Of course, he can name his impulses now, and the intensity with which they arrive isn't quite as riotous, so that's progress on both counts, he supposes. Still, he can feel the buzz, he can hear the music, it is familiar, it is directional, and he has learned to listen for the grace notes at the most unlikely of times.

Before heading back inside, where his tyrant father cranes for his last wisps of air, he looks up again at the towers, at the illuminated station building at their base. Somewhere in there, he allows himself to imagine, it is all stored on a console, the entire eighteen-plus years. He could call in one night and have them play it back for him, it would fill in the gaps, he could get his stories straight, maybe understand a little better how he has arrived at such a moment, or any moment, really.

He wonders if Jaime is still around, or Ricky Reese, or any of his other sometime friends, sometime nemeses. Or, like him, did they stumble out of signal range and keep going, as far away as they could, in his case to the opposite coast, where the distances are greater, the mountains higher, and it is easier to escape the noise. His brother, who stayed, would know. They'll have all night to compare notes. ∎

WAITING FOR A SHOOTING STAR
Alicia DeRollo

Once I saw a black hole
eat a star—
I was just sitting there
on that rickety old park bench
before the wet fog engulfed us
looking at the sky
waiting for a shooting star,
something to wish on
the way I always do
when the sky is clear.
That's when it happened.
Nobody believed me.
What's believable about a green burst
in the night's sky,
the kind that only happens
when a black hole eats a star?
But when I went online
there was NASA
tweeting about the black hole
that just swallowed my dreams.

POETIC INTERLUDE:
TINY LOVE STORY
Alicia DeRollo

We sat on dew-drenched stools
talking softly as the stars moved aside
making way for jet planes
and early rising birds.
You sipped coffee, black and steaming,
recalling stories of past loves
and childhood fears.
With my red wine still
from hours before, I
found a towel to sit on,
unwilling to damage my gift
of silky moss-colored pajamas
designed to control the sweat
that my body cannot
because my blood is bad.
Your voice sounded so gentle,
songlike. Have I not paid
close enough attention
to how lovely you are?
Somehow the sky lit up
and people were walking their dogs.
I know we will go too,
mark another day's tasks as done,
but before we go
our gaze holds and our pause whispers
Thank you,
I could never do this
Without you.

THE CRONUTS
Stephanie Hayes

She wanted a cronut, just one. It would be decadent and make Her feel vaguely French, if you squinted at France through a Vaseline lens. She had never been there, but she dreamed about it every day. She imagined that people walked around with baguettes sticking out of handbags while strolling home, that they wore berets and led white poodles on tiny strings, that the Eiffel Tower was visible from every location in the country. In Her mind, the entire nation was reduced to a bit of Parisian wallpaper from Pottery Barn. Sometimes, she put on a CD Dexter had found at Goodwill, *Café de Paris*, filled with songs by Maurice Chevalier and Edith Piaf. She tilted Her head back on the tattered plaid sofa, closed Her eyes and drifted away.

She first heard about cronuts via a daytime talk show hosted by three middle-aged actresses with frozen faces. The cronut segment, titled IT TAKES TWO, came after Mario Lopez made a frittata, but before the piece on how to style over-the-knees boots for fall. It was obscene, all those oozing foods in extreme close-up. Ramen noodle burgers, macaroni and cheese pizza, chocolate chip cookie waffles. But the cronuts were different. They looked lighter, fluffy and easy, like Her impressions of France.

"It's a cross between a croissant and doughnut," she told Dexter. "Have you ever heard such a thing? Huh."

When she saw on Facebook that Lorraine's Bake Shop had started selling cronuts, she wouldn't stop talking about it.

"Oh, Dex," she said, as he slipped into his Wellworths uniform. "I wish I could get out of the house for one of those. I would love to try them."

Dexter hated to see Her like this, housebound, wrapped in that pale pink crocheted shawl with holes near the shoulders where she constantly tugged. He couldn't give Her much on his salary, not trips to France. It pained him that he couldn't do more because she did so much for him. She made cookies for his co-workers. She packed his lunch. She offered a patient ear at day's end. She was his only company, other than the people at the mall. Sometimes, Dexter imagined what would happen if the mall closed. Every time one of those menacing envelopes showed up in Wellworths, he got a sinking feeling. Going to work every day knowing it could be your last was the American way, he supposed.

"In France, there's a safety net," she liked to say when Dexter worried, even though she didn't know anything about French unemployment policy. "It's not like here. Maybe if you lose your job, we can go to France."

Everyone in Pineacres lined up for cronuts. Capital C Cronuts had been readily available, almost passé, for years in New York. But trends took a while to trickle to Pineacres. It was six years before they got matcha lattes, four until Code started making Aperol spritzes. Now that cronuts were here, the queue wrapped out the door of Lorraine's. Dexter had attempted to buy them every day that week, but the store kept selling out.

Cynics called the cronuts thing a publicity stunt from Lorraine's, a ploy to get people in line, where they would be denied what they came for and forced to buy some cheaper facsimile of a cronut, like a cruller or, god forbid, a blueberry sour cream doughnut. But Dexter always believed the best in people. For example, he always believed in his father. It was a good thing he still lived in his childhood home. If he'd had to move, there was no way his dad would ever find him. Dexter flipped on the porch light every day, just in case.

When people stole things from Wellworths, Dexter figured they really needed it, maybe even more than the struggling store needed business. Companies could always make a comeback, but it was harder for people. Whenever he watched someone steal, Dexter ducked behind a display so they would not see him. It should have been the other way around.

"I think I might be a bad security guard," he confided in Her one night. She listened, the way she always listened. He waited for Her to object, but she didn't.

Anyway, he didn't believe Lorraine's was running a scam. He was sure cronuts were hard to make, what with the layers of butter and folding and rolling. He'd seen a video about it on YouTube. He believed the bakery simply ran out of stock each morning, not that there was some vast confectionary conspiracy afoot. A regular doughnut was a fine substitute most of the time.

But not today. It was Dexter's day off from Wellworths, and he had to get to Lorraine's by 8:00 a.m. if he wanted any shot at cronuts. He pulled on the same thing he wore every day off, black elastic-waist shorts, a Pineacres Mall T-shirt and a pair of bone-colored Velcro sneakers with black socks pulled up to his calves. He combed what little white hair he had left and spritzed on a touch of Échapper he'd gotten in a free sample at the store.

"Where are you going all fancy?" she asked from the sofa, tugging at Her shawl. "Isn't it your day off?"

"I've just got some errands to run," he said. "Don't you worry about it. Do you need anything?"

"Don't spend your money on me," she said.

Dexter leaned in and gave Her a hug. He could smell Her hair, powdery, a little like clay. He felt Her shoulders, small and cold through the shawl, and he lingered.

"Go back to France," he whispered. "Try some Jean Sablon today."

* * *

Dexter only ever wanted to be a dancer. In 1967, his mother took him to see Jacques Demy's *The Young Girls of Rochefort*, starring Gene Kelly and Catherine Deneuve. He was transfixed by the mod, candy-colored costumes, the sailor suits, the way the men lifted the women into the air, every pas de bourrée and pirouette, every flick of the wrist. When the dancers pointed their toes, Dexter pointed his in his seat at the Pineacres dollar cinema. Dexter practiced in his bedroom, the same bedroom he lived in still, sucking in his stomach before the mirror and standing with a proud chest. He smiled and went up on his toes, fell over, then did it again and again until he didn't fall anymore. Over time, his twiggy calves turned square and dense.

Dexter's mom wanted him to dance, too. She got him into Pineacres Dance Academy, which didn't accept boys at the time and cost more than the family could afford. She'd promised Patty Markowitz something or other in exchange for letting him join. Dexter didn't understand exactly what. It was something about not telling a secret to Patty Markowitz's husband. He'd heard his mother on the phone through the ventilation grate in his bedroom, which carried sound down the hallway like a pair of cups on a string.

"I've made my peace, Patty," she said. "I'm just asking for this one thing."

Dexter assumed it was a fight at bridge club. Dexter always sensed that his mother was somewhat jealous of Patty Markowitz, probably for the jet-black hair she wore slicked into a braided bun and the glamorous glass earrings that strained her earlobes, pulling her holes into vertical slits. Dexter's mother had dry, wiry hair and never wore any jewels. She had the hard face of someone who had not slept well in years. Dexter thought she was more beautiful than Patty Markowitz.

During Dexter's weekly ballet class, he learned about first, second and third positions, repeating them with militant precision. Every time Patty Markowitz said "Again," he was filled with joy and purpose. Dexter was thick and awkward, and when he attempted fifth position side, his knees bowed. Patty Markowitz snapped him with an extended metal pointer.

"Your knees must cradle each other as if they are secretly in love," she said, her orange lipstick seeping around her mouth. Dexter tried not to think about the stinging pain on the back of his hamstring.

Patty Markowitz was not about to change her whole curriculum for one boy who wasn't even supposed to be there. Dexter knew something was different about the way he was training, though. He had seen Rudolf Nureyev with Margot Fonteyn on The Hollywood Palace, struck by how masculine it seemed. Male dancers leaped from hulking quads and led with their chests. Females were taught to be light, perfect, featherlike, twisting princesses in a jewelry box. Dexter didn't suppose it mattered. He just wanted to dance. So when Patty Markowitz snapped him with the pointer on his croisé devant and said, "Your derrière has gone to Florida when it should be in California," he adjusted accordingly, thrilled to have such attention.

He was confused the night his father showed up at the studio. It was a Tuesday, and class did not end for forty-five minutes. His father worked late at the office most of the time. Dexter had no idea what his dad did, only that it required twelve hours a day. Dexter decided that when he got older, he would look for a job with more flexibility. He figured Gene Kelly set his own hours on *The Young Girls of Rochefort*. So, he assumed, did the Radio City Rockettes.

Patty Markowitz told the class to practice dégagés and turnouts while she stepped outside with Dexter's father. Dexter did as he was told, dread brewing in his stomach. He overheard Lila James murmur to Bernice Lopez, "Oh, this again." Dexter turned to find out more, and Lila sneered.

"Dégagés, you weirdo. You heard the lady. You want her to make us all stretch on the high barre again?"

He could see them through the glass, behind the pink pointe shoe painted on the window. His father looked irritated, and Patty Markowitz looked unsure, and Dexter was certain they were talking about him. His father was thrusting an envelope in Patty Markowitz's face. He was disheveled, his tie hanging open. Dexter had never seen his father appear so, well, old, and he wondered if it was his fault for dancing. Maybe his father was upset that he was learning how to plié when he should have been playing sports. Maybe he was threatening to pull Dexter out of ballet and send him away to learn baseball. Dexter didn't want to learn baseball. Maybe he could learn to like it, though.

He was relieved when Patty Markowitz came back into class, and when his father shot him a thumbs up through the glass, just like the dads at Little League. And he felt even better when his mom showed up forty-five minutes later to bring him home. She tugged on her pink shawl the whole ride home, her eyes puffy, focused on the road. She softly sang.

Give your heart and soul to me
And life will always be
La vie en rose

Dexter fell asleep in the back of the car.

He didn't see his father the rest of the week. His mother said he'd be out of town for a while on business, and Dexter didn't question it. When Dexter got back to ballet class, a short, severe woman introduced herself as their new instructor. And it was at that moment that Dexter realized the cruelest truth of all. It wasn't that his father wanted him to play sports instead of dance. It wasn't that his father had left on a train with Patty Markowitz and would probably never return. It was that, on the pavement outside the dance studio that night, the boy had had no residence in his father's mind at all.

* * *

Dexter did the math. He was fifth in line, and he could make out five, six, seven … about twelve cronuts left. If everyone ordered only their share, more people could have a taste. If people controlled themselves, he could finally get Her one.

Lorraine's was across the street from Pineacres Dance Academy, which had changed hands about four times since Dexter attended as a child. The short, severe woman was long dead and he had no idea who ran the place anymore. But he did know that the academy accepted boys, and Dexter liked to think he was responsible for this. A hero was in their midst, and no one knew it. He daydreamed about walking inside and telling all the children he was the first male ballet dancer in Pineacres history. He imagined them gathering crisscross at his feet to hear the tale.

He enjoyed watching kids come and go from class, but he had to do this from a distance, so the parents didn't think he was some kind of freak. Thinking about child predators made Dexter glad to be a security guard and not a real police officer. That kind of work would be so hard. He liked to drink coffee at the corner table in Lorraine's, which had an unobstructed view of the dance school. Sometimes, the kids even came into Lorraine's for a treat after class, which Dexter loved the most.

In line, a girl stood in front of Dexter holding her mother's hand. She wore a pair of Hawaiian shorts over her pink tights, plus purple Crocs with Disney charms stuck in the holes. She balanced up and down on her toes.

"I used to dance over there, too," Dexter said. "When I was little."

The girl and her mother whipped around and considered the old man with papery skin and a portly midsection. He was not exactly a dancer type, and he knew this. The woman smiled and turned away, but the girl was intrigued.

"Why did you stop?"

Dexter watched the bakery employee pull three cronuts from the case and box them up for a delivery driver from some app. He'd tried to use a meal app once when he was too sad to get out of bed and had no food in the house for Her, but he ended up sending spaghetti and meatballs to the mall instead of his house, and he was out $34.

"Oh," Dexter said. "Lots of little reasons. That's how life goes. But once you're a dancer, you never really stop."

Four more cronuts went to a couple wearing skin-tight athletic outfits, without an ounce of fat on their bodies. Dexter stood in fifth position side.

"Your knees must cradle each other as if they are secretly in love."

The girl giggled and practiced her own position.

"Honey, leave the man alone," the woman said. Dexter knew this was her way of asking him to please shut up. He was used to that.

A short, balding man in khakis and a blue BuyMore shirt had spent the entire time in line staring at his phone. He ordered black coffee extra-hot and three cronuts. *Three. For one person.* Dexter felt resentment, then pushed it away. Maybe this man was bringing the cronuts to others. He told himself to stop judging, that he didn't know everyone's situation. He thought about his mother and her puffy eyes, how she always blamed it on allergies to pollen.

"Oh, my," Dexter said quietly to himself. "Not again."

The girl in the pink tights gripped her mother at the hip and turned to face Dexter. She didn't say anything. She didn't have to.

"It's okay, sweetie," he mouthed. "Take them."

The bakery employee boxed up the last two cronuts. She flipped over a sign that said CRONUTS TODAY. The other side said CRONUTS TOMORROW.

* * *

Dexter's corner table was available, at least, and that was a small victory. He settled in with his coffee and blueberry sour cream doughnut. He had nowhere to be.

The guy in the BuyMore shirt stopped at the milk and sugar counter and emptied three packets of Splenda into his coffee. He took a steamy swig and punched his chest like he was swallowing a shot of tequila. He shoved nearly a whole cronut in his mouth, pastry flakes flying onto his shirt. Then, he left with the other two.

Dexter focused on the dancers to calm himself. So many more boys were dancing these days without fear, and it made him feel warm. A little boy in black tights and a stegosaurus T-shirt walked out with his father. The man, tall and chiseled with a sleeve of tattoos, carried the boy's dance bag, tiny straps on hulking shoulders. This was a good man. Times had changed and men were good now. Men were beholden to certain expectations, required to respect women, to participate in childcare and chores, to be fully present, to express emotions. Dexter's dad would not have been caught dead carrying a dance bag, let alone lifting a dish. Dexter listened to his parents argue through the grate, most of the time over his father's whereabouts.

"You're not my mother," his dad would say, which struck Dexter as odd. Why was it bad to be someone's mother? Dexter reckoned his dad had never had a good mother, but he'd never asked.

"Excuse me, sir?"

The woman had a neat, nut-brown bob. She wore salmon-colored pants, a printed top and ballet flats, but not the kind for dancing. He was pretty sure he'd seen her in Wellworths before. Today, she had bags from Ross and TJ Maxx on the chair across from her, and an iPad on the table. She nibbled a cronut.

"Would you mind watching my things for a moment? I need to run to the bathroom."

Dexter got this a lot. He had a trustworthy look about him, and complete strangers asked him to protect their belongings while they peed or stepped out to make a phone call. It made him wonder if he did exude characteristics of a security guard after all. Maybe he was more authoritative than he gave himself credit for. Maybe he was a bit dominant. More likely, he was harmless.

"Of course," he said. "Take your time. But I can't be trusted around that cronut."

"I don't blame you," she said. "I've been trying to get one for weeks."

He wondered what, exactly, it was about him that made people the opposite of scared. His soft face? His silvery eyes? The way he kind of looked like Santa Claus, if Santa was missing most of his hair? But maybe they were wrong. Maybe Dexter wasn't as responsible as everyone assumed.

A message popped in on the woman's iPad, and Dexter peered at the lock screen. His eyes had been getting worse lately. He'd been putting off the cataract surgery for two years now and could barely drive at night. He'd left his readers at home. He grabbed the device and tilted it toward his face. Touching someone else's stuff felt a bit brazen. The message was from Sarah.

I'm thinking of going to grad school.

That's nice, Dexter thought, nice for Sarah. Maybe it was this woman's child, or a longtime friend, or someone from church. Dexter wondered if he could go to grad school, too. He'd rather go to Paris.

It would be easy to take the iPad, hide it under his Pineacres Mall shirt and slip out the front door. He'd seen people do it a hundred times at the store. Dexter had been in his own grad school of sorts, higher learning in the art of thievery. There were lots of tricks. He'd watched people buy insulated coolers, which fooled the store alarms, then walk around the store dropping merchandise inside. He'd seen them carry umbrellas when it wasn't raining, sliding jewelry into the open tops. He'd seen them use windbreakers and strollers and yoga pants pockets and service dog vests. He'd seen women in long skirts walking strangely, pressing their thighs together. The real thieves never looked like the thieves in the store's training videos. They were not sinister, in trench coats and floppy hats. They were just people.

He knew the iPad had to be worth a few hundred dollars, although this one looked big, maybe eleven inches. He recognized it from Electronics. He might be able to get $800 for it down at Pineacres Pawn.

They could fly economy, probably with a few layovers, but that would be a perk. Dexter could finally say he had been to Amsterdam or Munich, even if it was only to the airport. Dexter had never been out of the country, and it would be so fun to build a list like that. He pictured his father and Patty Markowitz in a château somewhere, maybe Prague, wondering if they'd done the wrong thing. They probably felt bad. He hoped they felt bad.

Dexter closed his eyes, and he was with Her in Paris. They ate at a sidewalk café and drank Grenache and saw the Moulin Rouge and the Louvre. They took a picture of the *Mona Lisa* and gave other tourists directions to the Catacombs. In Paris, Dexter was different. Confident. Proud. In Paris, he asked forgiveness instead of permission. He danced in Paris, right out in the open on a moonlit bridge. The locals marveled as he plunged Her into a perfect dip. How did the fat old man, the hairless Santa Claus, know a glissade and a pas de basque? He had always been a dancer, he told them. *J'ai toujours été danseur.*

He thought of Her, shut in the house. Forget cronuts. She could have fresh croissants with real butter, not Country Crock margarine. She could stop listening to the *Café de Paris* CD, stop pulling the shoulders of Her pink shawl, and she could see the world. She could have this one thing before she died.

Sarah's friend still wasn't back from the bathroom, and Dexter started to sweat. He gave himself a deadline. She had two minutes to get to her table before he would slip away with the iPad and head to the pawnshop.

He walked to the counter of Lorraine's with his hands in his pockets and smiled at the employee, who was doing math on the back of a piece of receipt paper. She looked relieved the cronut rush was over. Dexter pretended to be very interested in the doughnut case full of Boston creams and chocolate frosted and cinnamon twists, peering past the counter to the ladies' room door. And that's when Dexter saw the most grotesque thing he had ever seen. Just through the kitchen, past the sign that said CRONUTS TOMORROW, on a long stainless-steel table, were rows and rows of cronuts. They were lined up, untouched, gleaming.

"Hey," Dexter said. "I thought you ran out."

"We make enough for the week and then sell a certain amount each day," she said. "If we sold them all at once, we'd run out in a single morning."

"But I want one today," Dexter said. "Please."

"Sorry, I don't make the rules."

"This is a scam. Everyone was right about you guys."

"If you think this is a scam, you need to get out more," she said. "We've all got problems. These are just pastries, sir. Come back tomorrow."

Dexter was on fire. Stabbed. Pressed to death. He saw Paris, the baguettes, the Eiffel Tower. He saw Her, sitting at home watching those awful daytime shows. He saw thieves in the mall slipping small purses into bigger purses. He saw his father and Patty Markowitz, and he saw the firing squad of cronuts. He saw the twin enemies of trust and belief, tied to a chair and shot in the head.

He turned back to the iPad. As he reached for it, he felt a tiny tug on the bottom of his shorts. It was the girl in Crocs. She broke off half her cronut and handed it to Dexter.

"Here," she said, and ran off.

* * *

"I've got a surprise for you," Dexter said.

He cradled the broken cronut in a paper napkin, a precious object, a bit of gold. *Café de Paris* blared through the house. Charles Trenet crooned "La Mer."

La mer
Qu'on voit danser
Le long des golfes clairs
A des reflets d'argent

"The sea that we see dancing, along the clear gulfs, has reflections of silver," he said. "Isn't it lovely when you translate it?"

The house was vacant and musty. The floorboards creaked as Dexter slipped off his shoes. He turned on the television to the daytime programs but left the sound off. There was a segment about miracle shapewear to help you shave off ten pounds. He pointed and flexed his toes.

"You won't believe what happened," he said. "The pastry shop is running a scam after all. But I did it. I got us one."

Dexter set the cronut on the kitchen table and wrapped the pink shawl around his shoulders. He tugged at the holes.

"I knew you would," he said. "I always believed in you."

Dexter lifted the cronut to his face. He absorbed the smell, sweet and buttery, and sunk his teeth in. The layers stuck to his molars and the flakes clung to his lips and he swallowed the lump in one desperate gulp.

His knees cradled each other as if they were secretly in love. He spun, whipping the pink shawl, and twirled all the way to the front door, polishing off the pastry and pressing his sticky fingers to the porch light. ■

A FIST OF MUSCLE
Sam Meekings

Today, wandering through the local supermarket, I see my brother. Again. He is leaving one aisle just as I enter it from the opposite end. Though I only catch sight of the back of his head as he turns the corner, I have no doubt it is him. He has the same red-flecked hair, the same languid and unhurried walk and, as always, the collar of his polo shirt up is turned up to cover the nape of his neck. Without a second thought, I hurry to try and catch up with him. A pair of doddering trolleys blocks my path at the corner, however, and, by the time I have forced my way between them, my brother is nowhere to be seen.

I consider calling out to him, but I worry that any loud noise might break the spell and so make it impossible for me to find him among the high-stacked shelves. I may have set reason aside for a minute, but embarrassment isn't quite so easy to part with. I put down my basket and begin to push past the slower shoppers, desperately searching each lane before rushing on to the next. I am moving so fast that I almost stumble and fall into a tall stack of buy-one-get-one-free cola bottles on display at the head of one of the aisles. Several times I duck back upon myself, and more than once I return to the dairy aisle for a second look between the stacks of milk and yogurt. Not for a moment do I even entertain the idea that the man I am chasing might be a figment of my imagination. In fact, I am convinced of quite the opposite—that the past few weeks have been unreal and illusory, and that there is a perfectly logical explanation (as yet unknown) as to why we have all fallen prey to the ridiculous idea that my brother has died.

Soon I'm confused about which of the lanes I have already been down and which I have yet to search. I am walking through some elaborate labyrinth and might remain lost within it forever. After completing my third or fourth circuit of the main aisles, I decide that my brother has to be in the pasta section, since for the last few years of his life he not only ate pasta with almost every one of his meals but, in order to aid his obsessive desire to bulk up, he also regularly ate a large bowl of it as a snack after returning home from work or the gym. When I find my way to the pasta aisle, I discover that it is completely deserted. I hover there for a couple of minutes, waiting beside the packets of butterflies, spirals, corkscrews and ribbons.

After a while I start searching again. I can no longer hear the heavy rain that was beating down on my way in. The stark glare of the supermarket lights seems designed to misinform the senses. Here it is impossible to tell whether it is the middle of the day or the darkest hour of night. It soon occurs to me that, without either phone or watch, there is no way of knowing how long I have spent in pursuit of my brother. Soon the supermarket light gives rise to the impression that the end of time has come and then passed and that this sterile place is all that remains of a forgotten civilization. Rows upon rows of tins and cans do nothing to alleviate the sense that something terrible has befallen the world outside and that the only people left on earth are a few anonymous survivors quarantined within. Even the hesitant and distorted voice crackling over the tannoy sounds as though it is, like the first phonograph recordings, the last relic of a distant and unreachable past. I start moving with increased urgency and, more than once, I pick up a packet or bottle to scrutinize its expiry date.

Ten years ago, this supermarket caught fire. The blaze, which started in the adjoining petrol station, was not extraordinary in itself, but what was amazing was that when the supermarket reopened some weeks later, it was impossible to tell which parts had been rebuilt and which belonged to the original structure. The reconstruction was, therefore, judged to be a great success, especially since it made it seem as if the events of the recent past had never happened. Supermarkets are designed to be uncannily similar to one another, and each time I enter one I take it for granted that I am setting foot within yet another copy and that the original was long ago lost among its countless simulacra. It is little wonder that so many people throughout the ages have posited that every life has been lived before and every conceivable action has already been carried out many times. Perhaps the world itself is a copy and there are an inconceivable number of other copy worlds. Perhaps there are more than a million copies, over a billion acts of creation abandoned by dissatisfied gods, a pluriverse of countless universes outside the limits of our vision, and no way to tell which was the first or whether all are duplicates.

I press on down the wine and spirits aisle, yet by the time I get to the fizzy drinks, I am convinced that the supermarket has been designed solely to unravel the loose tangles of my memory. Every shelf taunts me. First there are the fat loaves of bread that, as a child, my brother could not touch without falling sick, thus forcing our mum to spend hours every day making cornbread and gluten-free spaghetti. Next there are the protein shakes he drank each morning as though he was partaking in sacred communion with the savage and exacting god of bodybuilding. Finally, there are the fresh bouquets of flowers identical to those that have littered our house and garden ever since the funeral. I am dizzy and out of breath. I grab a bottle of water straight from a shelf. I gulp it down. The supermarket is a desert. This is my first drink in days.

Off I go again, off round the next corner, but my heart is no longer in the search. I am simply retracing my steps while my brother remains always a few aisles ahead of me, and it does not help that as I peer down each lane I encounter the same few faces staring back. But I must not give up. I begin to head back toward the dairy aisle and it is then, just as I am passing the pharmacy counter—where an old woman in an oversized raincoat is picking through a pile of crumpled prescriptions while the shop assistant toys with her nails—that I spot him. He is queuing up at one of the tills, his half-empty basket set down at his feet. I have to force myself not to run, as most of the shoppers around probably think I am sick or lunatic, though I cannot stop from increasing my pace.

He turns his head. I begin to raise my arm to wave to him. I have to catch his attention. I need to make him see. But then my rising arm falters. Stops midwave. It is not him. The man waiting at the checkout has a boxer's knuckle for a nose and bug-like eyes the color of wet seaweed. He is nothing like my brother. My arm slumps at my side. Only now does it occur to me that this man's hair is red, while my brother's hair had lost its fiery color and changed to a light brown. The person before me is tall and solid, as my brother had been in his adolescence and early twenties. He is not the bulky colossus my brother turned himself into during the last eighteen months. It is not him. I have been searching for my brother not as he was the last time I saw him but as he had been much earlier in life. It is not him.

I leave the supermarket in a hurry and dash through the rain to the car, without bothering to look for my abandoned basket nor the quickly scribbled shopping list it contains. After fumbling for a few moments unlocking the door, I climb inside and settle in the driver's seat without daring to turn the key in the ignition. How have I managed to become so confused? The ghost in the queue doesn't look like my brother at all, yet I have wasted close to half an hour attempting to track him down.

A world populated by doubles, I find myself thinking, would not be such a bad thing. In fact, the idea that every person might be a double of someone else is strangely comforting. Even though I know it will not change my own situation, I still hope there is a doppelganger of my brother somewhere in the world who has managed somehow to circumvent his fate. This twin of my brother would not have grown so obsessed by bodybuilding, would not have sought to become a titan, a demigod. And in the process, he would not have pushed his heart to breaking point.

More has been written about the heart than any other part of our anatomy. It has long been thought to be reckless and mercurial, the source of love, locked in battle with the more sober and restrained head. While the brain formulates careful plans, the heart gives sway to whims and passions. It is the enemy of restraint and rationalism, the furnace in which our desires are fired. The Romans even went so far as to formulate the idea that the heart is the place in which our best memories and ideas are stored. As for my brother's heart, I know it was saved, though not returned to us. In fact, I have no idea what happened to it after the autopsy. I know only that when his heart was removed, it was found to be close to three times the normal size.

The postmortem records that the walls and ventricles of the organ were so swollen that it was only with the most arduous labor that blood could be pumped through. His heart struggled, every day, until it could not go on. It was too big. So says the report. I read the same sentence again and again: *Histological examination of the left ventricular myocardium revealed widespread myocyte hypertrophy with replacement fibrosis as well as an element of myocyte disarray.* The words mean little to me, even after a day and a night with a dictionary stolen from a hospital. What, I wonder, do such words have to do with the active and inexhaustible person that was my brother? They are words that refuse to make sense. I simply cannot bring myself to believe that the statement is about my brother—it might as well be describing the orbit of a planet I have never seen, in a universe far beyond my own.

Is this all the heart is? A collection of ventricles, veins, valves, arteries, vessels, muscles, nodes and tendons? What about the rest? Everything else hidden within —his dreams and passions, his quirks and idiosyncrasies? The report tells me nothing of why the illness settled on him and not another—for example, myself. It will not tell me why he in particular was chosen. It does not hint at where the condition appeared from, or how long he might have borne within him such a fatal secret. It does not say how he might have felt, or how the disease changed him as time went on. The only fact that makes sense to me from the autopsy notes is that his heart weighed 886 grams. The same weight as a bag of rice. Or a small watermelon. The weight is important, you see. The weight of his lumbering heart. It is important not only because it must have weighed heavy inside him for many months until the day that it finally gave in, but also because it is by such criteria that lives were once measured.

The ancient Egyptians, preparing the body for mummification, would lay out the corpse and, after making an incision across the abdomen and cleansing it with wine both within and without, would remove lungs, liver, intestines and stomach. Even the brain would be removed, after which time the body could be coated with resin and bound tightly in strips of linen. The only organ left in place was the heart. This was for good reason: the soul could not travel on into the next world without it. At the very beginning of the journey into the underworld, this most vital organ would be weighed, it being well-known that all a person's sins and mistakes were written within the heart. Greed, malice, hatred, envy; all these were thought to make it grow fat and swollen. And on a great pair of scales the heart was to be weighed against a feather that stood for truth and fairness. If the scales did not balance perfectly, the heart was cast aside to be devoured by a terrifying creature with the body of a lion and the head of a crocodile. When this happened, the soul of the deceased would be trapped forever somewhere between death and life. Only those with the lightest of hearts were allowed to continue their passage on towards the next world.

My brother has travelled on without his heart. I suspect that he is better off without it. It only weighed him down, slowed his steps, until finally stopping him altogether. He had, as I say, a literally heavy heart, and it is tempting to think that his death was somehow connected to this. Did he sense what he was lugging around with him in those last months? Surely he must have felt it, the immense weight inside him like a stone, a cast-iron padlock, a fist of engorged muscle. Did he try his best to ignore it? Since his death, every time I wake in the night with my heart racing, I think instantly of him and wonder whether his heart's inevitable thumping ever scared him, or whether by the time he realized what was happening inside him it was already too late.

The word *record*, to note something down and store it for the future, is derived from the Latin *cor*, meaning heart. When we commit something to memory, we say we learn it by heart, and it was once believed that our heart recorded our longings, our ambitions, our regrets. It is not difficult, then, to see how a heart can grow heavy. And if his was weighed down, then now so is mine. I wonder whether my brother carried with him the weight of any regrets, or doubts, or mistakes. But what did he regret? I cannot say. My few guesses are feeble at best. Did he regret doing so badly at school? I am not sure. He had certainly been glad to see the back of the place, though in the last few years he worked hard at college courses to gain several advanced construction and design qualifications, of which he was certainly proud. Perhaps, though, he regretted his inability to control his temper. I think of the fights he and I often had in our teenage years, and of his legendary fits and rages that would cause us all to scatter and flee. Yet those were long in the past. In his final months he did not war with anyone. Not even me.

The more I think about the things that might have weighed heavy on his heart, the more I begin to think about how little I know of the person my brother had become at the time of his death. I cannot shake off the thought that I had lost or, if you will, mislaid my brother some years before he died. You will remember that the double in the supermarket looked not like my brother had in his last couple of years, but as he had been close to four years before. This makes me feel even worse. His heart was too big; mine, it seems, too small.

Not only have I now lost that future, but I also begin to worry that over time my memories of our shared past will grow increasingly hazy and that each day I will lose a little more of him. Yet at the same time I feel as though I cannot break away from him, and for many nights after the funeral, as soon as I close my eyes I am overcome with the sensation that he is still there, lying as ever in the bunk bed above me. If I listen closely, I can sometimes hear him muttering in his sleep. Occasionally I am even able to suspend disbelief enough to believe that at any moment he might swing his head down and suggest a midnight picnic, or ask me to tell him a story about the land of monsters we might find if venture through the secret tunnel found at the back of the cupboard. Sometimes I even open my mouth to reply.

He can only have been three or four when we shared a bunk bed. We were living in a cramped terrace then, a house where the pipes gurgled and babbled all night. My brother and I had a raggedy stuffed toy that served as a doorstop so that our room would not be completely given over to darkness. We also had a cassette player, which told us fairy tales as we drifted towards sleep, and I can still remember the first time that I managed to force myself to stay awake (by repeatedly pinching my arm) until the story came to an end and the tape clicked off. A horrible silence settled over the room, as if a great bell jar had been lowered over us. I could hear my heart beating louder and louder in my chest. If I listened carefully, I could hear the sound of a door being opened somewhere on the other side of the house, and even though I knew that this was probably nothing more than my parents coming up to brush their teeth before bed, I could not stop my mind from running wild. I had soon convinced myself that there were burglars creeping through the house and that they were heading for our room—hence the dull snuffle of feet on the stair, the sigh of floorboards and the hundred other odd noises that old houses possess in their armory. Each one my imagination seized upon as a sign of some approaching terror until, in desperate self-defense, I leapt out of bed, turned the cassette over, and pressed Play.

It is not, of course, so easy to calm an adult mind. My mum feels the same. Like the rest of us, she finds staying too long in the wreath-filled house oppressive and overbearing, and so this afternoon she decides to head to the beach. She spends a long time at the harbor, close to where the River Arun meets the sea, keeping the dog on the lead while she stands looking down at the bevies of swans and cygnets huddling in the crooks of shingle that rise up where the river swerves at sudden angles. When the restless dog finally succeeds at interrupting her thoughts, she turns and follows the river down to its mouth before walking east along the beach. The tide is slowly drawing in and the unleashed dog makes a frantic dash across the sand, darting close to the edge of the lapping waves and then sprinting back again, as though daring himself ever closer to the water.

It is the dog that draws the young child away from his own family. The little boy begins to follow our dog across the beach, zigzagging as the dog does and calling out to it in delight. Meanwhile, my mum is walking down the stony bank, looking out to sea and listening to the sound of each wave following on upon the last. Her eyes are trained on the distant point where the ashen clouds touch down on the dark-green sea, and so it is only once the little boy is close enough to snatch at the dog's tail that my mum notices him. He is perhaps four or five, though it is difficult to be sure, since he is dressed from head to toe in a Spiderman costume.

It is almost identical to the costume my brother wore at the same age. There were many days, in fact, when he would refuse to take it off, even to go to bed, his one concession being to remove the red-and-black mask and set it down beside him on the pillow. The only visible parts of the child on the beach are two blue eyes staring out from the holes in the mask. My mum freezes to the spot. When she finally starts moving once more, she finds that the boy is moving with her. For a few minutes he runs along beside the dog, and she starts to worry that the boy might attempt to follow them all the way home. It is only when his family starts calling out to him across the beach that he leaves the dog alone and wanders away. Once he is out of sight, my mum cuts short her walk and strides straight back across the sand. Towards the car.

She tells us that it is not the thought that it might have been my brother beneath the costume that has upset her but the knowledge that it was not. It is as though her heart is being tested. Wherever any of us goes, it is as though my brother is following. Time and again something moves in the corner of our vision, a flicker of color, a change in the light. Some days, in fact, it is almost impossible to leave the house without meeting someone who reminds us of him. The smallest thing is enough: a shock of red hair, a few freckles playing upon the nose and cheeks, or a laugh, or a boast. The rest of the day is then lost.

But at the same time nothing is lost. Because the certainty remains that the world is littered with the past, and so we will come across him—at the beach, in a queue for the cinema, in some cramped bar, at the supermarket—again, again, again. ■

ATLAS PEAK
Terri Drake

We fell in love
with the sky
at the top of the world,
worshipped manzanita and madrone,
damselflies, dragonflies, the red-legged frog.
Wine-drunk, we danced
in the vineyards,
slept underneath quilts
with the dogs at our feet,
woke when the sun rose over the ridge,
praised the red, rocky soil,
cursed the glassy-winged sharp shooter,
ate Zinfandel straight from the vine,
lounged under the sugar pines.
If ever there were a heaven
we found it under a layer of fog
hovering over the grapes,
their sweetness ripening the day.

HUGHENDEN
Whitney Watson

I picked up her naked foot. The smooth white marble was heavy in my hand. I lifted my own foot out of its rubber sandal. Bending, I lowered the sole of her marble foot against my own. In length, the two were nearly the same, but the marble foot was plumper, a foot that might kick out of a cloud in a Renaissance painting. The marble toes were straighter, pointing ahead with a conviction mine lacked.

Alarms did not go off, guards did not come running into Benjamin Disraeli's library. It was Mary Anne Disraeli's foot, and her sole cooled my swollen, warm one. Setting the marble foot back on the stack of books atop Disraeli's desk, I shoved my toes back into the straps of my sandal. A middle-aged couple wandered into the room with a docent. I was standing a respectful distance away by then, arms crossed, pondering the desk.

I wondered whether Disraeli had touched this marble foot after Mary Anne's death. Why did it even exist; was it an eclectic gift, some kind of joke? Or was Mary Anne's foot, in Disraeli's estimation, simply the most beautiful part of his wife's body? Such a tender, worshipful gesture seemed fitting. Disraeli was famously romantic about his wife. It was remarkably soothing, touching Mary Anne's marble flesh, so human and lovely. Would anyone ever cast my foot in stone?

* * *

When I was fifteen years old I found a copy of André Maurois's *Disraeli: A Picture of the Victorian Age* in my grandparents' library. It was not the type of book my grandparents would miss. Although people in my family owned many books, they rarely read.

From a young age, Benjamin Disraeli dreamed about the lands of his ancestors, who hailed from exotic places like Venice and Spain. Growing up in Southern California, I also longed for the land of my ancestors, but their land was northern England. To an Angeleno, England seemed exotic in its dampness; I wanted to run along the moors, face and hair lashed by rain. But my bedroom faced blue skies and antiseptic clouds, dry brown chaparral dotting the Simi Hills. It rained just a few times a year and then there were floods and mudslides as water rushed atop the dry earth. Below us were tracts upon tracts of houses built in the last twenty years. The houses all had the same floor plans; only the façades were unique.

Although I had never felt like I belonged in those mountains, I was a decent impostor to the people around me. I wore the sunny demeanor and tanned skin that signaled social and geographical suitability. We girls flipped our hair in the same manner as the trophy wives who controlled our town. But I felt darker beneath the tan.

The highest aspiration of any girl at my high school was to have her name spray-painted on the rocks of Malibu Canyon by older boys. Those boys, fogged with cologne, kept their trunks stocked with spray paint, flannel blankets, and condoms. They guided girls up dusty trails to arrive at a freshly painted boulder, towering in the sun. "Is that my name?" the girl would ask, in believing disbelief. She'd flush a little and drop down to the blankets. It was an aphrodisiac and all the boys had figured it out.

"Quit screwing around," my dad said if he caught me sunbathing. "Get down to brass tacks." My grades were good, but I didn't care for the subjects he did: economics, accounting. Each year for Christmas upon my reaching adolescence, my father gave me a fictional amount of money to invest in fictional stocks. If my stocks made money by the next Christmas, I got a check in the amount of the increase. If they did not increase, I got nothing. There was only one year my stocks did well. "If you spent more time on the *important* stuff," my dad said, "you could really be something."

But even Disraeli had set himself upon a course of financial disaster by investing in South American mining stocks as a young man, and the problems lasted almost until his death. He was pursued constantly by moneylenders and, were it not for his elected position in government, he would have gone to debtors' prison. Mary Anne saved her profligate husband, setting his financial affairs aright, though he continued overspending. Disraeli had a weakness for men's clubs, good food, fashionable clothing. There was something sweetly optimistic in the way he overspent, dressing in so much plumage. He modeled himself after Lord Byron, not other politicians. But Disraeli did not have Byron's income; he was often desperate. Perhaps this fuelled his dreams.

My father had debts but he did not seem desperate; he also did not have dreams. Although his finances spiraled down deeply at times, he gave the impression his affairs were perfectly under control. I was the one who felt desperate, waiting. I tried to adopt an air of mystery and impassivity, to read as much as possible, just as Disraeli had in his young life. I only had to wait for time to darken my own quaint hamlet, and I looked forward to that event. I was certain I was destined for a life more dramatic than anything my father, or I, could envision.

* * *

The summer I turned sixteen my father took me with him to England for a Lloyd's of London meeting. My father was an insurance executive at the time and also starting his own fund on the side. He hoped to find enough investors to leave his company and work for himself.

As soon as we debarked at Heathrow, my father asked "Catherine" to get her bag from the carousel. I almost didn't respond. He called me Catawampus at home.

The other person who accompanied us to London was an actuary named William, who worked closely with my father. He lived in Delaware but occasionally came to California. I had been to dinner with my father's business associates before, and my father let me order red wine. "Is she old enough?" the waiters sometimes asked. "Trust me, I know," my father responded. I liked William particularly well; he made eye contact and remembered what we'd discussed on previous occasions. He was also something of a history buff. His last name meant "knight" in a European language, and this suited him. His nose was aquiline, the type of nose rarely seen in the land of plastic surgery, and I found him aristocratic. He would not have looked ridiculous in a cape, except the cape might have smelled like mothballs, the way his clothes did. No one used mothballs in Southern California.

William came to London because his father was a "name" at Lloyd's. But William had worked his way up in the insurance industry on his own. "He's a smart, smart guy," my father said. "Understands all the fundamentals." I thought my father planned to make William a partner in his new company, even though William was more than a decade younger. My father said if I got my act together, maybe I could work at his company one day too. Nothing could have been further from what I hoped.

Our first morning in London, my father knocked on my door at precisely ten minutes till ten. I had never stayed in a hotel room alone; the room was cavernous and it contained so many things I'd never had before: a phone to call a butler, cloth bags to deposit shoes to be shined, a king-sized bed. There was no key to enter or exit, just a gray card embossed with the logo of the hotel. I unwrapped every bar of soap and opened every vial of lotion to breathe the scents. Nothing like the sweet, fruity perfumes my classmates sprayed in their hair.

As soon as I had received my wake-up call, I'd looked out the window, pushing aside the heavy curtains to see this new light. I was delighted by the small droplets of rain clinging to the windowpane, the wet pavement below, even the radiator at the window, warm to the touch.

My father and I rode the elevator downstairs. I tried to look bored as it dinged our descent, as though I was always riding in hotel elevators. Each time the doors opened, I caught a glimpse of the murals decorating the different floors. Oddly, they featured scenes of ancient Rome. The sandaled feet and fleshy peach skin of the people painted across the walls were in marked contrast to the polished leather shoes and dark raincoats of the people on the elevator.

We met William in the lobby restaurant for breakfast, then took a black cab to the Lloyd's building at One Lime Street, a huge modern complex in the city. It was my third time riding in a cab. My father wanted me to see the Lutine Bell in the underwriting room before he and William attended the conference. He explained that historically the bell was rung each time a Lloyd's-insured ship was lost at sea.

"If you really think about it," my father said, "insurance is the most exciting industry there is. It's risk and romance —teenage girls ought to like that." He handed me some Lloyd's annual reports, said we'd talk about them at dinner. I held the booklets awkwardly before shoving them into my backpack. To show off to William, I think, my father made a production out of giving me £100 and told me not to spend it all in one place.

"If I were you," he said, "I'd save it and spend my day studying."

"Regent Street," said William. "You'll like it there—you can walk all the way to Oxford Circus. Lots of stores. But," William added, to my father, "you've got to give her more than that." He winked at me.

My father pulled out his wallet again, gave me another £100. "Maybe buy some real shoes," he said, looking at my feet. My toenails were marble pink. Like most Southern California teenagers, I wore flip-flops in any weather, especially rain. They dried so quickly.

For a moment, I stared at the bell in its tall gazebo-like wooden cage. I imagined a man in Disraeli's day, letter in hand confirming a report of a ship lost at sea, marching to pull the Lutine Bell's long pale string. The bell would toll once, mournful, alarmed, and people would rush from the corners of the Lloyd's building. The drama was not based on the lives lost but on the money. I could not muster much interest in the loss of goods: fine china, spices, and whale oil. I wanted to know what was lost beyond the numbers on accounting sheets. I wanted to see the marbled feet in the water, floating.

* * *

I had already researched how to get to Hughenden Manor. Although I was tired, I knew I might never have the opportunity to go to High Wycombe again, so I took a black cab to Marylebone. The giant, arching station had multiple platforms and an announcer calling out the names of towns in the home counties. Stratford upon Avon was the end of my line, and I felt like a local buying a ticket to High Wycombe rather than the typical destination of Shakespeare's home. I wished my classmates could see me now.

When the train pulled out of the station and into the open air, I was surprised to see the daylit sky, which seemed to lift and vault the farther we got from London. As people boarded, they passed my row and always seemed to look down at my feet. I crossed my legs at the ankles. The train platforms became more rustic the farther we went. The iron and brick and concrete of London gradually turned to wood. Eventually, a teenage couple sat down across from me. The girl appeared to be about my age, but from the moment they sat down, she began sucking her thumb. Her boyfriend spoke to her as though nothing was amiss, sheltered her with his arm. I tried not to watch.

I was the only passenger standing near the doors when the conductor announced High Wycombe. I debarked as quickly as possible, afraid the train might start up again with me still on it, but it was still sitting in the station even as I pushed out the turnstile. There was one cab idling at the curb. "Where to, love?" the driver asked. This was a regular sedan, not a tall black cab with an orange light and a step like the ones in London.

"Hughenden Manor," I said, unsure of the pronunciation.

"Hughenden Manor," the driver repeated, dropping the "h," and he pulled away from the curb. I wondered where else tourists at High Wycombe station would be going. We turned down winding streets in the half-deserted town, past houses with laundry hanging in the yards.

We headed down into a valley, traveling a wide country road. At a stone church on the left, the driver downshifted and turned sharply uphill. "Disraeli's grave," he said, and I moved closer to the window but we passed quickly and I couldn't see it. The cab shuddered up the incline, through a narrow grove of trees and bushes that brushed against the sides of the car, until we made another left turn. Here was the circular driveway I had seen online. The trees were almost bigger than the brick manor house, which was smaller and less imposing than in photographs.

Inside, the house was comfortable; I could have easily lived there. Although the formal rooms had some ornate decoration, "to Mary Anne's taste," said the docent, they were sunny. After visiting the dining room and library, I climbed the stairs to the upper floors. There was a tour group in Mary Anne's bedroom; otherwise I might have lain on her bed. But in the adjacent office, where Disraeli wrote his books and letters, were no guards or visitors. I crept around to the back of Disraeli's desk and sat in his wooden chair. A sign said Queen Victoria had done the same thing after he died. Disraeli's chair was humble and personal, my size. Throughout the house, Disraeli's effects were simple. His home belied the witty quotes, glib comments, and boasting for which he was famous. "I have climbed to the top of the greasy pole," he declared upon being elected prime minister. Yet there was nothing too grandiose about his home. Perhaps inside he felt safe and calm, and, outside, protected by façade.

*   *   *

When I wanted to leave, there were no cabs at Hughenden. The woman at the desk seemed confused, as though visitors always arrived and left in their own cars. She disappeared into some distant office to use a telephone and I waited on a bench. The sky was still blue, but turning gray, a few wooly clouds moving behind the courtyard trees. It was getting cooler, and my toes felt numb. When the cab arrived, it was another sedan. "High Wycombe station," I said, and realized I wasn't sure of "Wycombe's" pronunciation either. The driver nodded but didn't repeat anything back to me. He looked at me in the rearview mirror, furtively dropping his eyes when we made eye contact.

We turned right at the church where Disraeli and Mary Anne were buried. I considered asking the driver to wait, suddenly deciding I shouldn't leave without seeing their graves. But he sped around the turn and I didn't want to ask to go back. Unlike the previous driver, this one turned off the valley road almost immediately and headed up the opposite hillside. I thought about speaking up, to make sure we were going to High Wycombe station, but didn't.

The car rattled over a pothole, then turned into a small drive. "I bet you'd like to have a good time," he said, with the same accent as the man who'd driven me to Hughenden that morning. He turned and put out his left hand, tracing two of his fingers over my kneecap. I jerked from his touch.

Clutching my backpack and scooting across the seat to the opposite side of the car, I opened the door and started running. But I had to run behind the car to go downhill, the same side as the driver. I kept expecting him to reach out and grab me.

I ran down the field, wet grass against bare legs, toward the long valley road. Why was it still wet, when it hadn't rained all afternoon? I couldn't get a full breath of air. I turned once to see the cab but it was hidden by a grove of trees, or had already gone. I imagined the cab plunging downhill through the grass, driving into the back of me, but the only cars I could hear were straight ahead. I stumbled in my flip-flops on the uneven ground, feet rotating and twisting. I tensed my toes to keep my sandals on. Wearing them felt like being home again, running along the ridge behind the house. I was halfway to the road when I realized I must have peed on myself; it was warm and sticky between my legs. I waited for a break between cars, then raced across the road to the stone wall at the edge of the church. I felt protected there, near Disraeli and Mary Anne, though I couldn't see them. A small pickup truck was driving slowly down the hill from Hughenden and I waved my arms until it stopped. The man inside was probably the same age as my grandfather.

"I need a ride," I said, stopping to pant, "to the station."

"All right, love," the man said. The truck smelled old but familiar, like rubber boots. The drying dampness between my legs was comforting, a secret, quietly sealed against the cracked leather seat.

* * *

I was so tired on the train ride back that I fell asleep, my cheek pressed against the plastic window. Somebody shook me awake at Marylebone station, the end of the line. I had two hours to rest at the hotel before dinner so I tried to nap but slept only a few minutes. I took a hot shower, rinsing my underwear in the stream of the water. I also rinsed my flip-flops; tiny pieces of grass had stuck to the edges and I let the water force them down the drain. There was a white robe on a gold hanger behind the bathroom door. I put it on—it was huge, sized for a man—and climbed in bed. I was filled with energy, my mind repeating questions about whether I had actually escaped anything in the cab. Maybe I could have just said something and we would have continued on to the station or turned around. Perhaps I could have assaulted the man, strangled him with the straps of my backpack. I wished I had stayed just a few seconds longer to find out. Maybe I'd spend the rest of my life running before anything happened.

That night I met my father and William at Simpson's in the Strand for dinner. The restaurant was full, and my father and William waved at a few of the other diners.

"And what did you do today?" my father asked, after we'd been served our drinks. "I see you found more appropriate footwear." They were the high heels I'd worn to the last homecoming dance in California. William told me about Simpson's, explained the different cuts of meat wheeled around the carpeted floor on trolleys. The restaurant was so old Disraeli himself might have eaten there. As William gestured, I was struck with the thought that William somehow resembled Disraeli, had William styled his hair in vain dark ringlets.

"Just wandered around the shops," I said, when my father asked again what I'd done. William was looking at me with interest, as though he was about to ask which shops, specifically, I'd visited. To that end, I'd memorized a few names in the cab back from Marylebone station. But I remained impassive, and no one pressed.

They discussed insurance. At one point, my father asked what I'd learned from the Lloyd's literature, which I hadn't read.

"Risk has its own rewards," I said. It was an inane comment but both men laughed.

"I'd say she's got the right idea," William said, and moved his chair a little closer to mine. Perhaps the fact that I looked at him differently now made him look at me differently too.

After dinner the men wanted drinks in the lobby bar. There was a skinny man in a red sequined tuxedo jacket seated at the piano, singing and playing. I wondered how singers could stand to be so intimate with their microphones, breathing, spitting into them, leaving a damp, personal smell on the metal tip. Each time the man was about to belt something, express some kind of emotion, he pulled away from the microphone so that the music had the strange effect of never really changing in volume.

At one point I left to go to the bathroom and my heels wobbled on the carpet leaving the dark bar. In the lobby, the polished floor swam in the bright lights so that it looked wet, though it wasn't. When I returned, two women were at our table with my father and William. One, in a sparkling evening gown, was posing on the banquette where I'd been sitting, the other, old enough to be her mother and wearing a dark skirt suit, was between William and my father's shoulders, as though instructing them. My father was holding a phone that must have belonged to the women. I'd never known my father to take a photograph in his life. My father looked a little wolfish; William seemed to be laughing. The singer was still leaning toward and away from the microphone, eyes closed.

"That's a lovely picture," the older woman was saying. She wore purple eye shadow and had a foreign accent. The younger woman on the banquette had a pretty, vacant face, just like the girls from my school, and all her features blurred when the phone flashed. She might not have been much older than me, though she was dressed in a floor-length gown with her hair up, sprayed into a tight chignon. I didn't understand why the older woman couldn't have taken the photograph herself, why she would ask my father and William to take a photograph of that young woman posing in the dark corner of our banquette. The older woman eyed me as I approached. "What a beautiful girl," she said, loudly enough that it was intended for me to hear. "Is she yours?"

"She's mine," my father said. I don't know why I felt such antipathy for the older woman, but I glared at her, and at the younger woman too. It was the kind of look other girls gave me, in school. But the younger woman just smiled emptily.

The older one had raised her eyebrows as if to make her face blank and friendly. "Well," she said, slowly, "I hope you enjoy your evening." She signaled to the younger woman with her finger and the girl slid herself out of the banquette. The two women glided toward the bar, as though that had been their destination all along. They never said thank you for the photo.

"You're far more attractive than those women," William said.

"Yes," said my father. "Certainly."

But the air was heavier and both my father and William seemed restless. I was tired, ready to climb into the large bed in my room. Maybe I'd sleep in the man-sized robe.

We passed a mirrored case in the lobby filled with rare books for sale from a dealer in St. James's. They were lit by tiny library lamps, and the chrome on the edges of the case sparkled. A small note card in front of a stack caught my eye: "First edition, Benjamin Disraeli's *Vivian Grey*, two volumes." I bent down to look at the mirrored glass case. I had never read *Vivian Grey* but knew it was Disraeli's first novel, about the rise and fall of an arrogant man. Hughenden had a similar set.

"Ah, Disraeli," William said.

"You know about him?" I asked.

"Of course," William said. "I'd say you're a very interesting woman to know Disraeli. Your father must be making sure you get quite an education." It was the first time anyone had called me a woman.

"I wonder how much they are," I said, although I could tell by the locked case in this expensive hotel and the fact of their age that they were expensive. Such a set belonged at Hughenden. It was laughable to think of them in my teenage bedroom.

"More than you can afford," my dad said.

William said, "I would be delighted to buy them for you." He sounded much more formal than usual. "Unless, of course, your father objects."

"No, no, be my guest," my father said.

William rang the bell on the reception desk for the desk clerk and she unlocked the case. I carefully withdrew the soft calfskin books, but as careful as I was still felt that I had pulled on the bindings too forcefully. My face felt hot but I saw, in my reflection in the mirrors at the back of the case, that I was actually very pale. And I saw my father's face in the mirror too. His wore an expression I had not seen in relation to me, only in relation to work, some kind of calculation in the horizontal lines across his forehead.

The brown leather cover was nubby, and tinged red. The pages opened with some difficulty, as though they had never been read, or, if they had, not in the last century. The endpapers were marbled in blue and purple and white, with no bookplates or script denoting ownership. The longer I held the books, the more I felt they were mine. They might be the closest I would ever get to such a man. William reached out to touch one, and, perhaps purposefully, his palm brushed my knuckles.

"Sold," said William.

My dad's voice boomed. "I'd say you owe William a big thank you."

William nodded to the clerk; she went to a back room to find the accompanying box. It contained dust bags for each book. The clerk dropped the books into the bags, settled them inside the box, and filled the edges with ivory tissue paper.

"Do you like them?" William asked, taking the box from the counter under his left arm. I nodded yes. The clock in the lobby rang for the hour. "I'll carry it up for you," he said.

"I'm going to leave you two to your own devices," my father said. He looked pleased, energetic. He strode off toward the elevator. William signed the bill presented by the silent clerk. My father had disappeared quickly, and we rode a different elevator. When the doors opened on my floor, there were the Romans again, stroking their beards, studying important documents. William took my arm by the inner elbow.

When we arrived at the door of my room, William held out his hand for my card key, slid it in and out of the slot above the door handle. I straightened my back; my ears were ringing a little. The light flashed green; William pushed in the heavy door, held it open with his back. How quickly this room, so foreign and exotic to me the night before, had become familiar, mothballed. I kept my head high, chin up. I was thinking about the women in the bar and Disraeli's own difficult ascent. No, I was thinking about Hughenden: that warm house in a quiet hamlet. My feet were sweaty in my heels, and I had to grip my toes to keep them on. I could have run; I could have said something, but I did not. ■

ON THE QUESTION OF PETS
Matt Polzin

Maria was small, and rather aloof. She had a little bell on her collar so sometimes I heard her before I saw her. I would be sitting at the concrete table outside the student-run café on my breaks, smoking cigarettes next to fruiting pomegranate trees and hibiscus, and I would hear her rattle coming up the main campus promenade. Sometimes she even came into the café, haranguing us for food. No one thought to bother calling the number on her heart-shaped tag. She was a cat doing exactly what she needed to be doing.

Then I encountered her on Highway 41. She stayed on the sidewalk, but I just got nervous, what with the speeding cars. If it was a betrayal, I was sorry. I referred to the number on her tag. Somebody answered and said he would be over in ten minutes. I told him I was waiting for the bus. He repeated himself and hung up.

The beat Camry came to a clunky, unpolished halt. I could see two people through the windshield, both of them wearing tank tops, pale skin heavily tatted. We all stared at the city bus, the hulk of its stiff metal body whining as it lurched down the street, clearly without me on it.

One of them asked, "Where did you say you needed to go?" Their name was Michael. I had seen them before at the café, where they ordered an almond milk cappuccino. They had a tattoo stamped on their right shoulder that just read HOMO. I liked that kind of forwardness.

"The orchestra," I said.

It was a thing I did from time to time, to the surprise of the people I lived with. I would put on a dress shirt and go buy a rush ticket for the second-rate orchestra in town. It was rare to find a place where I could sit and cry with little consequence. I felt like I had more privacy in a dark auditorium filled with well-dressed people than I did at the house where I lived with a bunch of students.

Orion was the one who'd answered my call. He was slightly older, with curls that were beginning to grey. He leaned over to address me through the window. "Do you want a ride?"

* * *

I could hear the frantic scraping of long nails on wood floors before I saw the skinny brindled dog turn the corner. Orion and Michael had invited me over to tea. The dog leapt, but Orion grabbed her by the collar. He sat her down, saying with a pleading voice, "Sit, Bailey," although she didn't want to sit. She immediately lunged and grabbed the treat he held out in front of her with her long, gymnastic tongue. Then he shoved her into the backyard and closed the double doors.

Their place had a kind of maturity to it, unlike the house I lived at. This was a midcentury ranch, with built-in shelves and cabinetry full of books and cheap ceramics and a picture of the Dalai Lama in a frame. The dark wood trim gave the rooms the feeling of being hugged. It was very Florida post-crash, that momentary renter's relief when the ruins of the housing bubble were falling into further disrepair and you could rent houses for relatively cheap. A buttery heat emanated from the oven.

"Where's Michael?"

"They're in the backyard, setting things up."

Orion opened a cabinet with, like, fifty boxes of bagged tea from Trader Joe's. Everything in my life felt utterly disposable, so hoarding of any kind impressed me. I dunked my tea bag and watched the red hibiscus bleed out while Orion started asking me questions.

"It was so hard dating at that college. Is it still like that?"

Every question had a real question behind it, which was the question I answered. I told him that I was single. I told him I wasn't interested in monogamy. I told him I thought exclusive relationships were rife with toxic heteronormative dynamics and patriarchal power grabs. I'm not sure I said it exactly like that, but my friends and I did think that. We had formed a queer action group that we called the Fruit Punch Collective with a mission of "subverting the American family with arts and crafts." It was basically non-active, and all we did was talk negatively about everything, although once we did crash a Defense of Marriage Act rally, standing on the sidelines in scandalous outfits, popping condoms we had blown up like balloons and filled with glitter, which wasn't as dramatic as we wanted: the lubricant turned the glitter into a pasty gunk and it sort of just fell to the ground. I told him I was interested in finding romantic structures that didn't feel possessive and controlling, like polyamory.

These answers seemed to satisfy him. Eventually, we started carrying things out to the backyard, where Michael was running their hand over a lace tablecloth, brushing off live oak leaves. They were wearing a top with glittery sequins. Others had started to arrive, using the gate in the chain-link fence. We sat beside clumps of lush bougainvillea and passed around a plate of shortbread and drank tea while playing competitive cards and saying snarky things to each other. I had never felt gayer in my life. Personally, I was coming from a more burn-everything-to-the- ground punk scene. I was enchanted.

* * *

I made plans to help Michael install their show at the student-run café. I was there mostly to approve moving furniture for the exhibition and nailing into the wallpaper, which later angered the café manager, an alum who disliked me (I was a horrible employee). I should say that bell hooks was in residence at the school for a few years and she personally told me that I made a great smoothie and also that I was cute. Later she even sat with me on the concrete table out front and let me cry about my living situation. She was modeling compassion that maybe only theorists without teaching responsibilities have the time for.

Michael had crocheted a bunch of cock rings with bright-blue yarn and dildos out of yarn, too. They were really into fiber art at the moment. Listening to them describe their feminist art practice, I realized this was precisely something the Fruit Punch Collective would have done, or talked about doing, as that was our speciality (talking, I mean). Michael's plan was to hang the cock rings and dildos in a triangle formation next to a sign that invited people to take one. I was actually kind of grossed out by the idea of a cotton dildo, which seemed too absorbent of a material. Who wants a cotton cock ring? Surely, not everyone. I was surprised my manager had approved the show, but then again everybody loved Michael. They were sweet and soft-spoken and smart and beautiful. They were extremely tall, but they slouched, as if sticking out in space didn't appeal to them.

I was thinking these things and I wanted to say something nice about their work, so I said that I was impressed by their commitment to replenish the supply of sex toys.

"Orion said you're interested in maybe joining our relationship," Michael replied. I stared at them, murmuring something vague, affirmative.

"Maybe you want to join us for dinner tonight?"

I invented some new vowel, a vocal glissando, gliding from one pitch to the next. We walked back to their house and found Orion sitting in a large wicker chair in the backyard, stiffly reading. He kissed me on the cheek in greeting, saying he was happy to see me.

We made a stir-fry, which looked promising. Then Orion dumped like half a bottle of hoisin sauce over it, so it just tasted like sugar. I don't remember what we discussed. I was apprehensive, nervous about what was to come. I was such a faggy bottom. Typically my strategy for sex was lying there and hoping somebody would do something. Now there would be two bodies I would have to figure out what to do with, and it would be quite obvious that I didn't know how to do that. But they pulled my hand to their bedroom, where they put on cheesy, synthy music. They told me I didn't need to worry. I didn't need to do anything. I just needed to lean back and they would do everything.

* * *

I showed up to Palm Court on campus a few nights later and saw her among the dancing students. Palm Court was this large outdoor space with dangerously slippery tile and geometrically spaced palm trees that students called "the center of the universe." Social life at our school revolved around those parties. Even Maria was there, sitting slightly to the left of the speakers, looking too good for everything.

I felt like we shared a secret, both of us inhabiting that midcentury ranch with exploding plant and animal life by Sarasota Bay. She would refill on kibble and then plow through the front door the first chance she got. I stayed longer, making soggy vegetarian fare drowned in sauce before crawling into bed, all of us in the queen.

I saw her in the library not so long after. I didn't think she was heavy enough to get the automatic doors at the entrance to open. The bell on her collar was the exact kind of persistent annoying sound you'd expect to drive students up the wall, but she didn't seem to be a bother. Maria was walking up and down the stacks, as if searching for something to read.

One day I went to a campus town hall meeting to announce that the café would have later hours during finals week. Students were sitting around Palm Court, listening to various speakers, looking lethargic and hot. The residence life manager took the bullhorn, berating us about what we were doing wrong. She even ranted about Maria. She threatened to slap students with fines if they brought her into the dorms. It was news to me that she was sleeping in people's rooms. She said, I remember it perfectly, "Maria doesn't care if you get fined!" Then she called my boyfriends negligent pet owners.

Orion was deeply in favor of keeping Maria indoors after hearing this. It was safer for her to stay indoors, he argued. What if the school called the pound? Plus, he had all this death on his conscience. Outdoor cats killed birds and lizards and things. As the human who tolerated her excursions, wasn't he responsible for that loss of life? It was the more compassionate thing to do, Orion said, keeping her inside.

Michael clashed with Orion, saying we were in no position to keep Maria inside against her will. They proceeded to tell us about the artist they worked for, who'd had a cat that needed to be prescribed antidepressants because she wasn't allowed outdoors. She would sit across from the door all day, watching it open and close as people went through. Then one day she crawled into the furnace, possibly because it was still warm, but who could say? The studio manager turned it on at the beginning of the morning shift. Another friend of Michael's in New York had a cat so desperate to get outside that she let the cat out on the fire escape, from which it promptly jumped.

* * *

I posted a letter to the student listserv on Orion's behalf with his number, imploring students to let him know if Maria was seen on campus.

It was useless, though. Maria spent every second at home by the door, waiting for an opening, which she got often. Bailey threw all of her weight at whoever walked through the door, licking us with her tongue and scratching with her claws. I almost wondered if it was conspiratorial, Bailey's timing, bombarding the door like that.

Michael wasn't very helpful either. They could not—no matter how many times Orion reminded them—they could not remember to check if Maria was lurking near the front door, ready to bolt. Sometimes they forgot to close the door, too.

* * *

I moved in January of that year. It made sense. My two partners already lived together, and so why shouldn't I live with them? We put the utilities under my name, just to make it feel official. I wouldn't be on the lease. Integrating my few belongings into their clutter was strangely molecular, like osmosing across a threshold. For a while the spines of my books jumped out from where I'd inserted them on the shelves, but their glow gradually faded.

We dumped my bright-red writing desk, which was actually a small vanity, in the garage.

That wasn't such an insult as it sounds. The garage was Michael's studio. It was filled with glittery fabric and crocheted oddities. Their current project involved gold leaf and paper and wax, arranged in a large triangle on a canvas. It was kind of like a collage.

"Do you know why I like triangles?"

I shook my head. They must have known I had no idea.

"The triangle is a really durable shape," Michael explained. "Builders use it as the basis for complex structures, like geodesic domes. I think that's a good sign for us."

Walking around campus, I started looking for triangles and other polygons in the buildings I passed. College Hall was mostly large square marble slabs, though. The Pei dorms were bunker-like cement blocks. I began to scrutinize the normativity of parallelograms. And why should love seats only have two cushions? Mattresses, with their two long sides, seemed to be exclusively designed for two people. Square tabletops were less giving than round ones.

Michael and I talked about things like this, how to remedy the exclusiveness of furniture. Even the phrase "I love you" seemed to be designed for two. So we wouldn't say it.

Then one day, when we were returning from a grocery run, Michael spotted a hideous curved sofa with five cushions on the side of the road, green with a metallic silver trim. Its long crescent shape meant there was really nowhere to put it in the house, but we found some room by pushing most of the furniture against the wall.

Orion was surprised.

"Matt likes it," Michael said, quickly.

"Do you really?" he turned to me.

I stared at the silver metallic fringe. The way it clashed with the green fabric made my eyes shake painfully. "I don't mind it," I said, diplomatically.

"That's two of us," Michael smiled.

"So it is," Orion replied, sighing.

* * *

Michael and Orion adopted animals like they got couches. They could fall in love with the design of a box of tea and decide to buy a dozen. The things Michael and Orion loved blocked other things from view and filled the backs of drawers. I haven't even mentioned the two ferrets at the house. Ferrets sleep for twenty hours a day and then for four they are alert Slinkies, bobbing around space. There wasn't much to say about them, but they were there.

Then Michael got a puppy.

I put my hands up, wanting no part.

"You'll do everything?" Orion asked Michael, making sure.

"I'll do everything."

One person doesn't a raise a dog. Michael kept saying it was easy, raising a puppy, basing that on their experience with Bailey, I guess, but Olli wasn't easy. It was a collective effort to house-train her. All day we stalked around the house to catch her so that we could tell her she was a bad dog, but she was smart and knew what we were up to. We would only later discover a gross turd somewhere. She fit into places I swear a dog could not get to. Her poops were like cow patties, shapeless and awful. Eventually Michael ripped up all the soiled carpeting without even consulting the landlord and there were beautiful terrazzo floors underneath. We were amazed at how all along there had been beautiful speckled stones there, cool to the touch and easy to clean. Why had there ever been carpeting?

One afternoon I was sitting in the bed, eating sauerkraut with red cabbage and reading for class. Olli, the little terror, nudged her nose through the crack of the door. I tried not to make a noise, but her nose was too smart for that, and she rushed towards the bed, yapping at me to pick her up. I put her on the bed and tried to tolerate her as I got back to reading. Then I thought I had spilled the pink juice of the sauerkraut all over. It was such a strong experience, the slow transformation of my understanding of the color all over the sheets. The sauerkraut seemed to transform in my mouth, too. She was having her first period.

Orion was insistent that we get her spayed when I told him. I knew Michael wouldn't be thrilled about it. I wasn't thrilled myself. Although I understood the importance, you couldn't get consent from a dog for a thing like that.

"Michael wouldn't allow it," I said.

"We don't need to consult Michael," Orion responded.

"She would have to wear one of those cones."

"Consult me on what?" Michael asked, entering the room. They seemed to process the soft faded bath towels draped over our shoulders. "Are you all going to the beach?"

Orion didn't look up from lathering his legs. "You should come."

"Were you going to wait for me?"

"I thought you worked," I said to Michael, which was true. I did think that.

"I had a half shift." Then Michael looked at Orion. "I told you that."

"Oh, come on—I forgot."

"It looks like it," Michael said. "Would there even be room for me in the car, with you, Matt, and your massive ego? You were really going to spay my dog?"

Orion clenched the suntan lotion he was holding so that half the contents of the bottle exploded across the space between them.

It was in Michael's hair, on their shirt. In their eyelashes.

"I'm so sorry," Orion exclaimed, slamming the bottle on the dresser.

* * *

Here's a story: Orion is driving on the highway. The car in front of him hits a small blurry shape and drives off, but he pulls over. Clouds seared with red are building up at the horizon. He can see the body of the animal dragging itself along the side of the road. The opossum is badly bleeding. If it doesn't die right there, it will soon. He kneels on the pavement. The animal knows it's dying. It runs into his open arms.

That was how Orion told it at one of those Sunday tea parties. But I had watched from the back seat, how Orion had actually walked to pick up the animal and then cradled it before we took it to an animal hospital. Michael didn't correct Orion's telling of the events either. They nodded along, emphatically. Both of them wanted compassion to be something that was magnetic, something that crossed lines, species and otherwise.

Once Michael and I picked hundreds of mulberries from a huge tree for pies. The purple juices of the mulberries stained our hands and clothes as we climbed through the branches. The air smelled yeasty and there were flies, but we weren't discouraged. We returned to the house with plastic bags full of sopping fruit, drenched in purple. It was only when we started washing them off in a sieve that Orion noticed there were the teensiest worms on the berries. They were so small they were almost not there.

Michael and I took the position that we could just wash them off and that would be fine.

Or we could do nothing, seeing how they'd probably disintegrate as the pie baked. Orion wouldn't let us. Not because he thought that was disgusting, but because the worms would die.

He spent over an hour trying to pick them off, putting them in a dish, which he then set in the garden. They would die anyway, we told him. The larvae fed on the fruit and without it they would starve. We couldn't say anything that would change his mind, though.

* * *

"The two of you always gang up on me," Orion said to me, as he and I walked Bailey out to the field of crabgrass near the bay.

I unclasped Bailey from her leash. The Florida I knew wasn't the powder-white beaches, but hostile, serrated grass, fire ants, and unruly fronds. The air smelled salty and acrid, due to rotting citrus and mangroves. The sun was searing, almost invisible in the white bleached sky. Cabbage palms reached up for it. We watched Bailey run in ellipses the length of the grass, circling us without paying us mind.

"I'm sorry," I said, feeling unsure of what to say.

"How long does it take to pick mulberries?"

"What do you mean?"

He listed a number of times that Michael and I had gone off together. "I think it's interesting, how you seem to look for every opportunity to do something without me."

I was confused. Weren't he and I walking Bailey together, while Michael stayed at home working in their studio? I said what I always said, that I cared about him, just as I cared for Michael. Really, that was the truth. We needed Orion to shape us.

"I want you to want to be with *me*," Orion stated.

"I do want to be with you," I repeated. Only I added: "And Michael."

Orion frowned. "It's like you want me to do all the feeling in this relationship, and then you get to just soak it up."

I stared at him, unsure of what exactly he wanted. "I feel strongly about you."

He looked back at me with a hawkish glare, as if the space between us had stretched and he had to locate me across all that distance.

We had started to head back. Ahead of us, someone was approaching the house. The person was a student: Pink Floyd shirt, oversized corduroy pants, messenger bag, no shoes. He was carrying

Maria. She looked plaintive in his arms, not even struggling.

Orion put his arm out. I didn't understand, but he shushed me, grabbing me by the wrist and pulling me behind a parked car.

It was strange. Michael answered the door and acted like they had never seen the cat before. They tilted their head in confusion and squinted. Then they pointed vaguely down the street with a flutter of their hand. They said that her owners had moved.

* * *

Orion suggested that we make a Concord grape pie. After days of not speaking, days during which I hadn't done much speaking either, as I found I had little to say, sleeping between two people who were not talking, he said it might be a good way to patch things up with Michael.

A Concord grape pie is an extravagance. I was enchanted by the idea of baked grapes, curious what would happen to their purple color and consistency. I fawned over the recipe in *Joy of Cooking*, written by Irma S. Rombauer with her signature brevity, that down-to-earth poetic compression. "Stem the grapes. Slip the pulp out of the skins. Cook the pulp until the seeds loosen. Press it through a colander. Permit these ingredients to stand for five minutes." Each sentence was like an invitation, easing us to act. Rombauer lent ingredients a magical animate quality, suggesting you "permit" them to stand there, as if the grapes desired rest. I read it aloud to Michael, to warm them to the idea of baking it. How could we not want to bake this pie?

We saw an entire display at the market filled with Concords, clumps upon clumps of the smoky, billowing fruit. We bought pounds, more than we needed, as well as an orange to grate for the filling, a bag of flour, and unsalted butter. With the sugar we already had at home, that was everything. That was the beauty of a pie.

I entered with the groceries. Bailey lunged at me, trying to lick my face, giving Maria the opening she needed. She ran out. Orion grabbed Bailey, throwing his free arm towards the door, as if to say, "Go!" I ran to set the groceries on the counter, and then I went after Michael, who was already running. Maria was a straight line over the ground, a brushstroke flying across the pavement. We were never going to catch up, but we tried at least.

Concord grapes are on a list of things, up there with chocolate and peach pits, to keep away from dogs. You'd think that Orion would know this, having raised Bailey. You would think that he would finish putting the groceries away.

Perhaps he had simply forgotten. Perhaps he'd put everything away except the grapes, which he thought to leave on the table. Perhaps Bailey had grabbed the bag with her teeth and carried the grapes into the sunroom, where she decided she didn't like the taste of Concord grapes. Olli did, though. She loved them. She ate nearly her size in fruit and stem and then her kidneys quit on her, although not before she crawled under the pullout couch, where she was out of sight. She made not a peep for hours, shitting her bowels out with her usual clandestinity.

We didn't know that the grapes were missing. We weren't planning on making the pie until the next day. We didn't realize Olli was missing. I only went into the sunroom when I heard Michael. I was unsure what to make of the mass in their arms, what was dog, shit, or blood. She seemed to rub away against their shirt. They stared at me and then tilted their head back and this spear of sound shot out of their throat, a horrible cry. I could hear it the entire drive to the pet hospital, where we were ushered into a small white room with a padded blue table.

Of course, it was true that I was the person who left things out, who mindlessly left burners on, who sometimes got an idea in the middle of cooking eggs, only to return when the fire alarm went off. I can't tell you that wasn't true, but I was disturbed how quickly Orion said this to Michael when we were back in the car. I didn't see how it was relevant.

"You dropped the bags with the grapes on the floor," Orion said to me. "You can't do things like that when you live with a puppy."

I stared from the back seat. "What?"

Michael hadn't spoken since the veterinarian had removed Olli from the room. But now they shifted slightly to look at me. "You left the grapes on the floor?"

Orion frowned. "I told him numerous times not to leave food around."

"I didn't leave them out," I exclaimed. "I put them on the table!"

"You don't need to get so defensive. It was an accident—an easily preventable one, but an accident nevertheless."

"I did not kill Michael's dog!"

"Not intentionally."

Michael dropped their face into their palms.

* * *

The sunroom had a pull-out couch, where I slept with the glass panes of the louver windows slightly cracked. The wet, sloshy air swept through at night, like a river rising up around me. Some mornings I would wake up to live oak leaves scattered on the seafoam comforter. Other days Bailey woke me, setting her head on the pullout mattress and sighing enough times that I got up. I let her out through the back door and followed after, picking up moldy citrus and hurling the oranges and grapefruits the length of the yard, generally in the direction of my old room.

I developed a new tendency to stay out late, wanting to avoid Orion, who had convinced Michael that I'd killed their dog. My old housemates were surprised to see me—being in a relationship was akin to dying to them. One of my first nights back, while we were sitting under the strung lights in the backyard of my old house, a friend quoted a line from a book that people were passing around at the time. It was a real grouchy text. "'The family only exists as a family, that is, as hell, for those who have renounced the project of altering its debilitating mechanisms,'" my friend said, reading the words from the chapbook.

Then she looked up at me. "But you tried to alter it, and it still was hell."

I remembered what Michael had said—that the triangle was the most durable form. That it was the basis for the sturdiest structures. That you could build out the most interesting architecture with it. I sat there, half listening to the people around me as they told jokes in that deranged, vicious way that happens when a group of otherwise nice people sit together in a circle. I didn't know if it was Olli or the failed relationship, but I had started drinking a lot.

Everybody was drinking. Then we climbed onto our bikes.

Campus parties were either fun or wholly depressing, and that was totally dependent on your talent for making a lot out of nothing. I wasn't so good at that, but that wasn't the reason I went. I had gone there searching, and so I searched. I looked among the dancing bodies and the clumps of students in the dormitory common areas for her small form. I half expected to see her appear beside the speakers. I expected to hear her.

"Maria comes and goes as she pleases," one student said when I asked. Others were almost put off by my questions. I knew that Maria could take care of herself, but what if she had been hit by car? What if a dog or even a Florida panther had gotten to her? No one had seen her for days, possibly weeks. Or perhaps someone had adopted her. The staff in the financial aid office had always used to joke about installing a kitty door so that Maria could come and go as she pleased. Perhaps somebody had gotten it into their head to take her home.

But the responses were the same there when I checked. "Maria? She's moved on, man."

* * *

I would stumble towards the bathroom after getting home and see the light underneath their closed door. If it was a faint blue, I knew they were watching a movie on Michael's desktop. If it was a bright, watery yellow, it probably meant they were up late bickering, or having sex. The three of us had always kept the lamp on. I had never understood why you would want all of that in the dark.

Now I felt differently. I discovered how pleasing it was, simply tossing out the utility bills, which were still in my name. At first it was an accident, a casualty of the breakup—I was too overwhelmed to remember to pay. When Orion asked if I was going to cash his check for his and Michael's share, I had actually forgotten. Then I did cash it, and instead of paying, I bought myself a new bike seat. It felt like a little theft, a little way to snatch something back. The next month, when he handed me another check, I cashed the check and bought myself new tires.

I had started biking a lot. I found that it relaxed me. As I waited for the power to get shut off at my own house, I liked to bike along Bay Shore, a curving residential street that ran beside the Sarasota Bay. The neighborhood was a swirl of overgrowth, all of it enveloped by sky and blue water. Trunks of live oaks dipped over the road, sprouting mossy bromeliads and orchids so that the bark was flecked with bright colors. Mossy roofs arched over the attics of bungalows, the branches of slash pines forked into smaller branches—it was incredible to me that I had missed all of these triangles months ago. I guess I had been looking for standalone shapes, when all along to see them you had to see everything.

I was thinking about that when I realized my front wheel was nearly flat. I steered the bike to the curb, unzipping the small bag Velcroed to the handlebar. I didn't have any spare tubes. I was three miles from the house, on the side of the road, under a sun that was smearing across the sky, turning it all a clementine orange, which was when I saw her.

Well, first, I heard her. She started out as nothing more than a sound, almost like a faint chime. I dropped my bike and crossed the street. I passed a massive star fruit tree. Once the branches were out of sight, I saw her. She was coming up the sidewalk, exactly how she always looked. Small and resolute, like a fist. She stopped about a foot away from me.

Then she started walking again. ∎

WHEN THE CLOCKS
D. James Smith

find these hours
at the bottom of my years

and a glacier moon
courting silence reveals

ants pillaging the purse
of a dead wren's chest,

when needles of stars pin me, stilled,
when I'm sure the mosquito is the fallen world

and my heart lurches like a frog out of wet grass
to rest three feet away blinking at me without recognition,

I sit on the wooden porch until morning,
old songs crowding the back of my throat.

ALL THE PLACES
YOU WILL NEVER BE AGAIN
A. J. Bermudez

Acamera is a little room, she's saying, a chamber, in Latin, you know, and then it's in her hands, thick with ink, bleeding onto the glossy square like an omen. She's towering over you on the mattress, shaking the Polaroid like you've seen people do in movies, her legs quivering for balance beneath a pair of popcorn-yellow underwear. She is steel and sweat, jacket but no blouse, all teeth. A man-made wonder.

When she touches you it's like a blister, the sensation dialed up too high to be real, and this is when you know, like when the earth shakes in Iowa or the moon rises twice, that you are not awake.

This is a frequent one, as is the one where you meet at that blush-brick, corn-scented all-girls school in the heart of true nowhere, a blur of plaid and touched knees and pencil lead speared, initial after initial, into the wood of your desk. You count this among all the places you will never be again. There and here.

The photograph's of you, of course, invincibly coy, an almost-smile frozen in time. She's blithering about *La tache aveugle*, some French film you've never seen, in which a figure materializes, nothing to something. Invisible to visible. Like you, she's saying, the Polaroid box slung across her bare chest. She presents the photo for inspection and she's right: that pinned-down smile of yours blossoms from sheer absence to a ghost, to something that looks exactly like you.

There are boxes of these things: little squares of you in a sundress, you at the grocery, you on a boat. Whose boat, you can't recall.

You've never understood why she took so many. Could she have been afraid, even then, of forgetting? Of missed pills and buried parents, years like rooms where the lights turn on and off without rationale, scattered faces and addresses, events softening and sliding together like dirt in rain?

She bites your ear at the top, the part called the helix, she's saying, the unruly dark blur of her hair in your mouth and your eyes, and there's another click and whir of the machine, a new square, another you.

When you wake up, she'll be her again and you'll be you. She'll be five times her age, the age she is now, clove smoke and chenin blanc, a knee on either side of you. You'll be immortal, a slew of you in the box.

She's asked for it to be brought here, to the hospital. This box of photographs. This box of yous. She's shown you a photograph with which she's especially thrilled, you smoking a cigarette, fresh out of the shower, fingers splayed as though to ward off the lens, but even in this moment, you're elsewhere. It's not real, you're saying, it's the false you, the you of the photographs, the impeccable you, the you of never again and bliss-stricken now. The you who is always awake.

The room is itself a little chamber, a camera (in Latin, you know), an angular box of single incidents. Announcings, acceptings, hand squeezings, tracheal insertions, shots, cures, last rites, last words, deaths. Births, maybe. This isn't that part of the hospital. Everything is eggshell plastic and recycled sheets, the knit blue blankets pale and rippled, like the ones you pretended were the ocean as a child. Her fingers are curled around the box in her lap, like roots around a stone jutting up from the earth, and this is how she sleeps.

You sleep, too, curled in the waxy pink shell of a chair beside her, although sleep is a strong word.

There are things you'll miss, she's saying. That's *la tache aveugle.*

But what if you catch them in time? you say. And there's nothing you can do?

She is unfazed. She's talking about silver halide grains, interlayers and image dyes. She has always insisted on the *science*, science above all, the way the pieces collapse on themselves, layer on layer, catalyzed by time. You remarked once, in a world other than this one, the real world, on the irony that science couldn't save her. Big deal, she had said. Science has better things to do.

She bites the pieces of you as though she could keep them, your neck and nose, your hair and little finger. She is magic and misery, a flicker of herself. The nimble, hazy goddess you imagine her to be, like a manuscript on which coffee has been spilled.

You look up and it's like seeing her through water. She wavers as though being shaken.

She's shown you the pyramids, dragged you to the exhibit of the mummified gazelle—the pharaoh's pet, can you imagine? she's saying, and you can. You can imagine.

She'll want to be buried with these photographs. At first you'll hate the thought of it, that much of you beneath the earth. But you'll come around, knowing that when she dies, so much of you will be down there anyway.

When she wakes, she'll ask for her favorite thing, which is to see the thin negative layers of plastic laid on top of each other, cell after cell, demonstrating the steady, greedy march of her condition. She never remembers which disease it is, what she has. Good for her.

She'll turn to you, not remembering that she's said this before, and say, Isn't it something?

It is, you say, it is something. Then she's back into the box of photographs and you hate how many are of you, they're all of you—why didn't you take more pictures of her? You're the one who will need them.

Still, she is transfixed by the thick greens and blues, the interlaced fingers and sheets, the summers of bangs and corduroy, the local politics, the attempts to kill a lobster you had not realized would be sold to you alive.

You have seen the pharaoh, and you are the gazelle. ■

THE MANSARD
Mark Duncan

The pantry looked like something organized by a marine fresh out of basic training. Pasta and rice bags tidy on the bottom shelf, canned vegetables flush across the middle, ketchup bottles and relishes second from the top, cereal boxes above. All labels facing forward, equal distance between rows. You didn't know whether to grab a can of petits pois peas or take a picture of it.

Mom had her obsessions. She had her hang-ups and her ways. Her pantry was only one of a multitude of quirks and rituals that ruled her daily life. At bedtime she ate three graham cracker squares washed down with three ounces of skim milk, but not before she measured the milk a level three ounces in a measuring cup. She folded underwear with the precision of an architect. Your dresser drawer was left with a perfectly aligned tower of Sears Best, all elastic bands in formation to the northerly side. T-shirts were folded in half lengthwise, then in three so the quarter-moon crew necks all faced west. Flawless. No wrinkles. Nothing out of sort.

She wore sleeveless blouses and stretch polyester shorts no different than Hugh Hefner wore silk pajamas. If Monday found her in green, Tuesday might have been blue or orange. She had seven sets in all, one color for every day of the week, and a dresser drawer that resembled a carton of crayons. She possessed no taste for fashion, no longing for jewels. She didn't sit for pedicures and manicures. Her hair, however. *If your hair looks good, honey, you look good.* My grandmother's words. Mom took them to heart. Every Thursday morning at the salon, dyed, fried, and teased with extra stiffener before being sculpted into the shape of a chocolate-brown helmet. She thought she had the world fooled, an eighty-year-old woman, nary a strand of gray. We finally convinced her to go for a silver fox pixie look, and the shock of the change made her realize she was old and damn near put her out of her mind.

We buried her on a chilly Saturday in November, seventeen months before Dad. A year would pass before any of us truly mourned her, mad as we were at how she'd played on death and what she'd put us through. Her body was strong. It might have sustained her another fifteen years. Her mind was a layered curse of nuttiness and drama, and it took her down with flair at the age of eighty-four. It was hard to watch her throw in the towel like that, long before her time.

Dad was very different. Low-key and direct, he decided things on his gut while she planned, second-guessed, and agonized. He was a fireman in his prime and ran a newspaper recycling business on the side. Nothing much fazed him. Mom's car broke down once while she and our sister were in Chicago. Nine hundred miles away, she called him to wail at length about the car and the costs and the disruption of her life. "What do you want me to do, Barbara?" he asked, even as always, and it was enough to tell her there was nothing he could. "I just wanted to hear your voice," she barked, and hung up the phone. Dad wasn't a man of outward emotion. He didn't say the three words. They were awkward and difficult for him, but his voice worked, calm and still as a burning candle, it worked for all of us. Mom figured her way out of Chicago.

He had no vices, our dad, no gambling or smoking. He'd have a beer or two at a crawfish boil, maybe a glass of sambuca in later years, but that was about it. No fancy cars, no fancy clothes, no expensive watches. Brand names weren't his thing. After Mom totaled the station wagon in '75, Dad drove the wrecked heap for another six months. He climbed in through the passenger side and scooted across. He didn't care what it looked like. In the old days, you could always spot him at our brother's basketball games, the lone white dude sitting on the visitors' side of a racially divided gym. He took no interest in the murmurings of people and their bullshit. He only wanted distance from Mom and her cackling mouth as it pounced on every rank injustice that occurred on the court. Her sound effects reverberated in your brain and shimmied down your spine. Not his. He knew his best medicines and knew how to roll. When the years finally caught him, the doctors gave him an expiration date. Two years, they said, his heart wouldn't last. Stamped it on him like on a quart of milk. He didn't blink. He held on for years past it without complaint and did it on balls alone, so what do doctors really know about balls and what do they know about death?

I hadn't given much thought to their old house really, I'd hardly the time. Among my divorce, the move, the kids adjusting, never mind running the practice, the only constant in my days was an appetite for distraction. Google Iceland Vikings, Google Bukowski quotes, Google into the grip of a vice. Facebook, Insta, the whole clutter; old friends looking old, birthdays of old friends' mothers, still around, walkers and wheelchairs, posing for a family photograph. My days passed like choppy seas. There was no time for meaning anymore and time was hemorrhaging away. *These are the limits of your life, man.* Steve Buscemi. *Fargo.* How old was Buscemi now? IMDb. Born December 1957. Bloody hell. *Reservoir Dogs* was 1992. Mr. Pink was no more than thirty-five. Not so long ago. I was living in the East Village and buying cannoli at Veniero's every Sunday morning. Life is short enough. Society was swarming with creepy phone addicts with curved necks and wired brains, and I was as guilty as anyone. Postapocalyptic was here and nobody heard the bang. The Kindle then, poetry. Every morning at breakfast. Just another screen to scroll. Yesterday was Robert Frost, today was Robert Hayden. "Those Winter Sundays." *What did I know / of love's austere and lonely offices?* Google Robert Hayden. He was a homely man, Robert Hayden, he with a homely face and goggly glasses, and from this homely, goggled man sprung a lasting ode to parental love. The world needs poetry. The world needs Vikings, too.

We listed the house in late February and dropped the asking price within weeks. I estimated the current market would have us waiting a good six months before we got a serious bite, maybe longer. The house has a look to it, you see, and it's not altogether pleasant. It's not a bad house by any standard. The size is decent, and it's located in a nice middle-class neighborhood. But what our mother built is in every respect a box. A squarely square. They both built the thing really, but it was her game from start to finish, Dad only wanted the key. He let her have her way with everything as long as she adhered to the budget. She behaved and gave us an anticlimactic rampage of right angles and equidistance fronted by a door and walkway as deadly centered as the crack of an ass.

"Oh, you designed this house yourself?" they asked at the Tupperware parties. "How wonderful." Mom was proud of her creation. She soaked in every compliment. But this was the early 1970s talking, and the early seventies I knew were a molded cheese with disco on the way. Mom relied on designers and builders with crooked moustaches and funky-fitting clothes, men whose every move seemed choreographed to the boogie sound. *Does anyone really know what time it is?* She relied most on the genius among them who'd decided the mansard roof hovering high and classic above nineteenth-century Paris would make a fine look wedged in a fifty-by-one-hundred rectangle in the grids of suburbia.

It didn't work. The domineering roof looks of a square peg hat pulled duncely below square eyes, its bridesmaid of red brick below. The house is at length devoid of charm; no woodsy grains to behold, no sweet-toffee browns, no flowy contours or sharply pointed gables. Never was it kissed by golden morning sunlight, nor its landscape dappled in sprightly spring blooms, or anything else from the dung heap of driveling prose a writer might summon to make more of something than it actually is. This house is dull. It is plain and it is characterless.

The innards, once hopeful, were equally doomed. Our packed holiday gatherings hummed and laughed within a dark pox of wood-looking panel, a coating indefensible in any place or age save a medieval dungeon. The carpets below, shag by name, conjured thoughts of a ratted urchin beast, a mongrel, and served as an able refuge for every mite and allergen known to science. Our sister grooved to the sounds of Leif Garrett and the family Gibb on a cake of royal blue while I, above fire-engine red, feasted my prepubescent eyes on walls hung in Farrah Fawcett and all her luscious pleasures. Our rooms were split by a hall cast in the green of the avocado flesh, a color that had Mom quite taken, for she splashed it about the master bath in motifs that resembled viral strains and microbes from biology lab. For our hall bathroom, we had yellow, inspired I presume by an Easter egg.

Mom roared through every swatch, every light fixture and every doorknob, each selection making its lone appearance in world history, never to repeat. We thought the look quite normal really, as normal as the yellow plaid couches and the rain lamp along the stairs. The lamp had little strings surrounding a statue of a half-naked Grecian woman trying to cover herself with a toga. Mineral oil rained down the strings in a weird, slow buzz. We had a dining set of round low-backed chairs Mom called "colonial." We heard this constantly, colonial this, colonial that. We dined high on corned beef and cabbage like we'd just marched in George Washington's fife and drum corps. She was a true patriot, our mother. She wept when the towers fell. Every time an account of Pearl Harbor came on television, she would grind "Those sneaky bastards" through her teeth.

We did it all with a smile in those days. Everybody did, the grandchildren that followed, aunts, uncles, friends. Everyone. People came over all the time. *This place is Grand Central station.* They thought the décor quite normal, too, as normal as we did. Mom remained ready to field any questions, as though others would be moved to duplicate the carnage in their own quarters.

The offer arrived early on an April morning. The numbers were in range, and it was a matter of time before the back-and-forth ended. The buyer was paying cash and set an ambitious closing date, leaving us less than three weeks to clear out all the furniture and accumulations of a sixty-five-year marriage. My sister sent a group text and we resolved to begin work the coming Saturday.

I rose early. My children were staying with me—my week, joint custody, all that. I made them wide bowls of Cream of Wheat with a side of thick-cut bacon, and cocktail glasses brimmed with freshly squeezed orange juice. *I have a sentimental weakness for my children and I spoil them, as you can see. The Godfather.* Everything is in *The Godfather.* Everything. I dropped them off with their plans and their practices and headed to the Southshore. My sisters and brother were there, hunched over photo albums and reliving sentimental nuggets of old. "Mark, do you want to keep this?" Some knickknack with a story behind it. No, I told them. I set to work in the coat closet. It has a secret panel door at the rear that leads to a storage space beneath the stairs. I went inside and began pulling out issues of *The Times-Picayune* from forty and fifty years past, all mint preserved in giant Ziploc bags. Mom's doing. They had not been opened or read. She hoarded shit like this. The space shuttle disaster, six copies. The assassination attempt on Ronald Reagan, four. Another four copies for the Pope's visit to New Orleans. Then one edition unremarkable, until I figured this was the last edition of the *Times-Picayune* before it merged with the *States-Item.* It became the *Times-Picayune States-Item.* That was important. Ten issues.

I started a trash pile in the driveway with the old newspapers at its base. I pulled out Hallmark ornaments. I pulled out Merry Miniatures. I pulled out scores of Beanie Babies. Collectibles, she used to say, they'd be worth something one day. How had the old man managed? I moved them to the area of the den designated for stuff someone might want. I found massive trivia and reference books, thick as fire logs, one on the golden age of Hollywood, another filled with mind-numbing data on every motion picture ever made. Mom relished the black-and-white films of yesteryear. Bogart, Bergman, Alan Ladd. She once saw Veronica Lake in the city and rode downtown with her in a streetcar. I uncovered stacks of Betamax videotapes labeled in neat print. *Casablanca, Gilda, To Have and Have Not—You know how to whistle, don't you, Steve?* She'd amassed a full library. I once committed the cardinal sin of recording a boxing match over the final credits of *The Blue Dahlia*. She never forgave me. Without those vital credits at the end, it was ruined, not worth watching. She insisted I write a compelling letter to Ted Turner himself, requesting that he run the movie again so she could restore her collection to its prior glory. Nobody plays Betamax tapes anymore. Nobody wanted them. To the driveway. By afternoon, the trash heap was piled five feet high.

"Mark, do you want Daddy's old fireman jacket with the captain stripes?" No, I said. I could hear my father's voice. *Throw that shit out.* I came across a collection of manila folders. They were thick and lumpy and smelled of yellowing paper. I opened one to find countless obituaries and clippings, the lives of local luminaries, parish priests, and former classmates departed. They had been cut out neat and straight with a pair of scissors. Another folder held prayer cards from funerals Mom had attended, loads of them, spanning decades. She was obsessed with death. She spent a lifetime obsessed with death. She had been dying for sixty years before she passed. Through her early life she harbored an unwavering conviction she would not witness life past thirty. She would be stricken with leukemia.

"Do you want Mom's blood pressure machine?" No, I said. She strapped herself to that thing countless times a day. And the notebook. We found it. She logged every blood pressure reading in the penmanship of a cinematic love note. Never would she be caught unprepared for the inevitable rush to the emergency room with a certain heart attack or stroke. She envisioned a team of doctors huddling around her notebook, absorbed in the great challenge of her condition and the vital information she provided. Medical exams, tests, diagnostics, these were riveting to her. Her arrival at the Ochsner clinic was like a kid arriving at Disney World. *Let's get a fast pass for a colonoscopy. CAT scan me, please, take my blood, give me a name, Doctor, something, anything, tell me something wrong with me. I will tell the world and you will etch your rightful place in the most prestigious journals to medical history. I told all you sons-of-bitches something was wrong.* Hiatal hernia. Nuclear stress test. Fibromyalgia. Everyone in the family knew the names. She had an eighth-grade education but could pronounce the most complex of medical terms with the elocution of a Harvard English professor.

"He doesn't want anything," my sister said. I uncovered collector magazines nobody was going to read, hundreds of old 45 records nobody was going to play. Gary Numan. "Cars." The label was water damaged, a reminder of the day we'd played it for hours until we heard the needle screech across the vinyl. Mom frisbeed it out the front door. It sailed in a high curling arc and landed across the street on a neighbor's lawn. It was quite a throw. We didn't know she had it in her. Old files petrified in their casings were pulled and tossed, worthless life insurance policies of a half century past, scores of them, yellowed, faded, and obsolete. She'd bought every policy available. The death obsession. Calamity. Remain vigilant. It comes for all of us and some of us young. I threw it all out, deafened to every hint of sentiment. *Don't give in to nostalgia.* Alfredo in *Cinema Paradiso.* Google Philippe Noiret. Long dead. Everyone was waxing it while I piled the junk heap high and wide. There was callous work to be done and opportunity at our feet. Someone, a subnormal apparently, wanted this box and would pay a nice coin for it. No chance would I imperil our good fortune on the wily trick of the past.

It was evening when we finished. My back and legs ached. My arms were gritty in the dust of a half century, my shirt soaked in a pool of gratifying sweat. I stood over the trash heap like a conqueror, pleased with myself, when all at once I was alive with a notion I hadn't considered before. There near the bottom, her golden age of cinema book, beneath her Betamax tapes, beneath the death files, beneath all the precious pastimes of her life reduced to ruins. These were the places she found comfort, I thought, the places she chased her unusual brand of happiness, and there was nowhere left in the world for any of them. And Dad's things—worn-out shoes, an old, dusty back brace, a strap he'd once used for his glasses, all useless. Everything looked lonely and empty and sad and there was nothing you could do.

We returned the evening before the closing, we the dozens, the generations, every soul spawned by these two very different people who didn't even have a photograph together from their honeymoon, only solo shots of one another on a chilly Biloxi beach. My sisters had the idea of a final sendoff, and everyone wanted a piece of it. Nobody had to explain. I brought my children along with a bottle of sambuca. The house was bare, empty of furniture, empty of everything. The walls were as naked as the day we'd moved in.

Room by room we roamed, first the kitchen, then the dining room. My children talked of freezie-pops and cookies and Mom's system for doling out treats. They remembered the jar of gummies and the old radio that hung from the cabinet and the toys they pulled from the closet nearby. Through the rear window I could see the stump of Dad's pecan tree. Hurricane Katrina had taken it down. He was proud of that tree, it was massive, grown from a single pecan he'd planted and nurtured himself. He would sit outside with his grandson's BB gun, waging endless battles with the squirrels. They robbed him of every pecan. I could see my friends and football games back there, once upon a time, the bumper pool matches beneath the carport, the places we buried our dogs. We walked through the foyer and up the stairs. This was Mom's photo studio. She had red photo albums shaped like rectangles. She filled them in perfect chronological order with a lifetime of images spanning decades. Opening day of Little League, ribbons from the playground, nights dressed up with friends all flashed before my eyes. Mom wouldn't let us leave until she had her pictures, ever in tune with the nostalgia the instant it was born. Years ago she'd given me a box of duplicates selected only for me, personalized for every step of my child- and young adulthood. She knew what the times meant. She knew what they meant to all of us. She was the most empathetic person I've ever known, possessed of a capacity to step into your experience and feel what you were going through.

Whatever my previous indifference, I could feel my parents in every room now, see them, she in her designated spot on the living room couch, equal distance from every wall, he, dozing in his recliner chair nearby. She, folding clothes like a boss in the master bedroom, her *Yankee Doodle Dandy* movie playing on TNT, he in his office behind the old adding machine, the paper roll spitting out numbers and figures of a week's business. I could feel the currents of so many parties, the heat of the crowded den, the movements and the bodies rubbing past. We'd go all day and into the evening, and finish with hours at the table playing back alley poker.

We went to my old bedroom. My roost. I had a built-in desk with cabinets and shelves, and a closet with louvered bifold doors. My room was on the second floor at the front corner of the house. It's the only bedroom near the street. I could still hear Dad's truck outside, his movements upon countless sunrises, the screech of the rickety driver's door, the chirrs and coughs of the engine as it rattled away into the sweat and the dirt and the distance. His life's work was his voice, and these were the sounds of the love and devotion that lived inside of it.

I found myself viewing the house with new eyes, and my parents, too. This was the place we breathed the daily fumes of family, the place they poured our foundation and assembled who we are. This was the place we formed our dreams and the place from which we set sail to find them. I said goodbye to my childhood within these walls, and all the things I do no more. I said goodbye to everyone I loved here, and this place welcomed me when I returned. From the kitchen to the couch to the foot of a bed, this mansard was home to everything I'd ever known growing up, to all those talks and every head poked in, and all the advice and understanding of a lifetime. They filled this home, our parents, filled it with the one word our father could never say. This was no mere box of right angles and squareness. What Mom and Dad built was a palace, and they never stopped, brick by brick laid in the unspoken poetry of the human heart.

We left through the side door and circled out front. We smiled for photographs on the porch, first the four of us, then crowded in with all our children, and the multiples that followed. Everyone knew. Scarcely a word was spoken. This was how we closed the chapter on them, so very suddenly it seemed, and what was left for us would live on in our memories and our stories.

I remember the ground beneath my feet as I walked away, how we pulled apart as though detaching from a vital organ. I didn't mind the feeling. It was good to sense life's stream taking me once more. The path had changed over the years, and seldom would my ways return me to this place that for so long had been all our own. This felt of an old-school goodbye, the kind you think of in the movies before cell phones and the web numbed us all and made us boring. The house looked majestic in the rearview mirror, the most distinguished on the block, and then it faded as a whisper beneath a sinking spring sun. ∎

CENTENNIAL PARK
William Crawford & Charlie Hahn

GETTING CLOSE TO VIVIAN MAIER

William Crawford & Charlie Hahn

CENTENNIAL PARK II
William Crawford & Charlie Hahn

THE LIFETIME MEMBER
Jack Norman

1

During all the middles of his long life, the often lonely Lionel Duck always felt as though he had *just now* emerged from the perfect timeline of his boyhood. He seemed to view the world as through the front window of his parents' Proserpine home, where everything stood a long way before him and a process of becoming was promised behind the focus of the glass pane (through which the lawn seemed greener in the soft tint, and relatives could materialize from somewhere much realer than the front room). If asked, he could still recall each Christmas, most birthdays, eventful barbecues, funerals, engagement parties, long stays with friends and family (and the reasons for), school excursions, extracurriculars, sport carnivals, rare trips to the beach, major and minor injuries, all the stories his father told, and the times he saw his mother cry—usually citing the year to go along with it (the month, and sometimes exact date, if given enough time to think). And although he had begun each morning of his late life with the same bedroom carpet he had chosen over thirty years ago (that was by now so worn by the simple fact of his repeat bare feet), or with the smell of wet dirt from the garden beneath his kitchen window as the soft mists sprayed on cue, none of it had ever seemed as real to him as the old suburban eucalypts that used to hang across his mother's garden hedge and whisper dryly in the breeze (to the white curtains of his parents' en suite bathroom) . . . for Lionel Duck, life seemed to travel forever through the long columns of sugar cane paddocks and cricket dugout tunnels he had known as a boy, and resume again in the moment he had finally arrived (and again in the next, and the next).

Only a short time after Lionel had received his initial diagnosis, he found himself surrounded by his immediate family, and he wished more than anything that they would all go away. His wife, Eliza, had nearly emptied the linen cupboard when preparing the spare rooms and she had shifted him from his room into hers so that they had to share a bed again for the first time in over ten years (where he felt compelled to hold on to his farts, as he had in their earliest months together). For what felt like the very last time, his whole family was under the same roof again (and the number of grandchildren had only multiplied in the years since anyone had visited regularly). His children had all come a long way from up and down the coast to make sure they each had the opportunity to say goodbye—without ever actually saying *goodbye* in so many words. Instead, they made safe conversation with him over the television and let the children run amok in the backyard and scatter his garden rakes and kick the football over the fence and make the homey sort of ruckus that young parents have become used to and arrogantly assume anybody else will want to hear.

Under strict observation, Lionel attempted his usual routine of waking early in the morning and starting on his first beer of the day, watching the races from his chair and craning his neck to the see the mounted television, enjoying cool afternoons alone on the patio and listening to the sound of the trees in the wind (which he had never tired of hearing or seeing written about in print again and again over seventy years).

Eliza, with her renewed license to nag, stressed openly and righteously about his drinking habits and recruited the grandchildren to her cause in a festive sort of spirit and had them set upon him whenever they heard the crack of a carbonated can.

His youngest son, Michael, was fixated on the poorly installed television and continued to insist that Lionel allow him to readjust the wall mount to a more suitable angle.

"It'll only be ten minutes, Dad," he said.

His oldest son, Douglas, could not seem to bear the sight of him alone in the afternoons (though it had never been a problem in the past) and he often came out to join him at the glass table and belabor the same topics of conversation they had shared for the last twenty years (and report later to anyone who would listen that his father seemed very distracted and was probably reflecting on the course of his life and dwelling an awful lot on death).

Lionel had begun to wonder if visiting family—in any household, at any point in time—had ever been anything other than a tolerated, stationary presence in the living room that had to be checked on now and again, asked if it was hungry, forgiven for any of its faux pas, arranged together after lunches and photographed for later.

Early on Saturday morning, after he finished inspecting the rainwater gauge, Lionel found his wife and daughters-in-law at the dining table, where they announced their plans to have a family dinner that night at the cricket club (the reservation had already been made).

"Well what about all the children?" he asked.

"What about them?"

"I don't know if they'll be able to take so many in the restaurant."

"I already told them about the children, they said it was fine."

"Well I just hope they don't go running around all night."

"They'll be on their best behavior; they know not to carry on down there."

A nice goodbye dinner, Lionel thought, something they could take home with them and remember they'd attended whenever they started to feel as though they could have done more in those last few months. People liked to pretend they felt guilty about things. Even his own mother had often said in that singsong, regretful tone she could affect (sat at their old table; tacky marble pattern chipped away) how much she wished they had visited her brother before he died . . . but her brother had only lived in Kuttabul, an hour down the way, and Lionel knew that the reason they had not gone to see him was because he told long, resentful stories and his kitchen floor was made of concrete and he only served bore water from the tap that whined loudly, and they had all preferred that he die through the telephone without a fuss (and he did).

It occurred to Lionel that that was how his father would experience his death as well. Lionel had called him on the same afternoon of his diagnosis to tell him the news before anyone else (Eliza not included). He remembered the call very well, as he did most calls with his father—visually—seeing the old man reclined his chair, startled by the sudden ring, slapping his thighs and fumbling across his pockets for some reason, finally finding the phone on the small table beside him (draped with a crocheted tablecloth; touch lamp with the finger-stained shade, stacked magazines, small silver case that once held something important). "Hello?" he always asked into the phone, never convinced there would be another voice on the other end . . . and he rarely managed to say much more. The old man had already made a dozen of the same calls himself, concerning himself, his own parents, and Lionel's late mother; they both knew that the real impact of bad news took days or weeks to feel (if there was to be anything at all). So, his father padded the conversation with questions about the doctor, the hospital, the procedure itself, and how Eliza was handling the news. It was otherwise a very ordinary conversation, except that he called Lionel *son* and wished him all the best and said that he would pass the news on to his sister that afternoon.

In the face of Eliza and his daughters-in-law, standing next to his reflection in the television screen (which now hung several inches lower on the wall), Lionel wished that his father could attend the night's dinner and felt sad that there was never enough room in a person's life for two immediate families.

The dinner was scheduled for later than Lionel expected and at six o'clock the children were still being dressed by their mothers. When he found himself alone with his two sons, he almost complained about it being such a big deal to everyone that he come along . . . but he could see by the way everyone was dressed in their best clothes (had packed them in their suitcase) that this was the reason behind their visit—something planned for the weekend, which no doubt included some element of surprise or ceremony (his sons had been speaking to each other in unusually cryptic phrases all afternoon), and he did not want to appear (or actually *be*) ungrateful.

"Are you all right, Dad?"

"Yeah, mate. I'm all right."

"We'll be going shortly."

"It's no rush, don't worry."

2

In the entry foyer of the Mason Park Cricket Club, an old woman with dyed red hair sat stoutly behind her front desk. Her name was Maxine. She was one of the establishment's most senior employees and an old friend of Lionel's. He used to occupy the small accounting office behind her workstation. There was a time when she had captured Lionel's imagination in a very safe and attainable way (particularly when she wore certain outfits he was fond of), but that was before she had gained her final bit of weight and cut her hair brutally short to match it. Now, and for the better part of their relationship, she was trusty old Max, smiling behind the desk, greeting his son Douglas (as an old friend, as well) and having them all sign their names in the guest book or scan their membership cards on the glass panel with the green glow.

As always, Lionel and Max exchanged a few familiar words with each other before he walked slowly along the curved desk. He paused at the far end to allow her to finish what she was saying and punctuated their conversation with a small joke at her expense (the gist of it being *I'm retired and you're not*). He followed his family around the corner.

The cricket club (which, in truth, called itself a country club) was a large, well air-conditioned establishment that mostly gravitated towards the bar in the center of its open plan (built like a large circle that all around encompassed all parts pub, café, and poker machine room in a gradient sort of fashion). It was very unusual for Lionel or either of his sons to spend any time at the club without running into someone they knew, and as a kind of courtesy to anyone this chance may have pertained to, it was customary for the family to drift around the bar and the general family area for a short time before sitting properly down to dinner. The bulk of the family filtered out onto the deck and ordered soft drinks to occupy the children, while Lionel and his sons sat in the middle thoroughfare of the bar area at a large, round table and nursed their beers slowly. Their postures seemed more alike now (and certainly their fleshy chins, which compressed against their chests the more they relaxed into their stools). For Lionel, Douglas, and Michael, that world seemed to have lost some of its significance. Time and distance worked against it in the way that they sometimes do, but for the old friends (and their fathers) whose hands came to rest on the edge of the table, there was still a great deal of concern about that cricketing community they used to share. Lionel made a habit of agreeing with anything they said by staring vaguely across the table, nodding and grunting, watching the condensation from all their glasses soak into the cardboard coasters that advertised a commercial painter around the local region. They spoke about old players (who were now officials and lifetime members), young and promising talent (usually related to friends and teammates), old grievances (with club managers, selectors, umpires, friends' wives), new business, new venues, state cricket, international cricket, and the deteriorating mental health of Eliza, whom Lionel placed the blame upon squarely for not knowing when to let go, how to apologize, how to pick her battles, or when to keep her nose out of other people's business (and they were soon left alone).

The club that Lionel had known seemed to be buried beneath all the different phases of renovation and forgotten at some point during a changing of the guard (there had been several, in fact). He wasn't sure there was anything left of himself at Mason Park and he began to wish they had chosen to dine anywhere else that evening. The young men he had once called *my boy* had all aged slowly and fatly and they lingered on like fleshy ghosts . . . he did not have time for them anymore and wanted only to recognize them through the front glass that still displayed field number one to the main room, where he had sat so often and watched them play. They used to wear grass-stained cricket whites and stand beneath a healthier sun; long, shaggy hairdos, innocent love for the game they played; the kind of boys he remembered being (the fastest runner in his year, who married the neighbor girl on the back step and coaxed her into his father's shed) . . . *Please! I want to go back!*

"Granddad!" she said from behind his arm.

"What's that, my girl?"

"We're sitting down now; do you want to come?"

"Righto. I'll be right behind you."

He followed her into the main dining area behind the trail of grandchildren and daughters-in-law. It would be nice if they sat him with the children. He watched them cross the floor at a brisk pace and they did not seem concerned with him as he began to fall behind. At the far end of the room, his son's wife opened the door to the function area, and it opened wide on a number of faces he was not surprised to recognize. He saw his old club manager, Gregory Fox, emerge from behind the door and shake hands with Eliza. When he turned to his son Michael, who followed a few steps behind him, he only ignored his questions and patted his father on the shoulder and encouraged him along the rest of the way.

"Good to see you, Lionel," said Gregory.

"You too, mate. What are you doing here?"

"Why don't you come in and see?"

The magnanimous smile on Gregory's face went a long way in agitating him. He looked to his son Michael for anything he could tell him but felt as though he was playing a character in doing so, he knew more than anyone else that he was not such a clueless old man yet. He passed Gregory through the door and feigned the right level of surprise when his grandchildren screamed the word at him in a practiced little routine (the best part of his good nature he still reserved for them).

3

Having heard the news about his health, the Mason Park Cricket Club had arranged with Eliza to make Lionel a lifetime member of the club. There would be no family dinner. It was, instead, a surprise function to commemorate him for an evening and officially welcome him into the small handful of lifetime members while they were all present. As Lionel collected his thoughts, friends and family hovered in his line of sight and asked him the usual questions about whether he had suspected anything and if he was feeling okay (seeming to hope that he might break down into tears and vindicate all their well-intended efforts). He told them he was fine and said that he only needed a few moments to take everything in and he stood quietly in changing circles of friends as they all enjoyed themselves and experienced the positive charge of a night out the gate and well on its way.

The room included four large tables that were furnished with rich cloth and sparkling glass. A guest list had been written in cursive font by the entrance and he saw that at least thirty people were expected to attend. At the head of the room, a modest stage took itself quite seriously, and a projector mounted on the ceiling displayed a slideshow of his life; he recognized the images as the same moments he kept in his memory.

Lionel was shown to his seat at the front center of the room, directly below the lectern, where he would be forced to make eye contact with each speaker. He sat at the table with Eliza and the rest of his peers (those lifetime members whose induction had not been subject to a terminal status), while the rest of his family settled in by the entrance and already the children played behind the large curtains along the glass wall. He felt trapped by the old faces that stared at him across the table; all in perfect health, smug expressions that pretended they had anything to do with it. Their eyes seemed to search his for something they recognized and he found himself quite able to stare back at them without any obligation to explain himself. They still longed to find the meaning in things, just as Lionel had, but he knew now that it would elude them all forever (a year at most for him). The images on the projector screen showed him as a boy, a young man, a father, and a grandfather (though not in any order) . . . his history had already been written and it carried him into each moment that followed the next, it was comforting to realize that it could only have led him here. The unwilling inductee. A lifetime member for a little while. When had it ever been in his hands? When had the young boy (who he still felt he was, more than any version of himself that appeared on the wall) who used to bolt through the cane paddocks and grow dizzy from the thick smell of the sugar mill ever decided that this was to be his lot in life? For Lionel Duck, life seemed to resume again from the dream of a life he had lived. There was nothing left for him to want.

Once they had all been seated, Gregory Fox took the stage and introduced the evening. He spoke almost directly to Lionel's table about the important figures of the club's history. The story had much less to do with Lionel than his family would have realized, especially told by one such as Greg. He could have warned them if they had let him know. The images on the projector screen began to concern the club in its earliest phases: long-dead cricket teams in black and white, faces of old administrators, certificates scanned and faded and of significance to no one. Solemn faces in the dark were lit by the projector's glow. Eliza's glasses reflected one of the first images of that plot of land that had been donated to the Mackay Cricket Association. He reached out and squeezed her wrist and it made him sad to see how surprised she was. He had not loved her enough. She patted his hand rather briskly and almost seemed to brush him off, but he knew it was only because she embarrassed easily.

After a small applause, Gregory invited Lionel's oldest son, Douglas, to the stage. Behind the lectern, Douglas unfolded several scraps of notebook paper on which Lionel could see he had written in lead pencil. Privately, Douglas had expressed his wish not to eulogize his father in front of him . . . but he began to cry as soon as he began to speak, and Lionel felt it difficult not to look away. His friends smiled sadly at him. The room sat patiently as Douglas regained his composure (which did not take as long as it seemed to) and after an awkward phrase or two, he began to speak very well. He spoke highly of Lionel, and he even called him his *father*, which could often be forgotten given the way they had worked together for so long and run so independently in the same circles and made enemies of each other's friends and friends of each other's enemies. Eliza began to cry quite openly. It was clear she felt that she could— whatever nausea Gregory had left on stage was being swept away by Douglas's sincerity and suddenly the room belonged to the Ducks. As he watched the cavalcade of anecdote and memory that Douglas led across the room, he remembered that his son had always been an excellent orator and he was ashamed that he had not had more faith in him (the countless functions and team events, thanks-for-coming speeches, the surprise birthday party they had held for Eliza just a few years ago). For all the time he had wasted living in the vivid memory of Proserpine and in his boyhood dream, he had not wasted nearly enough on the other lives he had lived, and it required a tremendous effort on his part not to collapse beneath the painted scenes that Douglas spoke of and coaxed now all together from the back of his mind (street carnival in Clermont, toy trucks assembled on the shag carpet, cyclone in Townsville, late-night birth of Douglas's youngest daughter).

The present rarely felt as real to him as it did then. He watched Douglas step carefully down the stairs and felt it wash over him as the audience gave him a fine applause. Douglas sat back in his chair and the hands of his family slid across his back and he breathed a visible sigh of relief. The applause faded gently, it left a ringing in Lionel's ears and a distinct vacuum of silence only a minute later. For all its imagined significance, the moment had been committed to the past already. A feeling of pride lingered for his son and just as he resolved to hold on to it for as long as he could, he was disturbed by the fact that it would slip away at its own pace whether he had noticed it or not. The illusion of Lionel Duck was fading with each moment . . . insight and fatigue worked hand in hand. He had no reason left to want.

After a few more speeches (friends mostly, one acquaintance), the room stood down from ceremony and ate a messy dinner and got up and down for drinks and swapped tables and entertained the fancy of the children. Lionel had been asked to say a few words in closing (but everyone would understand if he did not feel up to it and by no means should he speak longer than he felt he could manage), so he thanked everyone for coming and commented on the honor it was and he made special mention of the friends who had not made it this far along the way. By all accounts, the evening was a complete success and should not have been considered a *sendoff* for Lionel in any way. He kissed Eliza on the mouth for everyone to see (and the crowd went *Aww!*) because he knew that it was the type of thing husbands were supposed to do in public, and because she certainly deserved it for one reason or another for something he had definitely forgotten at some point in time. He shook his sons' hands firmly and looked them both in the eye and said to each of them: "You're a good boy."

A little after nine o'clock Lionel began to feel very tired and he struggled to breathe without concentrating. Without having to make a fuss, Eliza appeared by his side and asked if he wanted to leave. He did. It was time to go home. She made an effort to hunt for her sons and for anyone who really mattered to make sure they had the chance to say goodbye, but he knew they would all be off by the bar and involved in things that didn't concern him anymore. There was a long way to go in the night, and for some, there was still much to be done and much to be said. He didn't mind. They had three hours left in them at most, four maybe (if things got carried away). Tomorrow would wipe the slate clean for them and himself alike. He was not afraid of missing out anymore. He was not afraid of leaving them all behind.

"It's all right, let's just go," he said.

On the drive home, Lionel felt sore and empty in the muscles of his back. Exhausted, he anticipated climbing into bed and even began to nod off a little in the passenger seat of the car. He was good at sleeping, he liked to watch it approach in each of its small stages. The mind starts to wander, lucidly at first. A tide laps at the sand and climbs the shore inch by inch. Reds become blacker. Greens much stranger. There are voices, images stirred in thick mud. Where is the difference between imagination and memory? Is there a difference between sleep and death? He had the sudden feeling there was not, and he began to dream of his boyhood home and the eucalypts he could never climb and the smell of his pillowcase after his mother had treated it with mothballs. ∎

SNAKES
Susan Shepherd

M ia hung herself in her closet with a shirt.
This is the first for these girls, three friends home
from college. Within the year Vivian's sister will overdose
on heroin. In four years Elly's uncle will fatally crash a motorcycle.
Fifteen years later Naomi's father will die of a heart attack. Now they
move silently through rooms, speaking softly, or laughing or crying,
alone, stunned, bereft, disbelieving.

They are particularly soft with Elly, who was Mia's nearly sister
since kindergarten, when they'd sensed each other's kindness to the
point of skinlessness, like octopuses, tactile everywhere. Neither had
a sibling, so they clung to each other through the years, with a short
hiatus in middle school when another girl managed to pry them
apart.

Mia's mother, beyond grief, had told the girls to take all of Mia's
clothes out of the house. The girls obeyed, hauled piles to Vivian's
car. This afternoon will be the funeral and they sit in Elly's room
with bags half emptied, stuff strewn maniacally, haphazardly from
the closet to the bed. In silent communion they all simply understand
they will wear Mia's dresses.

They have been up all night. Vivian, gaminesque, sits on Elly's
bed, one long leg tucked under her, a dancer with perfect posture.
Her hair hangs in ropes down her chest. Her face is covered with
freckles. She's perpetually stoned and perpetually amused, with
none of the anxiety that riddles the others. She holds a red dress up
to her chest. Are these girls, best friends since forever, pretending
today is Mia's wedding and they're dressing to stand beside her as
bridesmaids? Is this another thing they do without words as they pick
through the piles and hold one or another dress up to test for fit, for
formality, for Mia's reaction, which they will no longer ever see?

And what is Elly doing? She lies on top of a pile of clothes
holding a shirt over her face, breathing in Mia's scent like a girl lying
under a tree that rains cherry blossoms. Her blond hair blooms out
the sides like a fan, her skinny legs, her large feet clenched.

Mia hung herself in her closet with a blue long-sleeved shirt.

Elly's stepfather calls. "I left the snakes in your closet." No *hello, how you doing.* "Can you girls put them back in the aquarium?" He'd separated the snakes into individual boxes to feed them and in his haste to pack forgot. Why he chose Elly's closet, no one knows. Elly closes her eyes and breathes. He and her mom are at the airport waiting to board a plane. They won't be at the funeral. A trip to France booked eons ago that Elly refused to let them cancel. She told them she'd be fine. She starts to laugh, holds the phone out, announces the snake problem. The closet door has been open for a long time. Naomi looks at her silently. Vivian nods.

"Okay," Elly breathes into the phone. "We'll do the best we can."

The three snakes, which eat one mouse each per month and swallow them whole, have gotten loose. Now they're hiding in sleeves of clothes, or boots, or coiled in pockets, a bulge of mouse midway. From the darkness the creatures listen without ears to the sounds of the girls rustling in the room, sensing their beating hearts.

Naomi's phone rings. Her voice gets tense and she leaves the room arguing. The never-ending fight with her mother starts again like a sound wave that's always there, rising and falling. Naomi grew up in a mansion, was made to change immediately on entering the house, to wear her inside-only clothes. Her mother had borne four extra children when the oldest brother had been diagnosed with leukemia, so he would be sure to have a bone marrow match if the cancer returned. Each child has a one-out-of-four chance to match. The children all know they are fodder for their brother's blood cells. It is part of family lore. Naomi holds the phone to her ear with her shoulder, pushing her glossy hair out of her mouselike face with an aggravated flick.

The girls don't want their mothers now.

Vivian puts on the red dress to catch the snakes. It's too big for her around the waist, so she goes in search of Elly's mom's sewing machine. She'd grown up making her own dance costumes since the dresses cost a fortune at the local boutique, and her mother's teacher salary didn't cover such things. She hauls the sewing machine into Elly's room and clears a space on top of the vanity. Expertly she winds a bobbin that blooms in fast motion into a pop of red. Threading the needle. Zip zip up one side and zip zip down the other, the sewing machine's motor racing with rapid thumps.

Naomi brings the oven mitts from the kitchen. Vivian doesn't think she wants to touch the snakes with her bare hands. The stepdad said they don't bite but she doesn't know if she believes him. He's from Kenya. As a kid he dug a snake pit in the "garden," as he calls it. In America it's a yard. And in Kenya the back of the house is called the front so there are always confusing conversations about things like Easter egg hunts ("There are more hidden in the front," he told Elly and Mia when they were six, and they searched fruitlessly on the wrong side of the house). Also, he was decidedly not part of an albino family from Kenya, which was what a kid whispered to Elly once after meeting him. No, she told the kid, amused, there are actual white people in Africa.

Elly has gone to Kenya with her parents many times, and once they took Mia, who fell in love with a young giraffe and stayed moon-eyed for weeks. They were camping on a river and woke up to take an early morning walk through the bush. Rounding a corner they startled a herd of giraffe. A juvenile, delicate in spite of its height, stopped following the herd, stopped to stare at Mia as the rest loped off in what looked like slow motion. Both animal kids stopped and gazed at each other. The stepdad, Mom, and Elly walked on before turning around to this strange sight. Mia, nine years old, her black hair in pigtails, a purple kikoy tied around her waist, face-to-face with the giraffe.

Naomi hands Vivian the oven mitts, looking concerned. Naomi nearly always walks with her head down, a constant frown, displeased or worried. When she lets out a rare laugh, everyone looks at her like they've forgotten that's something she can do. But she's the mother hen to them. Practical. Straightforward. Now she opens the closet door slowly, afraid of what she might find, and she and Vivian go in for the hunt.

Elly will speak at the funeral. As she lies on the floor with Mia's shirt covering her face, words rain down. Her mother used to tell her that they had to do one hard thing every day. Elly thinks, *The hardest thing I've ever done.* For many years Mia couldn't walk into a classroom alone. Only Elly knew this, and one or the other of them would wait to go in together. Finally they convinced their parents to carpool so neither girl would have to stand outside the door.

When Elly was summoned to the police station for questioning about Mia's death, she told her mom that she would allow her to come, but there were rules. No talking. Walk behind me. Elly would do this alone. In the elevator up to the detective's office they were silent. If her mother had been allowed to speak, she would have told her daughter not to do this. The detective was gruff but kind, pressed about the death. Why would Mia do it? Elly's thoughts whir, a cyclone—because they all had left her? But she couldn't fathom it was something Mia could do. She was drunk, yes, and fighting with her boyfriend. But Mia wouldn't leave them. The whirring in Elly's brain concealed meaning. She spoke to the detective quietly, evenly. Told the story as she knew it. Hoped he'd find the truth. In the elevator down, Elly leaned against the wall and sunk to the ground—wailed like she had only once before—the moment she was born.

Elly knew bad things could happen. Her stepfather had shown the girls before. It's why the snakes were in separate boxes in the closet. Two snakes can want the same mouse, can consume one half of the same mouse into each mouth, and can come to a standoff. Possibly, the stepfather told them when he brought them in to see, both snakes will grip that mouse until it rots and falls apart. This sounds like a terrible thing for a stepfather to show, but they were delighted at the time. It was third grade, and the girls understood both wanting something that much, not being able to let go of it, and the strange bravery in that. It felt almost biblical, and they'd taken to saying to each other, when they wanted the same toy, or food, or dress, or boy, "This is *my* mouse!" and bursting into peals of laughter.

Mia hung herself in her closet, wrapped a blue shirt around her neck, and didn't make a sound.

In high school the girls most often slept at Vivian's, because Vivian's mother took a sleeping pill every night. Elly's mother heard everything and woke at the smallest sound. Naomi's mother was erratic, sometimes stayed up all night or got up at the crack of dawn. Mia's mother was the kindest mother, so no one wanted to deceive her. The sleeping pill allowed them access to the night. These girls, all girls, are happiest and freest at night, like vampires, like bats, like owls, like mink. It's when they come alive. Breaking out into the night, they sang and danced and screamed. It was their best time. They piled into cars. They went into parent-free houses. They purchased fries at McDonald's drive-throughs. They smoked joints. They kissed boys. They didn't feel the heat or the cold. Even self-conscious Elly danced a few steps at night.

The girls, in Elly's room now filled with Mia's things, ask each other this: was Mia ever mean? For a while they can find nothing. No hidden daggers. No half memory of a hurt. Vivian stands in the doorway of the closet. "Once she told me my ass was too flat." She's picking up shoes, one at a time. She knows the snakes are too big to be hidden there. Is there a way to call a snake?

Naomi stands behind her peering over her shoulder. "No, *I* told you that." And, "Look under there," she demands. Vivian lifts the pile of clothes and a pink snake looks up at them. They don't move.

The snake disappears. They watch the last of its tail. "One time, she dragged me to the bathroom because her shit was in the shape of a question mark."

From under the shirt on the floor, Elly says, "Evil."

"Evil," Vivian repeats, nodding. "She knew you would never get that sight out of your mind."

Elly takes the shirt off her face and gets up from the floor. She sorts through piles of clothes, picturing Mia in every one, while listening to the bumps and screams from the closet. She finds some of her own clothes here, things she's lent Mia over the years and forgotten about. For Mia's sixteenth, her mom and dad took the girls out to a fancy dinner. The four girls shopped for dresses together. Elly finds Mia's dress now. She'd wanted it for herself. It was the best dress they'd found. But it was Mia's birthday so she got the best. This is what she will wear. Until Naomi sees it and reaches out. "I want that one." Elly pulls it close and twists sideways, putting her body between the dress and her friend. "My mouse," Elly says.

In Kenya Elly and Mia slept together in a tent. Beyond the green undulating ceiling illuminated by their small flashlight, the night was wild with hidden creatures talking. They curled head to head and knee to knee. The air was smoke and earth. In the morning they were woken before light. The Maasai had spotted a den of rare aardwolf, so they piled into the Land Rover and rushed off to find them, the stepdad expert at driving in the red dust, mowing over bushes that popped up behind them unharmed, like inflatable punching clowns. They arrived at the spot and tiptoed slowly from the car, the stepdad going first, moving silently, as he had learned to do his whole life. The aardwolf babies poked their heads out of their nest in the ground, while their parents were out finding termites. They looked like puppies, like baby raccoons. They darted out, checked out the foursome, darted back in. More assured with time, they came out together to see the world without their parents, to stare at the people who were staring at them.

The two girls stayed awake each night amazed. Once they heard a lion roar, but it was far in the distance. Once the sound of a large animal moving slowly through the camp, munching branches loudly near them. In the mornings the stepdad pointed out signs of life. Leopard tracks. Elephant dung. The dainty imprints of the tiny dik-dik that huddled near the camp for protection. During the day they went on walks, passing Maasai boys their age tending herds of goat. When it got hot they took a dip in a cow trough, which was fed from a well. The Maasai herding boys came to watch. The stepdad spoke to them in a strange language and the boys giggled, one hand on a hip, the other holding a stick, their lean legs bare, coated in the red-brown dust of Kenya. Their bodies made geometric shapes. All angles jutting out, bent knee, foot on leg, Pythagorean triangles. The stepdad told the girls, "These boys can't fathom why we are all sitting in the cows' drinking trough." This sent the girls into fits of laughter. The boys into fits of laughter. The girls could only imagine this kind of freedom for a fleeting second as they laughed. The boys could only imagine sitting in a cow trough for a fleeting second as they laughed. Nothing was scary to Mia and Elly in Kenya; back home nearly everything was.

Elly pulls on the dress. They are the same height. They traded clothes like cards. Each night this week Elly has dreamed of Mia un-lost, coming home.

The funeral will be held at the old stone building in the cemetery where Elly's mom used to take them to ride their bikes. They'd zoom around looking at graves, the names, the dates, imagine the lives of kids and grandmothers, look at the family tombs, some big enough to walk into. The cemetery has a pond with a pair of white swans and a willow weeping on the bank. Elly's mom would walk while the girls careened up and down hills, dropping bikes on green grass. The dead: McKenzie, Payne, Harlow, Wilson, Nelligan, on and on and on, lined up, peaceful, green, serene. A place for bikes and walks and bird-watching. Four girls giggling. One mother reprimanding. Tuna sandwiches. Apple juice. Mia's purple bike with white streamers shooting from the ends of handlebars. They passed the imposing stone building so many times, never noticing.

Throughout the night of Mia's death, the two girls were texting. Mia drunk and upset because she'd kissed a guy at a party and then told her boyfriend, or perhaps was caught by him, and they were fighting. Or he was upset. Elly typed—*Come here, climb into bed with me. We can snuggle and everything will be okay.* But Mia couldn't leave. She'd hurt him and that would make it worse. So Elly said she'd go there, just say the word. But, no. Mia said no, *It's okay, I'm okay, stay in bed.* These texts flew back and forth on text wings until 3:00 a.m., when Elly finally fell asleep, her phone clutched in her hand. When she woke in the morning, the last text from Mia—*Help.*

The closet door is closed, the snakes inside, still sensing the girls' breath. The friends are dressed in Mia's clothes. Red, blue, yellow dresses. Primary colors. They stand in a line looking at the closet door. Inside the darkness the snakes are quiet, happy, warm. It's time to go. The funeral is starting soon. Elly is strangely calm, will speak for them all.

The night before high school graduation they'd piled into Naomi's car and driven to Gloucester. The moon was full, the air warm, the windows down. Alanis screamed on the radio and they sang at the top of their lungs: *You oughta know . . . of the mess you left when you went away . . .* Their hair whipped out of windows, schnapps was passed. What God has joined together, let no man put asunder. At the beach they piled out of the car and ran onto the sand barefoot. Naomi had brought a fake log, which they lit and danced around, sang and screamed and put their feet in the cold water. Splashed each other. Tossed sand into the wind. Fell beside the fire and longed for and feared their lives apart. Mia's head on Elly's stomach, Vivian's feet on Naomi's legs, Naomi's head on Mia's chest, they lay like that for hours. They passed the bottle. The fire warmed them. This would be their last summer. Vivian would be off to UMass, Naomi to UT, Elly to George Washington.

The three leaving girls didn't talk about what was ahead. Mia staying behind. Going away to school wasn't something she wanted. She would start a few classes at community college, and work, and live at home. Elly wondered: If they were going to the same school, would Mia want to go too? If they could walk into stranger-filled classrooms holding hands? Put on makeup, and share clothes, and pick each other up and set each other down, and, and, and, and?

On the way home they drove past the elementary school. In a unanimous unspoken decision, they pulled over and piled out of the car and ran for the swings, the slides, the climbing structure. The sun was rising and it alighted on the girls—they shimmered in undulating waves. No one was tired. They ran like crazies. Climbed the structure Elly had fallen off, third grade, broken her little nose. Mia holding her hand, as teachers ran. So much blood! Atop that structure, they relived all the fights, all the games, all the laughing, all the sobbing, jealousies, wishes, furies, hurts, kindnesses. They ran around absorbing and emitting all of this time, through all of the years.

Mia hung herself in the closet, wrapped a blue shirt around her neck and didn't make a sound; no one knew for half a day.

The azaleas are in bloom. The stone building is surrounded by deep pink, which makes it more solid and silent. The girls arrive together, their bright party dresses bobbing among the dark suits. The early June sky is bracingly blue. There is not a stir of wind. They stop at the door. A look travels from girl to girl. Then Vivian nods. They go into the building, the stone holding the chill like fists.

Elly stands before a silent crowd, Mia laid out in a box behind her. Naomi and Vivian sit in front, faces impassive. Elly's voice echoes in the stone room. Her eulogy covers: Elementary school. One beloved teacher fought over by all. Jump ropes and sword fights and hopscotch and princess dresses. Stuffed animals for way too long. Running away around the block. Every possible allowed sleepover. Middle school: Flurries of hair spray, blow-dryers, too much concealer, shouting, dance recitals, fencing, stacks of chocolate chip pancakes, scary movies. Benny liked both Mia and Elly and that caused a fight. Neither girl even really liked him, but his house was big with a swimming pool. High school English class: Mia copying Elly's exam about the plague but reading it wrong and writing, "all of the townspeople developed oils." High school math class: Mr. Woo begging Elly to coax Mia up off the floor where she lay, stubbornly refusing to do her equations.

Mr. Woo is here now. He hears his name and leans forward. These girls were with him two years in a row. He loves them. They make no sense to him. What he wanted in those days was to lie on the floor beside them, refusing. To Mr. Woo the four girls are one organism that communicates instantly when separated. Un-split-apart-able. Einstein's spooky actions at a distance. Entangled particles. They were hilarious. They all did well in math but didn't put in any effort—only Mia had trouble. But they carried her along and acted like they were home in their living rooms. They made teaching math fun.

Elly knows this: they felt more than they will ever feel. This was how they operated. Every day. Every hour. Every second. In the closet the snakes sleep, coiled tightly, waiting for the rustle of clothes, the murmur of voices, the beating of hearts. When the girls return, Vivian stands at the open closet door. Elly and Naomi lie on the floor. They've agreed without words to leave the snakes alone. Vivian pulls the chain, snapping off the closet light, and closes the door on them. This is how it ends. This is how the rest begins. ■

GOING BACK TO WHERE I'M FROM
Dipika Mukherjee

is to return to women who are goddesses,
incense smoke, and drumbeats & women
who bury infant girls in the ground, into
milk vats to drink until they drown;

to many-armed goddesses who slay
demons, and darkness, and scarcity
of thought & women who are womb
and vagina, never brain or mouth;

to stargazers who send probes to Mars,
mathematicians of cosmic poetry & women
raped in temples, strung from trees,
disemboweled in a dark-tinted moving bus;

to Bengal and Indus Valley and Chittaranjan Park
& Texas and Ohio and State Street in Chicago;

to meals beginning with bitter gourd and ending
in milky sweets & sweet-water fish, and mountain
goat, and homemade cheese strained through muslin
so fine it passes through a child's golden ring.

The mind travels as a flume,
belonging here, rooting nowhere;

the hunger for roads packed with parched
red earth; July, the monsoon cool of runny
streets, clouds paused for the miracle
of light on water, the sky's tandav;

rains feel amniotic as the nomad
breaststrokes through alien streets
for electric air, even as a belligerent
hunger pushes the boat away from shore;

I am more than a dress or a sari,
more than henna and bindi & more
than skin scabbed with regrowth.

                                  Still so far to travel,
                                     higher to climb,
                                so much to uncage.

BENIGN NEGLIGENCE
Dipika Mukherjee

My parenting style is benign
negligence; plotting books,
poetry, busy at the stove,
half-listening to talk
of soccer goals or how
the senate council will
make money this year.
I know too well those
other times—when home
is the only place to melt
from cool, the tantrums,
the door-slams—
yearning to be free.

Then, he leaves. I remember
light in his eyes when words
tripped almost incoherent.
I see in the child the man
he is becoming; I see him
so rarely now. That toddler
who stretched out expansive
arms all the way back
to show how much he loved
now uses that gesture on video
to silently say, *I miss you.*

Childbirth doesn't prepare
you for this. I am an owl
touched by the light—
yearning for the moon.

HOW TO IDENTIFY A PIGNUT
Ann Voorhees Baker

I t was a good thing Joette was alone, because what happened to her would have scared the holy spirit out of people.

From her armchair she landed on a YouTube video called "How to Identify a Pignut," and when she found herself, as if from above, looking down at a pair of tan leather boots standing amid the green undergrowth of a forest outside Belfast, an all-consuming desire came over her to *be* there. The yearning ached in her chest, and then it suddenly pulsed through her entire body, so forcibly that there was a roar followed by a long *whoosh*, and she was transmogrified.

Just like that, Joette disappeared from her chair.

Her feet were now inside the boots, and the man in the video, speaking in the Irish lilt, said, "Look, Joette." (The *t* said in that barely tapped tongue, a soft *th*.) "There," he said, which came out as *dare*. "And *dare*," pointing at the delicate flower clusters.

He burrowed his finger in the dirt, then put a soiled lump of sunset-colored tuber into the palm of his hand, a crooked root trailing off.

Joette and the man dug up a fine sackful of pignuts from the earth and then walked through the forest, leaves scattering ahead of them, until they came upon a gargantuan wooden box. The surface of the wood was darkened, as if it had burned at some time and then cooled, and it now sat charred and silent under a cluster of tall trees. A stovepipe sent a wisp of smoke into the branches above. Through the enormous glass wall that was one end of the box, two fat honey-colored chairs and a cast-iron woodstove could be seen within.

This was Joette's own place in the forest.

She pulled open the heavy door and they took off their boots and stepped inside in stocking feet. She lifted chunks of a tree limb out of the wood box, opened the creaking stove door, and added them to the coals. The wood snapped and a scatter of sparks floated upward.

They cleaned the pignuts and balanced a small tin box of them on top of the embers, and then settled into the soft brown chairs and nearly fell asleep; but when the warm smell of maple syrup reached out to them, Joette roused herself and turned the pignuts into a dish;

they pinged like tiny bells. which pinged like a tiny bell. They burned their tongues on the first honey-brown lumps. They ate them all.

Later they went back through the forest and walked down the way to the pub, where they sat at the dark and deeply pitted bar and drank frothy pints. They ate plates of mutton with mashed potatoes, onions, and carrots.

Outside, the night was starry and cold, and inside the pub glowed the color of brass. The locals filled the pub one by two by three; called greetings, slung insults, laughed loud and red-faced. Joette half turned into the room, propped her elbow on the bar. The fire in the corner hearth pressed a warm hand upon her chest.

In the midst of it all, the town drunk fell asleep on the shoulder of a pretty young girl, drunk herself and smiling sweetly, not a new thing, not at all, and no one gave it a second thought.

Then a man stood up, and everyone paused, and they leaned slightly forward.

The man began to sing, of childhoods and mothers, springtides and lovers; of how sad it is, time falling away, life. All the faces, nodding, were like, oh, it is, yes.

Joette's eyes filled with tears. How could she feel such an aching longing to be right where she was? How could she feel such grief to be so happy?

She did not even wonder how to get back. ∎

THE TABLE IN THE BACK
Prad Aphachan

Every restaurant in Bangkok always had one table that was permanently reserved, often wooden and often broken, usually in the back corner of the room. It was not like we actively forbade customers from sitting there, but the amount of objects, often strange and random—piles of old newspaper, a pack of unopened firecrackers, a toy water gun, empty water bottles, used metal mugs, an unfinished bowl of noodles—always discouraged anyone, us included, from sitting there. In our restaurant, that was Grandma's table. She always sat there when she was alive and even after she was dead, to monitor the operation, as if an egg-noodle shop (not a very good one at that; we were never featured on any magazines or newspapers) required constant vault-like surveillance.

Her matriarchal vigilance when she was alive was disquieting for our customers, especially those who crept around with uncertain, squirrel-like gaits, seeking the bathroom (complete with broken floor tiles, perpetually clogged urinal, about three to five spiders, the works), which someone, probably Grandma, had decided to put inconveniently inside the kitchen. She didn't want the customers contributing to our water bill. "They always leave the faucet running!" she used to say to my father, especially when he was trying to get her to agree to renovate the place or relocate the bathroom (he only got around to it after she died). She was always harassing anyone who came out of the bathroom with her grunts and glares, as if the customers could understand those vague gestures of discontent: a reminder to check the faucet.

After Grandpa passed away, she made it her mission to oversee the restaurant, erecting her watchtower on that dusty table, barricading it with things that seemed imprisoned in the past, those undeserving of the lucid colors of reality, capable only of possessing those long-faded black-and-white portraits. The pile of newspapers dated to the time when Grandma and Grandpa had first moved to Bangkok; the firecracker and the water gun were my gifts to her when I was four. For the longest time, her existence, like a kind of shackled benign spirit, was only capable of oscillating between the table and her bedroom, both of which left her with a distinct smell of ash and stale flour like a bowl of overnight noodles.

It was my father who was in charge of preparing the noodles now, while my mom was the one going back and forth between the storefront and the kitchen, repeating side dishes and drinks orders. Those jobs used to belong to Grandpa and Grandma, who'd opened this mediocre shop immediately after they had saved enough money from odd jobs here and there. It was only because egg noodles were easy to prepare, even with their scant cooking ability, and very profitable due to the (back then) low cost of ingredients.

Beside her physical manifestation (which grew less disturbing and more depressing the longer she sat there), there were also her occasional grunts, drone-like, permeating, like a distant rumble of an old air conditioner, capable of disrupting any nearby conversation, even the most lighthearted or romantic. She was not aware of it herself, but she would always grunt her low, husky grunt when the waitresses (often naive and young, recruited from the neighborhood) misplaced their orders or dropped the noodle bowls, or when they accidentally stuck their thumb in the soup or miscalculated the change (her eyes and ears had only gotten sharper after she turned eighty, and I think that they got even better once she was dead, through a kind of miasmic spectral omniscience). Her grunts, though soft and harmless, and her glares, through those matte pupils that would suddenly blaze with the intensity of the noon sun if only for the briefest second, always had me in shivers. The effect lessened somewhat once she was dead, as if those gestures had attained to a condition of lightness, becoming weightless in both their expressions and intentions.

I felt bad for the waitresses (most of whom were friends I invited to wait because they said they were bored during the holidays), so I made sure they knew that Grandma meant well, that her meanness was not just a mere dissatisfaction of old age or, after she was dead, of simply being dead. I knew because I was the closest to her in our family. Though we never really talked, not even when she was alive. Our unspoken bond was more a product of proximity than intimacy, created when I would glance at her from time to time while working on my algebra homework on the table beside her. Even after she was dead, as I worked on my calculus homework or helped my mom with accounting, in the corner of my eye, I would still see Grandma sitting there, and when she saw me, with her deceptively solid pair of eyes, wallowing in her intense stillness, which she occasionally, quietly, directed at our new waitress through her gaze, she would cease for a moment her eternal contemplation (probably on the fate of other dead people, Grandpa or her parents) and give me a nod with the side of her head, a simple gesture that served as our only form of communication when she was alive, the tiny and imprecise movement that encapsulated her contentment, anguish, and uncertainties, as if to announce to her only audience that she was still conscious, that she was still alive, that she was still there and resigned to any fate that would condemn her. That was the kind of bond we shared, one I couldn't put into exact words, and I'd like to think, with a strange kind of despair (that there was, after all, more living to do after death), that she would continue to transcend death and time until, perhaps, we all met the same fate as hers. Or at least, until Father finally got around to renovating the place.

At first, I did not understand why everyone in the family continued to ignore Grandma. We did not talk about her when we first got back from her funeral, much to my consternation. Though I knew they could see her as well as I could under her pale-grey bush of hair and her skin wrinkled like thin linen. My mom told me never to mention Grandma because she took Grandma's own saying to heart: "Talking to a ghost is a bad omen." Mom only ever said that "she should just pass on already." Yet, she was always forced to acknowledge Grandma's existence every other lunch service when an innocent customer would try to sit on top of Grandma. Oftentimes, the businessmen were just too hungry to be discouraged from barging into Grandma's fortress. Grandma, however, never seemed to mind. She didn't even flinch when their knees swept through her body or when their bottoms slowly submerged in her spectral face, their crotches coming close to occupying the exact coordinates where the pair of intense, once-burning eyes were, much to my mom's horror.

My father took a different, albeit a more successful approach: refusing to talk about her at all. With his usual nonchalance of an old-fashioned patriarch and his workmanlike attitude (more of a philosophy), it wasn't difficult for him to ignore her existence, both physically and through words. Every time I asked him about Grandma, he would give me a strange look as if to say that Grandma was just a dream or a hallucination of mine, even when she was sitting right behind him, staring vacantly at his sweat-soaked back.

Father was the only person in our family Grandma would scold when she was alive. She hated it when he overcooked the noodles or added too much salt to the soup. I couldn't remember too well how they'd treated each other when she was alive, but I liked to believe that there was no real animosity between them. After all, Grandma was the one who'd taught him how to boil noodles after Grandpa died, and I would like to think that their relationship extended beyond necessity. My father was just too concerned with "reality" to entertain, as he himself put it, "such strange fantasy." Father always did his best to deny her existence, but it seemed he was still occasionally affected by her lingering influence and strange whims. It was his habit to leave the toilet in a hurry during lunch services to go back to his station. As he passed by her table, he would hear or imagine himself hearing her grunts, which, in a Pavlovian way, made his hair stand on end. And that was how he always remembered to go back and turn off the faucet.

Unlike my parents, my younger sister not only acknowledged Grandma's apparition but actively tried to avoid her. She was always nervous to walk past the table in the back and could only do so by talking long, jerky steps, then leaping into the kitchen as fast as she could, the way children run up the stairway at night when the darkness instills in their imagination an unspecified sense of dread. It was also because my sister wasn't old enough to retain any memory of Grandma when she was alive. With their brief interaction (much less than nods and grunts), it wasn't surprising that she was initially scared of Grandma's ghost. The family portrait hung on the wall also didn't help. Seeing her infant self on Grandma's lap did not evoke in my sister any familial bond, the infant in the portrait being as strange and distant from her as Grandma was. It seemed that everyone in our family was, at one time or another, incapable of reconciling our past with the present and treated those in our past, those now existed solely in memory, just like Grandma treated those old newspapers. To my sister, Grandma (and, to that extent, her apparition) was something unfamiliar, uncertain.

Similarly, her apparition also saw my sister as a stranger. To Grandma, my sister was probably still the crying four-month-old she'd had to quiet with head pats. Grandma probably had no idea who this young woman with a blue streak in her hair was or how she came to occupy her old bedroom (which, as my sister always complained, still smelled of ash and stale flour). Perhaps time did not exist in the ethereal plane Grandma inhabited, and though she could still remember who I was from my somewhat underdeveloped face (judging from her nods), I wondered if she would still recognize me if I were to gain more weight or wrinkles. But I, for one, would still recognize her, only because she could no longer change. As

Grandma could only see my sister as an eternal four-month-old, Grandma would remain to me, to anyone else, eternally eighty-four. No one would miss, of course, the forms of her past, once expressed, tangible, warm, like the nostalgia piling on her table, a hoard incapable of silencing its own regrets. No one would miss the newly married lady who first read those newspapers many decades ago nor would they miss the grandmother who'd once received a water gun from her grandson. She would remain, to me and anyone else, forever the grandmother who couldn't finish her last bowl of noodles, whose sunken, hollow chest collapsed over that table in the back, some years ago.

Since everyone in my family refused to talk to her, I had to be the one to ask Grandma to be a little softer on my sister or, at the very least, to try not to scare her. On one holiday when my sister was left alone to tend the place (she was starting to get sick of the beach in Hua Hin where we spent every single vacation), Grandma finally made an attempt to communicate. She waved at my sister with her sinewy fingers, trying to get her closer, to which my sister reacted by backing farther away and hiding behind one of the other tables. When she found her courage, probably within the broom she was clutching, my sister drew closer and saw that Grandma was pointing at a pack of unopened firecrackers. She must have wanted my sister to have it.

But my sister didn't take it. In fact, like Mom, she dared not touch anything on Grandma's table. Yet, Grandma continued to insist that she take the firecracker, and when I asked her why she hadn't taken it, she said that she might get cursed. "Besides," she said, "I'm too old for firecrackers anyway." I thought it was quite amiable of Grandma to give firecrackers to a stranger. I thanked her by lighting one of the firecrackers beside her chair when everyone had gone to bed. She gave me the usual nod. Contented, I left in that warm, quivering light a body so light it refused to cast a shadow, not even on those peeling whitewashed walls.

I found myself wondering sometimes if she spent every night alone in the dark, whether she could at least reread those old newspapers or eat the bowl of egg noodles I left for her. I used to leave them hidden under the newspaper every other day. That was before Mom caught me and forbade me from leaving food to waste. "Grandma would not approve of this," she said. Still, I had never known or asked if Grandma liked our noodles, whether they still tasted the same after all these years. After my father went wild with it after he had fully taken over the place. He made changes to the recipe and ingredients, replaced all the old utensils and kitchen supplies, even planned for renovation. Grandma would have been grunting in her grave had we buried her. No matter how good the noodles were, no matter how little or how much the soup deviated from Grandpa's recipe, Grandma could no longer do anything about it. She would have to give up her old, strict flavor. All because she could no longer change. She had ceased to be volatile, unlike the noodles and the soup.

It was nice to have her around. We could always count on her constancy through all of our problems, those domestic, mundane, benign, but they still felt to us, to each of us, at the time, like they were the death of us and of our world. We all knew that every argument we had, every suffering we bestowed upon one another, would eventually make it to Grandma, and like the high judge in the court of heavens, we could count on her impartiality, her disinterest with our puny, mortal problems, a judgment so pure as to transcend all of our petty bitterness for one another. Even in death, she was still—somehow—the family's matriarch. I believed everyone else appreciated her for it too, all of us: Mom, Father, my sister. No matter what happened, we could count on her stillness and the table and her mementos, which maybe slightly displaced once in a while (should some customer bump into the table) but were never any different from how they'd been the day after Grandpa died or the very day she herself had lost her physical form. But in the end, Grandma still could not overcome time. Perhaps that was why Mom didn't want me to be attached to Grandma so much. It wasn't death that took her away from us; it was our inability to hold on to her. Old things, dead things, once designated as such, could only fade, initially only in importance, then in images, sounds, feelings, colors, flavors.

I saw Grandma for the last time before I left for university. In the first and last conversation we had, I told her that I would be back in the summer. My mom seemed a little worried that I was still treating Grandma as a person, even after I had gotten myself into some graduate program overseas to study physics. During my first year, Father finally got around to renovating the shop. They were just finishing with the cleaning when I came home for the break.

For a little while afterwards, my mom and sister were visibly saddened, and while my dad didn't really give it much thought, he probably felt some kind of guilt for dissipating Grandma's manifestation, the oddity that so closely resembled her, as if it was constructed from our impressions of her, melded and frozen into the most comfortable and familiar form. Maybe we were the ones clinging to her all along. Or perhaps it was created through Grandma's sheer will, in the moment when her heart gave in to the fatigue collected over eighty-four years, while her consciousness clung desperately on to the shop, to the table, to those old newspapers, to the bowl of noodles she couldn't finish, and perhaps (I liked to think) to us and to me. We threw away most of her stuff. We sold her old newspapers, which were worth quite something, to the secondhand bookshop next door. I took the water gun and the rest of the firecrackers. No one saw who took her chair and table or whether she went with them, but we were sure she did not even flinch or move from her spot, or perhaps she had given them a tiny, imprecise nod, signaling her resignation and acceptance before she became lost, like all of her stuff, like her ashes, which we'd scattered in the sea many years ago.

As easily as she'd lasted through death, perhaps with her soul latched on to those mementos, the chair and table, the whitewashed walls, the restaurant itself, she disappeared without a single grunt. Yet sometimes, as I listened to businessmen telling their crude jokes over their unfinished soup, their elbows resting on the squeaky white vinyl table, the very last table in the back of the room, I would occasionally catch a whiff of ash and stale flour, which had long sunken into the floor and walls, before I had to go to the newly renovated bathroom (somehow still inside the kitchen) and, with a subdued grunt, turn off the faucet. And when I came back to my table, I would make sure to quietly observe one of our new waitresses, following her uncertain movements, as if to assure myself that she wasn't about to drop a bowl of noodles. ■

SHORE SIGN
Michael Trocchia

We have only to speak
of hours like these

waves rushing up
to meet what is

always unlived
in us. Everything

we could mean, barely
touched and receding.

TOP BUTTON IS ALWAYS BUTTONED
Banzelman Guret

Even though Peter and Annie had both been Whirl Corporation Level 2s when they started dating four years ago, Annie was now a Level 7, working all the way across Whirl Village. And Annie said that things were different now. Level 2 and Level 7 were very different.

Annie's most recent Evaluation Report mentioned "Poor Personal/Social Choices" and "Lack of Romantic Ambition" and "Sub Level 3 Sex = Kinda Gross."

Annie explained to Peter that it was possible she agreed with the report. He fought back his instinct to panic, and he made sure that his face stayed somewhere between Neutral Nonthreatening and Stern Yet Absorbed.

But then, Annie told him that she didn't want to be engaged to him anymore. And she didn't want to live with him anymore either. And also, it turned out, she actually did love DerrickFromHerWork after all—a Level 8 with chest muscles and pants that snugged.

When she laid it all out, Peter looked around their kitchenette to think of what to say—but the perfect idea didn't appear in front of him. And he couldn't just stay locked/frozen forever. He needed to say something reasonable and Positive to ensure a successful Relationship Termination Evaluation from Annie. And if his natural default reaction would have been to snap out some defensiveness, he had to push that back down. He had to reassure her with Genuine Positivity.

If he seemed upset or angry, Annie might suspect that he was planning to Evaluate her negatively. And she might retaliate against this assumption/suspicion with her own Negative Evaluation. So to guarantee that they'd both give each other Positive Evaluations, he stayed calm and outwardly supportive of her decision.

He didn't want to have future/potential romantic partners turn hesitant because of a past Negative Relationship Termination Evaluation.

"I'm proud of you for telling me exactly how you feel," he said, showing a face that was Genuine Heartfelt.

Inside, though, his heart was rubble.

Annie explained that they both wanted her to be happy and maximize success. And that maybe this could be good for Peter in terms of long-term success/happiness/motivation—that this was best for both of them, not just for her.

But it seemed to Peter like maybe it was just best for her.

Annie packed up her belongings and left their shared Whirl Living Structure—even though the cereal she'd picked out was still in the kitchenette. And it was the healthy cereal that tasted like Styrofoam.

Peter had four hours to move from their Living Structure one-bedroom to a Living Structure studio—which he Evaluated as Fair.

* * *

It had always been her phone alarm that they'd used. And when Peter realized this—still half-asleep—it was too late. He jumped out of bed four minutes before he was required to log into Station J. He'd had a hard time falling asleep the night before.

Per the Whirl Corporation Policies and Procedures, he'd be fired. There was no gray area. He rushed to work—swirling mouthwash instead of brushing and sprinting across the ForLookingOnly Whirl Meadow, which could have gotten him a Negative Citizenship Evaluation on top of all of this, but he felt it was worth the risk.

He didn't need to rush, though. A little bit late and very late were exactly the same.

Desi Genk, the Human Resources Director for Stations H–L, didn't revel in firing Peter, but his hands were tied.

Peter explained what had happened, but heartbreak wasn't an Approved Excuse.

"If only she had died," Desi Genk said. "Then, you would have received forty minutes of preapproved grieving/mourning."

The Policies and Procedures were very clearly spelled out.

For four years, Peter had been rewarded with continued employment. He believed this was due to the intense effort he put into his job as well as his natural instinct to follow every rule, policy, procedure, guideline, and mandatory suggestion. His Work Performance Evaluations consistently rated his overall performance as "Fair but Underwhelming" and sometimes even as high as "Technically Meeting Expectations."

Now that he was losing this job, he felt like his internal organs were slowly compressing together into one. They were Jell-O Jigglers being vacuum sealed. He wanted to projectile sob at Desi Genk, who couldn't possibly be so strict that he wouldn't make an exception for a person who was wailing and heaving. But Peter knew better—because of course Desi Genk would be so strict. That was his job.

Peter couldn't project his sadness/frustration/shame for fear of a Negative Employment Termination Evaluation. He had to act as though he were completely on board for all of this.

Desi Genk said, "Here are five things to describe how amazing you are: wonderful, tall, top button is always buttoned, hard worker, prominent nose."

Desi Genk officially noted his Positive Attitude, which would help with finding future employment.

Peter thanked and smiled and handshook and left. He fought every impulse he had to react honestly, which might have been crying or begging or screaming out white-hot vitriol. He was so used to tamping it down that he wasn't even sure what he was tamping anymore.

Desi Genk's assistant, Lisa Gripp, said that she needed Peter's EmployeeFob, since he no longer worked for Whirl. She impatiently stomped her feet in what was supposed to be a jokey way. She snapped and clapped and said, "C'mon. C'mon. Hurry, hurry." When Peter finally handed his EmployeeFob over, she smiled and said, "Just being a dum-dum for ya."

Two Whirl Officers escorted him from Human Resources to Employee Housing. They let him into his apartment. The officers Evaluated him as he moved his boxes outside.

Officer One said, "Ya know—if everyone were like you and played it fast and loose with official work times, we'd have a really terrified Free Market and practically zero National Happiness. What even goes through your head?"

The Officers, of course, knew that Peter would be evaluating them, but they also undoubtedly knew that any Negative Evaluation from Peter would be labeled as Post-Termination Bitterness and dismissed from their official Performance Evaluations. So, they must have felt confident that they could say whatever they wanted to Peter without any real Evaluative Repercussions.

"My fiancée left me," Peter said, holding a box labeled *Ill-fitting sweaters*.

Officer One scoffed and said, "So what, ya weiner? You think anyone likes being dumped? You think I like being dumped?" He pointed to Officer Two. "What about him? You think he likes being dumped? His wife left him for another man just four days ago. You think he showed up late to work? Fat chance. And even though that other man was me—you think that ruined our Positive Working Relationship? No way," he said. "Right, Thomas?"

Officer Two said, "Right," but barely. Officer Two wouldn't look at Officer One.

"I said I was sorry," Officer One said.

"But you never *act* sorry!" said Officer Two.

"We can discuss this later."

During their Lunch Hour, Annie and DerrickFromHerWork helped Peter load a rented pickup truck.

In an ideal world, Peter would have been able to make some devastating remark about DerrickFromHerWork, but, of course, Peter couldn't.

And there wasn't much to criticize, even if he could. Being a Level 8, DerrickFromHerWork was somewhat powerful and fairly wealthy. Peter could tell that he was muscular. He probably had forearms so veiny that when nurses were doing a blood draw, they needed a minute to calm down and compose themselves.

Annie said, "Isn't DerrickFromMyWork so nice for helping out?"

DerrickFromHerWork said, "He sure is," trying to be all silly and fun.

Peter noticed that some of Annie's older stuff was snuck-loaded onto his pickup too. And also DerrickFromHerWork's broken NordicTrack.

But for the sake of his Relationship Termination Evaluation, he pretended not to notice. Ruffling feathers was a bad idea—even if it was only in response to other people's ruffling.

* * *

Peter would need to head south to his parents' condo—hours and hours down Route 32, through all that pathetic Non-Whirl Land and past the Sutherland-Dowd Bridge. His parents would ask him again and again how long he'd have to stay and whether it was absolutely necessary that he eat the food that they'd bought and he hadn't.

He didn't factor into their retirement funding or their 55+ Community.

He wouldn't be outwardly upset with their frustration, though. Keeping a Positive Mother/Son Relationship would help with securing future romantic partners. When he eventually got to their condo, he would pretend to understand all of his parents' concerns— even when they were about something as insignificant as leftover hot dogs that were "selfishly eaten" by him.

He put the truck in drive, and he left the Whirl Complex.

He could still see the Whirl Towers in his rearview mirror.

It was chilly, and the roads were quiet.

It almost felt good to be alone, defeated, and fired. Because it was all over. Once a person gets herpes, he doesn't have to be afraid of getting herpes.

There wouldn't be an Evaluation of his Driving Attitude. He could shake/rage or blubber/wail, and only he would know about it.

With this freedom, he decided that Annie wasn't some perfect, unblemished diamond. And he wasn't loose gravel.

"You don't even floss!" he said to the windshield/Annie. "Your eBay Feedback Score would be nothing without me!" Saliva flecked out of his mouth and his nose crinkled up. It all came out in a rush.

It felt good to be petty and small and honest.

He pressed on the gas pedal harder and harder—until a little flashing light on the dashboard told him not to. ∎

BLOOD MERIDIAN, AMERICAN ADDICTIONS, AND MY FIERCE RIDE OFF OPIOIDS

William Roebuck

I had back surgery in late May of 2021, the second surgery in a month, to address some painful sciatic nerve issues. If sitting is the new smoking, I had developed a two-pack-a-day habit in my twenty-eight-year career as an American diplomat, where long hours and proximity to crisis-addled bosses—helping them deal with all the problems that inevitably erupted in managing our relations with 193-plus countries—were the currency of advancement and promotion in the Foreign Service institutional culture (along with lots of sitting at one's desk mainlining voluminous email traffic and drafting political reporting and briefing papers for senior officials). The hazy stink of that "two-packs" sitting habit hung over my offices—in the State Department in Washington or in various U.S. embassies in the Middle East—all those years, doing the devil's work on my spine, as vertebrae slowly sagged and curved, squeezing out whatever remained of precious cartilage that prevented bone and nerve rub. In the euphoria of that addiction to work (and hope of scoring an eventual ambassadorship), I remained oblivious to the quiet devastation being wreaked on that neglected, troubled community known in the vernacular as my lower back.

An initial, less invasive surgery, described as a laminectomy, performed a month earlier, in late April, had not succeeded in reducing the sharp pain I was experiencing in my left leg, although it did provide the initial introduction to postoperative painkillers. The second surgery, actually two surgical procedures, spread over three days, was described somewhat picturesquely as a double spinal fusion. It required an initial four-inch abdominal incision—performed by a vascular surgeon—to allow my orthopedic surgeon frontal access (after some temporary moving aside of all those pesky organs) to my spinal cord to insert two small titanium disks between two sets of vertebrae known in medical parlance as L3 and L4, and L4 and L5. They had been diagnosed as impinging on the sciatic nerve. The two-stage operation was designed to recreate the space between vertebrae that healthy cartilage and correct positioning of the vertebrae normally provide, before aging and wear and tear do their work. It was the impingement that caused the fierce sciatic pain I had been experiencing in my upper leg. The nerve pain had become so intense in the months prior to these surgeries that it prevented me from sitting down for more than a few seconds at the time, confining me to bed for much of the day, as desk work, sitting to watch TV, and riding in a car (unless I was lying down, all six foot three of me, uncomfortably, in the back seat) became impossible.

The second stage of this double spinal fusion surgery took place two days later, with a five-or-six-inch entry through the lower back by the orthopedic surgeon to fix these metal disks with the unfortunate adjoining vertebrae, collateral damage of my sitting addiction, permanently in place with screws and a rodlike bracket, so the vertebrae on each side of the disk could heal into one solid unit (over a three-to-four-month period). Some bone graft material, grown from cells, was applied as coating on the flat, roughened surfaces of the disks, I'm told, to speed this fusing of the vertebrae. A slight loss in spinal mobility is the price one pays—gladly, assuming the operation is a success—for getting rid of the sciatic pain and getting one's life back. In my case, the surgery seems to have worked. "Seems" slipped into the fearful assessment I offered those first few months, because some residual nerve discomfort remained in the upper leg postsurgery (although it did not prevent me from sitting). And I can say this now, nearly four months removed from the surgery, the discomfort in the leg gradually diminished and, after a long ordeal and some helpful physical therapy, the operation has finally given me the sense that I am on the way to recovery.

But in the midst of this appealing arc towards recovery was a necessary, and helpful, but ultimately terrifying second arc—one that moved from months of critical pain suppression to gradual reduction of intake as the pain subsided, and finally, to what felt like the cliff edge of addiction to incredibly useful opioids: in my case, morphine and oxycodone. That second arc involved, as well, the tenacious effort to taper off these drugs and withstand the symptoms of withdrawal they, particularly the oxycodone, inflicted upon my body upon being notified the monthslong pharma party was being shut down.

As I started this difficult tapering process off opioids, recorded in a simple medical journal I had kept by my bedside since the surgery, I began by happenstance to read Cormac McCarthy's dark Western *Blood Meridian*, a novel first published in 1985. I had purchased but failed to read my copy in the early 1990s, when McCarthy gained fame and a wider readership. As I read, with increasing admiration that transitioned to awe and readerly trembling, I discovered it to be in a masterpiece category with a few select works of American literature I had come across over the years. Among its peers, I would include first and foremost Melville's *Moby-Dick* and a cluster of unforgettable Faulkner novels, such as *Absalom, Absalom!* and *The Sound and the Fury,* among others.

In addition to the spare medical journal, I kept a reading journal—or more accurately, a stapled-together (and ever-expanding) number of pages torn from a legal pad and folded into quarters, forming four mini-pages I could hold against the paperback and easily record my observations on in short breaks in my reading of *Blood Meridian.* I started with three sheets of white paper but barely five chapters into the novel, I had filled all my Lilliputian pages with fierce scribblings about the physical and temporal setting (1849, in the borderlands between the U.S. and Mexico, just after the end of the Mexican-American War, as fierce "Indian Wars" still raged), as I gradually pieced things together, and atmospheric description (instances of darkness, night, and blackness noted on nearly every page, for example, regardless of the time of day). I had fun trying to track McCarthy's allusions to the Bible, to the Argonauts and Gorgons of Greek mythology, and to past geologic cataclysms.

For the next month, I maintained these two journals: the medical ledger recording my daily intake and slow tapering off of morphine and oxycodone and the alternating yellow and white (depending on which legal pad I had borrowed from) reading pages recording my progress in *Blood Meridian.* The medical notebook entries were spartan and blunt. I had started it the day after my late-May spinal fusion surgery, to keep a record of the medications taken. At the late-May return from the hospital, I was taking five milligrams of morphine twice a day and fifty milligrams of oxycodone to address the intense pain, largely related to movement and transfers into and out of the bed and the throbbing miasma of aches caused by someone having carved, yanked, and hammered at or in my body over the course of three days.

I noted the early-morning and evening times for the morphine and the times in between when I took the ten-milligram light-pink oxycodone pills. I less regularly noted the extra glasses of water I was supposed to be consuming and the regular changes in position I was enjoined to assure, to avoid lying down all day. But for the most part, regardless of admonition and advice, the medical notebook consisted merely of the bleak notations of the times and amounts of the opioids consumed. I was only aware that they seemed to be blocking pain and keeping it tolerable (sensations that diminished, to my regret, whenever I got distracted and forgot to take the medication).

As I began my notes on *Blood Meridian*, helpfully noted as July 3 at the top of that first folded page, I had already begun the tapering process, initially reducing the oxycodone by ten milligrams a day and tentatively headed to further reductions until the physician's assistant helping me with the process suggested tapering off the morphine first. Somewhat frustrated but fearful of embarking on actions that ran counter to the medical advice I was receiving, I halted the effort with the oxycodone and focused on the morphine, using a small pill cutter obtained at a local pharmacy to cut the deep-blue pills into halves and then quarters and reducing my intake by a quarter of a pill (a bit over one milligram) a day, after an initial failed effort at a much bigger daily reduction that had left me dazed, throbbing in pain, and a bit of an emotional wreck. The slower taper off the morphine worked better and by July 3 when I started McCarthy's novel, I was making good progress. On July 21, I took the final quarter pill of morphine, feeling a huge relief, and, perhaps because the taper had been quite drawn out, felt no adverse effects.

During this period I had immersed myself deeply in *Blood Meridian*, reading the first third of it. I had already recognized the power of the writing, noting that it seemed to represent the work of an extremely talented writer writing at the height of his artistic powers and tackling a subject fully worthy of those talents. I had previously read a number of McCarthy novels but none of them compared in terms of assured artistry. The trajectory of the plot was clear: a rump effort by a group of ragtag American mercenaries to extend the fighting at the end of the Mexican-American War for the purposes of spoils and plunder collapses after the group is attacked by Commanches upon crossing the border, with blooded remnants of their group promptly jailed by Mexican authorities. The main character (one of two) named only as "The Kid" and a few others are released when they agree to join a reprisal campaign against Apaches being organized by the other main character—one of Ahab-worthy character flaws—Judge Holden, which plays out in the relatively sparsely populated border area that stretched from Texas westward to the Pacific. The Apaches stand accused of relentlessly preying on settlers and others trying to cross or homestead on Native lands.

I had come to know these main characters and a supporting cast of violent misfits, fellow members of this patrol of privately contracted fighters, financed by a mysterious "Señor Riddle" and paid by the scalp, ear, or other bloody trophy brought back to initially grateful Mexican communities in the borderlands. But already in its early days the shadowed hues of this mission have darkened, as its men become addicted to violence, mayhem, and bloodlust that intensifies as the chronicle moves forward. For McCarthy, these men seem to stand in—as he subverts the cowboy mythos and once-cherished ideals of our expansion westward—as founding fathers of the West, bathed in blood and corrupted by coin for mayhem and curdled glory. As the thematic references recur and begin reinforcing, it becomes clearer the novel is, among other things, a monument to what McCarthy elaborates as the rapacious nature of man, so evident in the novel in this westward founding of the full United States. McCarthy eventually wrote softer versions of the cowboy West in his trilogy of Westerns focused on the final days of that era, works of high escapism and elegiac nostalgia woven into their still undeniable artistry, particularly evident in the first volume, *All the Pretty Horses.* But *Blood Meridian* is a scalding-hot, antimythic ride of the Valkyries, motivated by vengeance, gold, racist and ethnocentric notions, and most of all an increasingly addictive bloodlust that turns this patrol into something near rabid in ferocity that eventually also slaughters and scalps Mexican villagers who had initially viewed the men as protectors and unfortunate Mexican soldiers bushwhacked before they realize the danger they are in.

From this first third of the novel, with scenes of episodic, intense violence and hints of further mayhem to come, McCarthy in the final two-thirds of his masterwork paints a grand canvas, a canvas filled with a novelistic rendering of our history and our ideals, embedded in escalating scenes of carnage and atrocities on both sides, with Apaches and Yuma countering with brutal ferocity of their own the mechanized violence—and savage trophy-taking—of the Colt-armed American mercenaries. As this blood-dimmed tide mounted and McCarthy's personified philosophical debate on the presence of evil in the world, the nature of man, and the place of war in society registered on me as reader, I continued my humble but increasingly fraught efforts to taper off of opioids and free myself of an invasive substance I had initially welcomed as savior from pain but that I no longer wanted or needed, and that seemed to be turning on me. Like McCarthy's now-unwelcome marauders, still grimly insistent on exhausted gratitude and payment from beleaguered, fearful townspeople, the oxycodone did not seem to want to depart.

As noted, I got off of the morphine rather uneventfully, in a long, drawn-out process that wore me down and made me anxious to expedite the similar journey off of oxycodone. But that proved tougher and more frightening. When I reached thirty milligrams of the drug and tried to continue reducing intake, my body rebelled, an insurrection that revealed itself in a creeping restlessness that stayed with me during the day; this was accompanied by feelings of depression, irritability, intense fatigue, and lack of mental acuity. At night, after I would fall into an initial, fitful slumber, the restlessness reemerged in a quietly menacing manifestation that prevented much further sleep, regardless of how tired I was. After several nights of this, I was beginning to panic as I realized this was a telltale sign of physical addiction and withdrawal, twin vultures of a reality I had been warned about repeatedly but that I thought I had avoided because in the four months I had been on opioids I had detected no "high" or other pleasant sensation attributable to intake, which would have made it seem like I was confronted with an addictive temptation. But the battle was joined nonetheless. And I was unable to get enough rest at night to function during the day afterwards with even the basic level of mental acuity I needed for my work or to maintain the emotional stability to prevent family members from worrying about my difficult journey to extricate myself from this tenaciously gripping and seemingly vengeful drug, friendly and soothing until one tried to stop taking it, and then relentlessly insidious and frightening in its insistence on further consumption.

In the end, I learned to just push through these restless nights, reading on my Kindle in the dark for distraction from the jazzed, restless fatigue that keyed me up to near-panic levels, until my breathing would gradually slow and exhausted sleep would come for an hour or two, before another Valkyrian wave of restlessness dragged me back into wakefulness and the awful cycle repeated itself. I wavered at one point and considered raising my oxycodone intake level back up. In fact, I did so at one critical juncture, as I gauged my emotional and physical reserves for the final push I saw coming. I slightly elevated the oxycodone level by a few milligrams, back towards thirty milligrams of daily consumption, and held it there for a few days, taking a breath, and then began the final taper—dropping a milligram and a bit each day (one-quarter of the now-five-milligram pills I was taking). My nights were unpleasant—not painful but disturbing and sometimes frightening if I let my panic and paranoid fears of addiction seep in. But I continued the descent, and soon, in an emotional sign to myself of how tough—I knew—this fight was getting for me, I invoked my mother, who had battled deforming, painful rheumatoid arthritis for decades before she passed away. She had had her own fierce ride to avoid addiction to painkillers and stay lucid and engaged with her family while trying to medicate the pain and cope with the disease that was slowly wrecking her body. I quietly begged her for the strength to get through this ordeal and not have any slipups that would lead to long-term addiction. I felt myself those weeks in July and early August in 2021 walking along an abyss—all flowers and heather of pleasant family life and work, doing a job in postretirement life that I loved on one side, and a hellscape drop-off to addiction and loss of control on the other.

Worried about what I had gotten myself into, I began reading up on opioids. Of course no one half-sentient over the past decade could have remained unaware of the painful realities, spelled out in detail on websites like the one operated by the Centers for Disease Control and Prevention (CDC):

- 38 people in the U.S. died every day from overdoses involving prescription opioids;
- over 70 percent of drug overdose deaths in 2019 involved opioids;
- about 80 percent of people who used heroin first misused prescription opioids; and
- about 8–12 percent of people prescribed an opioid for chronic pain develop an opioid use disorder [i.e., get addicted!].

It was not very reassuring to learn that the worst of this epidemic had crested a few years earlier, as the result of growing public awareness and concerted federal- and state-level actions to exercise more oversight over these powerful, addictive drugs.

My withdrawal symptoms intensified a bit as I made the final push, reducing intake daily, without holding for a day or two at each stage before reducing again. I found myself quietly sneering and cursing at the white five-milligram pills I sliced into quarters and eighths to at least get some reduction each day. I reviewed the entries in my cheap little notepad, purchased at a local Walgreens, noting the total daily intake, seeing it descend from 27.5 milligrams over time to 14.5, then to 12.5, registered a bit of loss of ground but then steadily on down to 5 milligrams, then to 3.5 milligrams (a quarter of that last pill three times a day), and then over the next three days (and sleepless nights) to nothing: no intake. On August 16, I made the simple notation "Salvation. Day One, No painkillers," and belabored it with a column of three zeroes where I had normally recorded intake amounts.

The withdrawal symptoms did not stop immediately. Days later I was still having jaggedly restless, sleepless nights. But they diminished over time; my fears that I would become an opioid junkie slunk away in one final spasm. I nervously contemplated how to get rid of the remaining pills, researching the matter to discover experts counseling discarding the pills (without any container or labels) in "unpleasant" daily garbage like coffee grounds. Taking a decision as I walked my dog one morning, I cleaned up his business in the little green doggie bag, and then stormed into the house, canine excrement in hand, dumping the remaining oxycodone in the bag, sealing it up, and tossing it in the garbage. For a couple of days afterwards, silly, paranoid thoughts flitted through my head that I would sneak out of the house at night and, in some excrement-smeared pharmakonic collapse, would retrieve the sodden pills and readdict myself. The once-weekly trash removal service capped this well of leaking emotional sludge, transporting this feared pharmaceutical detritus to city-dump oblivion.

During the determined push to the opioid finish (silly, paranoid final fantasies and all), I completed reading McCarthy. In my reading notes for August 16, my first day in five months without opioids, I noted, "*Blood Meridian*, by Cormac McCarthy, completed August 16, 2021." One should not overly seek or claim to find parallels. The one major commonality was addiction. These American marauders of McCarthy become addicted to violence, carnage, and rapaciousness, the founding elements in their messy progress westward; survivor Kid and a few others eventually make it to the Pacific Ocean. It is a movement, McCarthy hints broadly, that manifests in accent notes, America's westward destiny. An imaginary longitudinal meridian helps mark the steady westward progress of this band of mercenaries and misfits, their ranks gradually diminished by Apache counterattacks, as well as Yuma reprisals for having been betrayed by the double-dealing Americans.

At one point, McCarthy clarifies the unflinching reality of these Native peoples that, outgunned by a more technologically advanced society, "the destruction of these people would be erased. The desert wind would salt their ruins and there would be nothing, nor ghost nor scribe, to tell to any pilgrim in his passing how it was that people had lived in this place and in this place died." McCarthy's powerful, beautiful novel is not a political tract, however, scoring cheap points with some schematic view of America's founding. It is an artistic nightmare vision brought to life, with elements of Dante, Conrad's *Heart of Darkness*, and Céline of *Journey to the End of the Night* sharing in the inspiration, or at least drawing from the same artistic wellspring. The struggle throughout the novel—between the older, sly, and psychotic Judge Holden, glibly philosophical and an inveterately cataloguing student of nature and history (collecting butterflies and plant specimens and sketching rock paintings in his notebooks), and the illiterate, stubborn, flawed Kid, inarticulate but deeply skeptical of the judge's rationales for violence and war—animates this canvas. Notions about the presence of evil in the world; man, particularly western, American, modern man as the most predatory of all creatures; and knowledge that seeks to catalogue, dominate, and (at times) obliterate creation flow in a danse macabre with McCarthy's symbolic obsessions with darkness, with earth as terra damnata or a purgatorial wasteland, and with landscapes stained with blood and haunted with the spirits of previous, now-effaced inhabitants. Deep in that artistic vision is a sense—beyond whatever knowledge of good and evil lies buried in America's past—of a half-articulated, fully felt ecological terror, a notion that man has made himself suzerain over the earth and become, in his own eyes, god. McCarthy's wise admonition, cloaked in a novel of astonishing power and beauty, is that man needs to taper off of that addiction to exerting power and controlling knowledge over nature. Part of the force of McCarthy's art derives from an insistent realization, even obsession, that man is incapable of this transformation and, like "the troubled sect" of missionaries slaughtered at one point in his novel, will disappear "in the coming darkness like heralds of some unspeakable calamity leaving only bloody footprints on the stone." McCarthy's always somewhat overheated prose has found at last the subject worthy its power and scorching prophetic vision.

A cryptic epilogue (with exceedingly cryptic spoiler alert!) in compact allegorical language hints that the artist is capable of "striking fire out of the rock which God has put there," while the others accompanying him on the journey are focused on scavenging or just surviving in a dark, despoiled landscape. It isn't exactly a message of redemption or soaring hymn to the powers of art but a fiercely determined note that the artist persists in their work, even in the midst of man's powerful, destructive addictions to violence and dominion over the earth. I stuffed my bloated notes in the novel, after spending some days trying to make sense of them, put my medical journal away as well, pending a decision to either discard or make a shrine of it, and headed to the basement and my first real exercise in the past eight months, a smooth ride on my American spin bike: sleek, exhausting, and, in its own way, addictive. ∎

SIX STRINGS
Federico Garcia Lorca
-translated from the Spanish by Wally Swist

Guitar,
you make dreams cry.
The sobbing
of lost souls
issues through
your round mouth.
And like the tarantula,
you weave an enormous star
that hunts our sighs,
one that floats in your dark
cistern of wood.

LAS SEIS CUERDAS

La guitarra,
hace llorar a los suenos.
El solloza de las almas
perdidas,
se escapa por su boca
rodonda.
Y como la tarantula
teje una gran estrellas
para cazar suspiros,
que flotan en su negro
aljibe de Madera.

A SELECTED EXCERPT FROM A FORTHCOMING (UNAUTHORIZED) BIOGRAPHY OF DR. HIDEKI MATOSHI
Andrew Schofield

The apartment that Dr. Hideki Matoshi shared with Olga Savenko at 1834 Rue Rennequin was an old maid's quarters, a small studio sitting atop a narrow staircase on the sixth floor of a six-floor building not far from Parc Monceau in the 17th Arrondissement. There wasn't much to it: a kitchenette, a bed, a small dining table, and an old armchair. The only flourishes were the three skylights that dotted the slanted ceiling, each of equal size and each equidistant from the other. And in the afternoons, when the sun rose above the neighboring buildings and pierced through the cloud cover, as it did the day Matoshi and Savenko moved in, the room swelled with light.

Many ask me if they were happy, which is not a question I quite understand how to answer. But I can say that until the unfortunate events that came to pass in the spring and early summer of 2012, they did not want for much more than they had.

At a point indeterminate in early 2012, Savenko began to hear, in the dead of night, the sound of something scampering on the roof above them. In the beginning, she would wake Matoshi and ask if he heard it as well. Sometimes, he would think he did—he would listen, and between the sound of the cars passing on the street below or the drunken laughter of the Parisian night, he would hear the pattering of something like feet. But at others, he wasn't sure, believing perhaps that what he heard was the sound of something he wanted to hear— namely, the sound of anything at all—a cat, a raccoon, the clanking of a radiator breathing in new life, the reverberation of something deep within the building itself, the echo of metal on metal, the collision between one object and another.

In the mornings, he would tell her not to worry. In the good sense of daylight, he found the confidence to declare, beyond doubt, that it must be a cat—a stray hunting pigeons under the cover of darkness. At first, she would argue the point. They would sit at the small dining table under one of the skylights, which filled the room with a warmth that Matoshi would one day remember and find unsettling, incongruous with what was to come, a motif left over from someone else's story, and she would list all the reasons she thought he was wrong: the steps were too heavy, the gait too irregular, too stilted, too inorganic. And what was a cat doing up there, six stories from the ground below, scampering for pigeons when, surely, she told him, much easier prey could be found in the dark alleyways or in the little park down Rue Cardinet on the corner across from the karaoke bar that spilled out laughing happy people at all hours of the night. And one morning, she asked him if he had ever had a cat (he had not) and she told him of the cat her mother had adopted when she was younger. Her coat was all white and her mother loved her above almost all else, perhaps even Savenko herself she wondered. Until one day, the kitchen window was left open and the cat was never seen again. Isn't that sad, she asked Matoshi. And as he started to clear the table, collecting the crumbs and wiping them neatly onto his plate, he said it was.

In the early spring, Savenko continued to hear the noise and Matoshi continued to rationalize it. But Savenko no longer had any interest in arguing. When Matoshi presented a new theory, she would simply agree. I'm sure you are right, she would say. But in the middle of the night, he would wake to find her looking up at the skylights, craning her neck in an attempt to catch a glimpse of whatever it was she was hoping to find. He would call out her name and tell her to come back to bed and she would smile and say of course.

On other evenings, he would wake to find their bed and their apartment empty. On the first occasion—on a particularly cold, windy evening—he had the strange feeling that something horrible had happened.

It is perhaps worth noting that Matoshi was not a religious man, but it can be said equally that he was no atheist. He was, as he mentioned once in a passing lecture, "a man of faith in spite of [himself]." And so when met with the slow deterioration of Savenko's well-being, it was greeted not with the logic of the psychoanalytic clinician he was, but rather by a certain fear that would not leave him until his death. And yet, perhaps it is not altogether surprising. His life's work—most notably *In the Eye of the Beholder* and *Fear and Loathing: The Self-Destructive Nature of the 21st-Century Automaton*—always entailed a devotion to all that is unseen and unsubstantiated but that is felt, and deeply so, within the lived experience.

I have devoted little of the chapter thus far to Matoshi's work. Much of this is due to my belief (one shared by many close to Matoshi throughout his life) that his relationship with Savenko and the nature of its undoing came to shape the vision of his later work and, in large part, spurred an obsession that would lead to his untimely demise. But this is also doubtlessly due to the transitional period that Matoshi found himself in at the time. The coinciding of his romance with Savenko with the completion and successful defense of his doctoral thesis (*In the Eye of the Beholder*, which would, years later, gain both popular and critical acclaim after Matoshi had become more of a known commodity within the industry) and lack of a fellowship or other academic positions that he would later hold meant that little is known of Matoshi's intellectual life at that time.

However, there is one particular episode in the email correspondence between Matoshi and his close mentor and advisor on his recently completed thesis at University College London, Dr. Pearlman—once considered something of an enfant terrible within psychoanalytic circles for his reinterpretation of several early works by Melanie Klein. The two were purported to be quite close, so much so that their relationship was often subject to some particularly distasteful rumors regarding an alleged romance between the two. But by all the accounts, their relationship was platonic and the two held each other in quite high esteem—Matoshi even going so far to describe Pearlman, in his famed lecture series at Berkeley, as the "true unappreciated genius of the twenty-first century."

When reading the correspondence between Matoshi and Pearlman, one is, at first blush, taken aback by how little is said of their personal lives. Their conversations inevitably, as if in the presence of some unseen force, gravitate back to the question that consumed any two self-respecting Lacanian scholars: the nature of desire, where it comes from and where it goes and how it is to be satisfied. And yet, there are moments when the personal cannot help but breach the surface. This past summer, I spent a week in a small cabana on the coast of Ecuador. Upon arriving, I was told by locals it was the one month of the year that the humpback whales pass by their shores. They come north from the Arctic in search of warmer waters in which to raise their young. One morning, a man in a fishing boat told me that for a modest fee, he would take me to the whales. And when we arrived in the deep water off the coast, chasing the tips of the tails seen in the distance, I was struck by how quiet it was until the moment came when the humpback jumped from the sea, rotating slowly in the open air—as if to admire this newfound element—before landing with a crash. This is what I think of when I think of the email sent by Matoshi to Dr. Pearlman on March 29, 2012, at 10:42 p.m.

In it, Matoshi tells Pearlman that he has been rereading Freud's *Totem and Taboo* and offers a short commentary that would later make up the thesis of a minor, little-known essay published by a friend of Savenko's coworker in *Le Revenant*, a short-lived Paris-based publication devoted to the "exploration of the intersection of culture, psychology, and current affairs." And then, breaking the train of thought mid-paragraph, he writes:

> Yesterday afternoon, I walked past one of those small independent theaters not far from the Latin Quarter, the ones with the uncomfortable seats that you seem to become wedged in and the sticky floors that do not seem to have been cleaned in quite some time. I bought a ticket for the first film I saw listed on the bright board above the ticket kiosk. It was a documentary about the migratory patterns of Canada geese. It was fine—nothing more—but wholly satisfying in a way that only movies seen in a theater can be. The last fifteen minutes were devoted to a mother whose wing had been clipped by oncoming traffic after she'd rushed out to push her gosling to safety. And when the flock took flight at the end, she could not join them. They say that geese mate for life. And that when her mate returns in the spring, he will remember her and search for her. Olga is not well and when I think of her, I am sometimes struck with a terrible guilt.

Just as quick as the sudden personal revelation came, it left. And Matoshi concluded the letter with a short summary of his professional and academic plans in the near future, inquiring as to whether Pearlman had any advice.

When Matoshi found Savenko that night she left the apartment, she was sitting on a park bench not far from the studio. The two sat together for quite some time and it was decided concrete action would be taken. They called the landlord and asked for the roof to be inspected—for what, they were not sure. Evidence of rodents perhaps, maybe feral cats, or the nest of a bird much larger than a pigeon. They asked the super if the boiler in the basement could be to blame, perhaps even a radiator from a neighboring building. They asked their neighbors down the hallway if they had heard anything in the night, something like footsteps on the steep tiled roof. But they had not and nothing could be found and all the while, Olga became more withdrawn, quieter. She would call in sick from work for days at a time. She no longer complained of the noise, even so far as to become surprised at any mention of it—as though it were an old friend whom she had not thought of for a very long time. Which is perhaps why, despite the event's treatment by other journalists and biographers, Matoshi deserves some sympathy for what would follow in the summer.

To summarize in brief: On the night of June 3, 2012, the Paris police dispatcher received a call from a resident across the street from the apartment rented by Matoshi and Savenko. The resident claimed a woman was on the roof. A patrol in the area was dispatched to the apartment building, where it was soon confirmed, with the help of the building superintendent, the woman was on the rooftop above Apartment 6E—the one belonging to Matoshi and Savenko. The patrol responding to the call quickly informed dispatch of the situation and the Suicide Prevention Unit from the nearby Seventy-Fourth Precinct soon made their way to the scene while the officers from the patrol proceeded up the six flights of stairs.

From that point onward, there is much we don't know and I find it unreasonable to speculate on Savenko's motivations and intentions or the otherwise unknowable contents of another's mind, but here is what has been established with some degree of certitude:

In the middle of the night, Savenko, using little more than a step ladder and a screwdriver, removed a skylight from its frame and hoisted herself onto the roof. Matoshi had taken a significant dosage of cold medicine earlier that evening, which was, as he later speculated, a contributing factor as to why this did not wake him. What happened next is unclear and subject to wide speculation. Savenko herself never commented on the matter. It has been widely hypothesized (most notably by Hernandez in *The True History of Dr. Hideki Matoshi*) that Savenko had intended to commit suicide. This thesis purports to draw from anonymous sources from the Sainte-Anne psychiatric facility that Savenko was soon thereafter committed to. Matoshi never commented on the matter throughout his life (refusing to answer related questions in the few public interviews he agreed to), but those close to him maintain that she went on that roof in search of the only thing that interested her: the noise, the dull vibration pulsating through the ceiling, the rhythm of a song you recognize but cannot name. The officers climbed up the stepladder with Matoshi close behind and when she looked across at them and noticed their arrival, it was said she did not stir. She sat there, looking out across the city and watching the trains pull into Gare Saint-Lazare, and did not offer much in response to the inquiries into her well-being. They asked her if she would come back down with them. She said she would.

Arrangements were made for her to be committed to the aforementioned Sainte-Anne psychiatric facility in the 14th Arrondissement, not far from where she had once lived as a girl in a small one-bedroom apartment with her father. Matoshi was told by authorities on the scene that Savenko would simply be kept overnight, but following her initial psychiatric evaluation, the chief resident psychologist—one Dr. Jean-Paul Bouffard—petitioned the presiding judge for a twenty-one-day extension towards her involuntary commitment, citing in the June 6 request that "the subject's mental state entails a clear and obvious danger to herself" and that "her past actions cannot be ignored or, without a clear psychiatric treatment plan, said to be the object of recovery."

As well may have been expected given Matoshi's extensive psychoanalytic background, he took exception to Dr. Bouffard's recommendation to the French circuit court, lodging an official complaint with the presiding judge and arguing that Savenko's actions could not be proven "to constitute an act of self-harm" given the suspected presence of something on the roof above their room (the true existence of that *something* notwithstanding). Matoshi's dissent, however, was ignored.

It should perhaps be mentioned that for as much respect as Matoshi found within the more academic-leaning psychoanalytic field, his expertise was not recognized within the more clinical, medically minded domain of psychiatric care. In fact, according to certain rumors that unfortunately cannot be substantiated, Matoshi arrived at the Sainte-Anne facility on Rue de la Santé, with its tall iron gates and limestone walls, once a soft yellow, but now, after decades of existence, more a dirtied grey, and attempted to confront Dr. Bouffard and gain the discharge of Savenko into his care. But it was to no avail.

Matoshi, as the rumor has it, was denied admission and only found his way onto the grounds the following evening after he impersonated a psychiatric consultant called in from London at the request of Bouffard himself. But upon his arrival, he found Bouffard's office empty for the night. He searched for Savenko instead, but the orderlies on staff were insistent he could not be granted access to her wing without supervision from Bouffard himself. Dejected, he left. His attempts to contact Savenko's only next of kin, her estranged father, who lived a remote existence in rural Prince Edward Island, also proved unsuccessful and so Matoshi resorted to petitioning what few contacts he had within the psychiatric community.

Sources within the Sainte-Anne facility described Savenko as "quiet" and "withdrawn," perhaps even bordering on "dissociative." She was housed in the Magnan Pavilion, the facility's main wing, and spent most of her time in her room, a second-floor dormitory on the corner of the building that, in the afternoon (and weather permitting), received all the sun. Below her window was a garden maintained by members of the staff and the more tenured patients of the facility. When Savenko was asked to leave her room, to perhaps spend time in the common area or to participate in a group therapy session (the likes of which were very in vogue at the time), she obliged, but only for a time—excusing herself in a quiet, polite manner and announcing that she had to use the bathroom. Minutes, sometimes hours later, when members of the staff became aware of her absence, they would search for her and they would find her behind the closed door of a bathroom stall and they would ask if she was okay. Yes, she would tell them, she was fine.

In the first days of her stay at Sainte-Anne, she would speak to Matoshi on the phone every day at two o'clock in the afternoon. Matoshi would walk to the corner store at the end of the street and purchase more minutes for his prepaid cell phone plan, aware the minutes were not likely needed but anxious nonetheless that the phone call would be cut short, that a breakthrough would be suspended, trapped on a cell tower with no receiver, and lost forever. He would then walk to Parc Monceau and speak to her as long as time would allow. In the beginning, they would speak of their life: errands Matoshi must run, trips to take when she was better, a new film that Matoshi had seen a preview for. Matoshi noted in his private correspondence at the time that Savenko seemed better, more herself. They agreed they would leave that sixth-floor studio and, later, Matoshi would report to her on the apartment listings he combed through in the late afternoons. He toured one in Montreuil, a suburb just outside Paris but still on the metro line, not far from the Bois de Vincennes. It was cheaper and bigger too and there was a small patio with a space for a garden where they could grow herbs and flowers in the summer. Matoshi finished his journal entry for that day with the words "excited to tell Olga tomorrow."

The following day was June 17, eleven days after Savenko had been admitted to the Sainte-Anne psychiatric facility. Upon calling at 2:00 p.m., Matoshi was informed that she was unwell, nothing serious, but that she would not be able to come to the phone that day. From that day forward, there was something different about her. Matoshi began to express concern to mutual friends. All her earlier enthusiasm was gone. He attempted to contact Dr. Bouffard but was forwarded instead to his junior associate, who assured him Savenko was doing fine, that they were happy with her progress, that such "episodes," as he well knew, were well within the confines of what could be considered "a healthy depressive state."

And yet, to Matoshi's ear, she continued to deteriorate. Their conversations became shorter, more punctuated with long moments of silence and gaps in understanding. She would lose the threads of conversations and introduce what seemed to Matoshi as non sequiturs: the identity of the facility's namesake (the mother of Louis XIV), the Magnan Pavilion's most storied guests (Paul Celan and Louis Althusser among others), etc., etc. And when told of the suburban apartment he had seen, Savenko failed to understand why they would move, ignoring any attempt by Matoshi to recollect the noise they had heard above them or the episode on the roof.

If you have been to Paris in the summertime, then you know what a difficult place it is to be sad. Hemmed in on all sides by what begins to feel like a disgusting joy, you feel guilty for failing to enjoy all that is being offered. And that guilt only serves to remind you that you are standing outside of something, which is to say of course, you are alone. It is with that in mind that I think of Matoshi—surrounded by all that laughter that lines the streets—on the day he received the phone call informing him that Savenko had accepted a transfer to a facility in the small Mediterranean town of Argelès-sur-Mer. She was to leave the day after tomorrow, they told him, and her admittance had been extended, as per her instruction, indefinitely.

It is from this moment forward that what little we know of Matoshi's already protected private life is mostly reduced to conjecture, hearsay, and half-truths. Although we know that Matoshi remained religiously devoted to his journal keeping until his death, no records of them can be found. And his correspondence with close friends and family decreased precipitously in the months and years that followed Savenko's transfer to Argelès-sur-Mer.

We do know from sources at the Sainte-Anne facility that Savenko refused Matoshi's calls up to the day of her departure. However, Matoshi petitioned Dr. Bouffard and the hospital authorities for a personal visit. Despite their initial hesitation, given Savenko's perceived unwillingness, they granted him permission to do so in the afternoon before her departure the following morning. What follows next has been the subject of considerable mythmaking in no doubt due to the attention paid to it by Gay Talese's long-form feature in the *Thw New Yorker* on Matoshi following his death ("But of Course It Is Only the Insane Who Speak the Truth").

As Talese writes:

> It is June and unseasonably cold. Matoshi sits in a long, empty room with high ceilings, next to an open window through which he can hear the sounds of chatter from the garden. He watches an orderly at the opposite end of the room methodically clean the tempered glass of the high windows and rehearses all that he would say to Olga—all which can be summarized with the brief plaintive phrase: "Please come home." A door opens. Olga walks through the doorway, then pauses, looking behind her and then back across the room towards Matoshi at the far end. Matoshi rises from his chair and smiles. He walks to her and moves to hold her, but she pulls away just slightly. Matoshi asks if they can sit and she says yes. They walk back to the table by the window.
>
> Matoshi does not know where to start. He fumbles with his words. He begins with that studio apartment on the sixth floor, where they were once happy. He apologizes, though not entirely sure for what, perhaps for a vague sense of guilt that he had failed her. He continues—he speaks of their neighbors and of other shared acquaintances and when he reaches something of a crescendo, arriving at the point of his plea, she stops him. She apologizes. But she does not remember. She wishes she could but she can't. And she gets up from the table—repeating those words like a prayer: she doesn't remember, she's sorry, she wishes she could but she can't. And then the door clicks shut behind her, sending a vibration through the window panes, and it's a return to the silence, the chatter from the garden, and the unseasonably cold June afternoon.

There has been no shortage of theorizing on these events, especially following Talese's infamous account of the exchange that is, to my knowledge, uncorroborated. Sources at Sainte-Anne claim that the official diagnosis at the time was a sharp dissociative event brought on by the return of repressed trauma. Others claim that Savenko was subjected to an experimental drug therapy that spurred her loss of memory. Some, however, go as far to say that Savenko had no memory issues at all. She did remember and remembered very well. And her insistence on the opposite was, they speculate, the only way she could distance herself from a commitment to a man whom she could no longer love in the way he, or anyone for that matter, needed to be loved.

Last summer, I visited Argelès-sur-Mer. Nestled between the Pyrenees to the west and the Mediterranean Sea to the east, it's a quiet fishing village—the silence of its night punctured only by the waves reaching shore and the music dancing out the open windows of the town's only discotheque. In the day, I interviewed the townspeople. I asked them if they knew of Matoshi or of Savenko. I showed them photographs and newspaper clippings. Some were familiar, but the townspeople's knowledge ended there. It was nothing but a story to them, something they had read, something that existed somewhere else.

Many, instead, asked me what had brought me to Argelès, what exactly was I hoping to find. And I am not entirely sure, but I can say it was something involving a hope: I would go to a café and sit at a table in the shade under tall oak trees and would dream that someone—the busboy collecting plates or the florist in the window across the street or maybe the clerk at the small hotel at which I was staying—would come to me, perhaps in the romanticism of the final hour, the last afternoon, the moments before my departure (the trunk of the taxicab just about to be shut), and they would tell me that the story was not over. That, maybe, Matoshi had come to Argelès. That he'd sat with Savenko at a table in the back corner of the recreation room and they'd played checkers and spoken of nothing of Paris, or Sainte-Anne, or that studio on the sixth floor, and certainly not of that unknown rhythm scuttling across the rooftop. ∎

THE LOOP SERVES UP SILVER
William Crawford & Charlie Hahn

THE LOOP REQUIRES SWITCHES
William Crawford & Charlie Hahn

URBAN CANYON
William Crawford & Charlie Hahn

DIRTY JERSEY
Amy Kiger-Williams

I lured squirrels and pigeons in the park with the Pop-Tarts and potato chips my mother had packed in a brown paper bag. A whole battalion of squirrels hovered around me and my chipped green bench, manipulating bits of frosted blueberry pastry and barbecue Lay's in their clawy hands. In my backyard, squirrels did the same with the acorns that littered the ground from the tall oaks that shaded our house. It seemed wrong to feed these squirrels junk food, but I kept tossing them more tidbits of my lunch. I drank the carton of orange juice my mother had packed for me and ate the turkey sandwich. The squirrels and pigeons hung around, waiting for the food I wasn't yet sharing. I kicked them away with the toe of my Doc Martens.

I had never cut school before, but I thought that day I would try. I didn't really have a good reason for cutting class. It was a whim. Instead of walking to school, I headed over to the train station and stood on the platform. All the fathers had already gone to Wall Street, and the mothers were in the places where the mothers go when the fathers are gone. I put the hood of my black sweatshirt over my head to hide my pink streak. People knew me because of my hair. People talked about me because of my hair, and this is what enraged my parents. I fought with my parents over my hair, my clothes, my piercings. My parents asked why I'd had to choose, out of all the styles in the world, the one that made me look like a truant, a freak, like someone who should only come out on Halloween? Eventually we gave up fighting, but the subject of my appearance hung between us like a force field, something we couldn't get close to without getting hurt.

The train pulled into the station. I stretched across a three-seater and let New Jersey Transit deliver me to Hoboken. There I changed to the PATH train, which took me to Manhattan. I thought, *Dirty Jersey*. The station was light blue and dark blue and covered with a thin coating of grime. The PATH was dingier than the New Jersey Transit train, which was clean but had an air of vague use, like the auditorium after an assembly at school. I knew New Jersey had a reputation, but I had lived here all my life and I'd never quite understood it. I knew there were leaky refineries, the stinky air of the Turnpike, cities slowly crumbling and decaying. But my Jersey was the Jersey of lush lawns, tall trees, the backyard barbecue. The grass grew tall and rangy, and men would spill from lawn service trucks with industrial-sized mowers and edge trimmers. They'd cut the grass, then blast away the debris with leaf blowers, scurry back to the trucks, and disappear. The neighborhood would be quiet and manicured once again, as if they'd never been there at all. New York City had homeless people and vagrants, and corners that smelled like piss and shit, and neighborhoods I was afraid to walk through. *Dirty New York*, I thought.

My father worked in the city, downtown, in a big office building on a trading floor. I didn't fear bumping into my father here in Washington Square Park. The only time he'd ever venture up to the Village would be to have drinks after work. Right now he was probably sitting behind a bank of computer screens, watching the market, ducking out quickly for lunch. I looked south toward the gap in the sky where the Twin Towers used to be, and I wondered if my father would even care that I had cut school.

It was October, a grim, sunless day, and I tugged at the zipper of my jacket, even though it was already zipped to the top. I jammed my hands into my pockets and rubbed them against the thin fleece lining. The sky was dreary and I wondered why I was here, if I should just ride the train back home and crawl into bed, pretend I was sick. I pulled a pack of Marlboro Lights out of my backpack and lit one, shielding the flame with my cupped hand.

"Can I bum one of those from you?"

I looked up and saw a guy wearing a baseball cap and a backpack and holding a big black art portfolio. He had an accent that sounded European, though I couldn't place it, and he looked as if he hadn't shaved for a few days.

"Sure," I said, tapping the bottom of the pack against my leg until one of the cigarettes popped out. He pulled it from the pack and placed it between his lips. He leaned forward, and I lit it for him with the burning ember of my cigarette. He leaned the portfolio against the edge of the bench and sat down beside me, placing his backpack between us.

"Crappy day to sit in the park," the man said, dragging on the cigarette. He had deep dimples in his cheeks, flecked with stubble.

I kicked at a pigeon. The pigeon skittered away, then returned to the same spot. "Yeah, I guess it is."

"You live around here?"

"No, I live in Jersey."

He raised an eyebrow. "Ah, a Jersey girl," he said. "I've never really been there. Except Newark Airport. Much better than JFK."

I shrugged my shoulders. "I've never been to JFK."

"Not missing anything," he said. "When I go home to Poland I try to go through Newark Airport now, but all I've seen of Jersey is what I've seen from the cab."

"You're from Poland?"

"Kraków. Heard of it?"

I nodded my head.

"Beautiful city. I like New York, though. So, you go to NYU?"

I shook my head no. "I go to school in New Jersey. I'm taking a . . . day off today."

He nodded his head. "What do they call that, a mental health day?"

"Exactly." I crushed the cigarette with the tip of my boot.

He took another drag. The ember glowed close to the filter. "A pretty girl like you shouldn't be smoking. It's a dirty habit."

"Then why are you smoking?"

He raised his eyebrows. "I'm not a pretty girl."

"Neither am I."

He flicked the cigarette butt through a low iron fence into a scrubby patch of grass. "Thanks for the smoke."

"No problemo."

"Say, can I get you a coffee?"

I shook my head no. "You don't have to do that."

"Why not?" He smiled. I noticed how one of his front teeth was darker than the others, how his laugh lines swallowed up his dimples when he smiled. "You gave me a smoke. The least I can do is buy you a coffee."

I thought of my father, how when I was little he would wake me up on the weekends by rubbing his five o'clock shadow across my cheek, how he would smell like last night's cigarettes.

"Sure," I said. "Let's go. But what's your name?"

"Jan," he said.

I extended my hand. "I'm Beth."

We headed over to the Starbucks near Astor Place. The wind swirled around us, sending dry leaves into the air and fluttering the pages of the magazines that the street vendors were hawking along Eighth Street. Jan's legs were longer than mine, and he walked at a rapid clip. I struggled to keep up with him.

"Should I slow down?" he asked.

I shrugged my shoulders. "It's better to walk quickly, I guess. We'll get there faster."

The place was full of students, writing papers, drinking coffee. I ordered a grande chai tea latte, and he ordered a double espresso. We found a small table that overlooked the Astor Place subway stop, and I watched as people emerged from underground and others descended back into it. I pulled down my hood and ruffled my hair a bit to get the flatness out.

Jan popped the plastic top off his cup. "So, tell me, what is this with your hair?"

"What do you mean?"

"Why do you have the pink in it?"

I shrugged my shoulders. "I don't know. I like it."

"It's good that you don't have white, like that little animal, you know, the one that smells bad."

I laughed. "A skunk?"

"Yes, a skunk," he repeated. "So what do you do for college in New Jersey?"

I laughed. "Oh, I'm not in college. I'm in high school."

"Oh. How old are you?"

"Seventeen. I graduate this year."

"Will you stay in New Jersey for college?"

"I don't know. I'm applying to a bunch of different places. I could really end up anywhere."

"It's good to keep your mind open. Have a sense of adventure. That's how I came here from Poland."

"How long have you been here?"

"In New York? Just a year. But I came to America to study. I went to school in California. I lived in Chicago for a while, Seattle, Austin. I used to be a computer programmer, but now I do art photography." He patted his portfolio. "Want to see my pictures?"

He zipped open his portfolio and pulled out a black binder, flipping through the pictures. They were all of teenagers, like me, standing on street corners, against brick walls, on the subway. The teenagers wore black studded leather jackets, combat boots, ripped T-shirts. Their hair was gelled, spiked, streaked, fluorescent. One guy had his cheek pierced. Many of them had tattoos.

"Cool," I said.

"You have a great look," he said. "Very photogenic. Has anybody ever told you that?"

"No," I said. I had been told plenty of times that my look was tragic, an embarrassment, that I needed to get a new haircut, a new wardrobe. That my allowance would be cut off if I didn't do these things. That I made our family look bizarre.

"I'd like to photograph you," he said. He put the photographs back into the portfolio. "Would you be up for something like that?"

I shrugged my shoulders. I had spent the last year avoiding cameras, while my parents avoided recording my image. They didn't seem to want photographic evidence of what I had become, so they didn't take many pictures of me anymore. My senior picture was a compromise. I wore a dress my mother had purchased especially for the occasion, and I pulled my hair back so the pink streak wasn't as noticeable, but I didn't hide it. When the photos arrived, my parents framed one of the shots and put it on the mantle, tucked unobtrusively in an arrangement of other photographs of me, nestled toward the back, unnoticeable.

"Really, I would love to photograph you," he said, and he reached out to clasp my hand. "Would you allow me to?"

I thought of my mother, of shopping at Lord & Taylor with her for the dress that I wore in my senior picture. We'd shopped at Lord & Taylor for every special dress I'd ever owned, dresses for the Girl Scout dances that I went to with my father, who stood beside the punch bowl talking about football or the market with the other dads, while I scurried around the darkened gymnasium with my friends. Lord & Taylor dressed me for awkward middle school dances with boys whose braces clinked against my teeth when they leaned in for a kiss. Dresses for my grandparents' eightieth birthday parties, dresses for their funerals. My mother had just gotten off work when we shopped for the dress I wore for my senior picture. She was wearing her real estate agent clothing, a silky blouse, a crisply pressed pantsuit, shiny black pumps. Her makeup was freshly applied, as if she were meeting an important client and not the daughter who habitually disappointed her. She had just been to the hairdresser. Her short hairdo was puffy and smelled of hairspray. I thought of the dress I allowed her to pick out, a black dress that she could probably borrow for her next open house, a very tasteful, expensive crepe shirtdress with a thin matching black belt. I threw it in the back of my closet as soon as I got home from the photographer's. It probably still lay crumpled beneath shoes and boots and the other assorted crap at the back of my closet.

"I don't have to dress a certain way or anything?" I asked. "You just take my picture?"

Jan nodded.

I looked down at my cup of tea. "This is weird. Nobody has ever asked me to do anything like this before."

Jan laughed. "It's good to try new things!"

I nodded. "Okay. I'll do it."

Jan raised his paper cup in a toast. "To new things."

* * *

Jan pulled his camera from his bag and hung it from his neck by the strap. He hoisted his backpack over his shoulder, picked up his portfolio, and we started walking east. We went down St. Mark's Place, past the vendors selling woolen hats and gloves, old vinyl records, tattered paperbacks, whatever could be made or found or bought for cheap and sold. The street was a mix of things being torn down, put up, or staying exactly the same. Handbills on buildings looked like they'd been there for hundreds of years, curling, ripped, scored, abraded from the sun, the rain, the air itself. We walked past a scaffolded building, the sidewalks blocked to prevent bricks from raining down on passersby.

"Stop there," Jan said. He balanced the portfolio between his legs and lifted the camera to his eye. He started to click the button and I heard the shutter.

"What should I do?" I asked.

"Just do what you feel like doing. Act natural."

I stood there, afraid to look directly into the camera. I looked up at a light pole. Someone had thrown a pair of shoes, laces tied, up there, and they hung on the pole, rotting away. A sparrow was perched on top of the laces. The sky was no clearer; it looked as though someone had painted it with a mixture of milk and dust "I feel funny just standing like this," I said.

"Then just feel funny," he replied. He put the lens cap back on the camera and picked up the portfolio. "Go with it. You look good. Let's keep walking."

We crossed Second Avenue and continued walking down St. Mark's. As we kept moving east, I watched the other pedestrians, walking quickly, going places. People sat on building stoops, talking to other people, reading the newspaper, writing notes to themselves. Cars and taxis flew down the street. Parents pushed their children in baby carriages. I felt a raindrop on my cheek and I imagined myself here, older, one of these people with places to go. I felt another drop on my hand, then my ear. I turned my head to say something to Jan, but he wasn't there. I turned around. He stood further up the block, camera in hand. He was photographing me as I walked away.

* * *

Jan walked me back to the PATH station at Ninth Street and Sixth Avenue. I gave him another cigarette. "Give me your address, too," he said. "I'm going to send you a picture."

I wrote my address in my math notebook and ripped the page from the spiral binding. "Don't forget," I said. "When you're a famous photographer, I want to have proof that you took my picture."

He looked at the paper and folded it into quarters, then slid it into his jeans pocket. "I won't forget, Beth." He hugged me, and I could smell the coffee and smoke on his breath as he pulled back, and his stubble scratched my cheek. I looked at him. I noticed a thin, hairless line on his cheek, a scar, amid the short brown growth. I reached out and traced the scar with my index finger, then I kissed it gently. Jan smiled and pulled away.

"You're a good kid," he said. He patted my shoulder. "You be good."

"You too," I replied, then descended into the windy train station.

* * *

By the time the commuter train emerged from underground, the rain pelted the cars. The windows had steamed up on the inside, and water streamed down in tiny rivers along the outside of the panes. The sky was gray and dark, an evening sky in the afternoon. Rumbles of thunder vibrated the car and flashes of lightning illuminated the landscape, the factories, the tanks, the railway yards.

We moved into the gray suburban landscape. Wet backyards and swing sets strung along the railway line like one long banner. The rain had forced many of the leaves from the trees, and bare, spindly branches reached into the blank sky. When we finally got to my station, the thundering and lightning had ended, but the rain was steady. I picked a discarded newspaper out of the trash bin and held it over my head as I ran through the parking lot, cutting across backyards and down side streets till I reached my house.

Nobody was home. The house was quiet. My father wouldn't make it back from the city till at least seven. My mother was probably still at the office, playing matchmaker with buyers and sellers. I untied my boots at the door and placed them in the wicker basket that my mother used to corral wayward shoes, then I hung my soaked jacket from a doorknob and threw the wet newspaper in the kitchen garbage. I opened the refrigerator door, dug an apple out of the crisper, and sat in the quiet kitchen, looking out the window at the backyard, the slick flagstone patio, the empty birdfeeder. I went back to school the next day. I handed my homeroom teacher a note on which I'd forged my mother's signature, excusing my absence. My teacher took the note without a word, filing it away in his planner. That day was the same as every other day at school, as was the next day, and the next.

I continued filling out my college applications. My parents encouraged me to apply to their alma maters, small, quaint local schools. I started the applications but never finished them. Instead, I completed applications to faraway schools, in places like Seattle and San Francisco, places where the country could stretch far and wide between me and my parents, places that would require an effort to visit, places in which I could effortlessly hide myself away.

* * *

The holidays arrived. We put up a tree, an oversized fir that consumed half the living room, and my mother decorated the house with garlands and porcelain Santa figurines. The mail arrived every day, the postman stuffing the slot in the front door with Christmas cards from my parents' colleagues, neighbors, relatives. My mother replaced the photographs on the mantle with the greeting cards, until the mantle was full and she had to place the extras on the coffee table. One day, mixed in with the cards and catalogues, a large manila envelope arrived, addressed to me. "Do Not Bend" was written in large block letters across the bottom of the envelope. I handed the rest of the mail to my mother, tucking the envelope under my arm.

"What's that, hon?" my mother asked.

"Just something from some college." I raced up the stairs to my bedroom, closing the door behind me.

I opened the envelope. There were two pictures inside, nestled between two stiff pieces of cardboard. One photo was of me looking up toward the sky. The other photo was also me, walking away from the camera, my entire body framed by the shot. I flipped the photographs over. Jan had written in black Sharpie on the back of one photograph, "To new things. Jan."

I looked at the photos more closely. The girl who was looking at the sky didn't really resemble me at all. She was unrecognizable, even though I knew her features, her hair, her profile. She was a girl I hardly knew. The second photograph, the girl who was walking away from the camera, was the one I recognized. I had been getting to know that girl for a very long time. ■

BEACHFRONT
George McDermott

The dredges are saving the beach again,
pumping sand to the shore from the sea,
sand that once was part of the beach,
sand the storms will wash back out—

the surging tides, the punishing surf,
waves reshaping the water line—
hundreds of yards of coquina sand,
weathered remains of pulverized shells,

of Pleistocene lives memorialized
in sun-warmed sediment, reddish
and barren. A thousand years ago,
the beach had the space to save itself—

adjusting the coast to suit the currents,
shifting the sand to match the weather—
but now the beach is real estate,
paved and covered with condos and bars,

crowded with revelers, shallow as swamps,
wading, unthinking, through discolored tides,
denying truths submerged in the flood,
fractured beneath the pounding lies—

belief or suspicion, known or imagined,
the curse of inevitability,
the residue of numberless lives
coarse and warm as ancient sands.

LITTLE SPECIAL
E. Nolan

Charlie learned that his son was gifted when he picked him up early from school on Friday. Richter's kindergarten teacher pulled him aside, and, after commenting awkwardly about how it was nice to finally meet him after half a year of instuction, said, "He draws with both hands."

"He's ambidexterous?"

"No, you don't understand. He draws with both hands at the same time."

The teacher pulled out a sample from a file cabinet and handed it to Charlie. It was a bunch of scribble marks that conveyed a distressed, yet confident monkey. Charlie recognized something in the drawing that made him uncomfortable. An ease of the talented.

Charlie asked the teacher, "He drew this with both hands at the same time? Like he drew the tail and the head at the same time?"

The teacher enthusiastically said, "Yeah!" then looked confused when Charlie didn't reciprocate the excitement. He got red and seemed to scramble a bit. "He could ride this to a specialized high school . . . I've never seen any child ever . . . I've been teaching for fifteen years . . . just look at the emotion in that monkey's gaze . . . I'm sure he's going to be very successful at whatever he chooses to pursue."

Charlie wasn't so sure. He knew that disappointment accompanied talent more often than success.

Richter peeked up from his play and came over to his dad and they went home.

* * *

Richter drew something at Charlie's request. Richter used both hands, but not at the same time. It was a dinosaur drawn in tiny segments, like a poster of a cow at a butcher's shop showing the various cuts of meat. Charlie watched from over his son's shoulder and didn't realize at first that Richter was crying. It obviously had nothing to do with the drawing, but Charlie tried to make him feel better by complimenting his artwork because anything else would have just been too complicated. "It's a great drawing," Charlie said.

"This is exactly the kind of dinosaur sketch I wanted." He took it from under Richter's tiny hands and made his way over to the fridge to hang it up, but there were no magnets so he just folded it up and put it in his pocket. Richter protested with a "Hey!" but Charlie's mind was elsewhere suddenly, gripped with anxiety about his approaching weekend plan to attend a math teachers' conference upstate. He put Richter in front of the television, and with the door propped open, sat on the front stoop and smoked a cigarette, waiting for his ex-wife, Maddy, to come pick up her son.

She arrived toward the end of Charlie's second cigarette. She parked her car at the edge of the driveway and left it running. The sun was coming down and the wind blew the white pines to the left and right of her as she approached. Charlie was still very much attracted to her and struggled with accepting that their intimacy was lost. He got up and threw his cigarette on the lawn like a dart before heading back inside. He called out to Richter and nodded to the door. He wanted to share with her that he was sober now. Three months. Hard to imagine, him being clean, but he liked it. He helped the boy put on his coat and pushed him out toward his waiting mother. In the bustle, he forgot to say bye.

* * *

Charlie's colleague, Mort, drove the Jeep and Charlie slouched in the passenger seat. "You can do this," Mort said. Cars were passing them by on the left. Mort's Jeep Comanche had been relegated to the slow lane ever since the engine bolt had cracked thirty thousand miles ago. Driving with Mort was like driving with an apostle who'd somehow survived the centuries and had picked up a few bad habits along the way. He looked the part: grey, bearded, hairy, old, scuzzy. "Do the conference, eat the shit pastries, talk math with the other teachers. Simple."

They were making the 250-mile trip to South Fallsburg for the New York State Association of Math Teachers of Junior Colleges Convention. The convention was to be held at a small campus with accommodations at a nearby family-owned dude ranch, but they'd chosen to make reservations at a small motel outside of the compound, in order to have more access to cheap food and booze. The reservations had been made several months ago, when Charlie's life was utterly different.

"You wanted to stop drinking and you did. Pat yourself on the back. But you're leaving me out in the lurch, man. I baked a batch of pot brownies and you tell me you're straight. Here's your chance to smoke cigarettes till you're blue in the face while I eat my brownies. I can eat brownies in front of you, right? Or is that considered *déclassé?*"

Charlie sank back into the seat and stared out the window. Mort had the wiper speed on high even though the falling snow wasn't that bad.

Charlie's lawyer, a scrunchy-faced guy in an outdated baggy suit, had been the one to tell him to quit drinking. He was able to size him up as a chronic alcoholic and his suggestion was so that Charlie could look more presentable in court. But he had then pulled Charlie aside to a quieter part of the hallway and asked, "You know you don't *have* to drink, right?" It was the first time Charlie had ever heard that before and hearing it from this lovable creature made the message a hope that he could latch on to. And he gave it a shot. It was rough, since he was used to drinking every day, but he did it. There were no physical withdrawal symptoms, and he took this to mean that it wasn't too late for everything to turn out okay.

What exactly that meant, he had yet to understand.

"Am I pissed?" Mort asked rhetorically. "Yes, I'm pissed. Will I get over it? Sure, man. No hard feelings. No fucking hard feelings at all."

Mort put on the radio and Charlie nodded off. He woke up an hour and a half later as they pulled into a wide-open parking lot. Charlie took one look at the shitty motel and wanted to go back to sleep. The whole thing seemed like a bad idea.

He had the awful sensation that he should be doing something completely different and that it was of the utmost importance. He'd get these feelings every now and then but he'd never follow through on them. It was his understanding that normal people listened to these inner voices and that this was the main difference between him and them. He knew he should be home with his boy. Even Maddy had said on the phone that he should've canceled. Why did he insist on coming?

Stepping out of the truck, he remembered the drawing. He checked the pocket of his jeans and pulled out the drawing. Sheilding it from the snow, he was struck by its quality as if seeing it for the first time. He was an artist! It was obvious! How could he have not known about his talent? Since the divorce, he hadn't spent enough time with the kid. And the truth was that before the divorce it hadn't been much different. He folded up the drawing and put it back in his pocket.

Standing in that oversized parking lot already accumulating snow, Charlie knew that he would either remember everything about this trip or not remember it at all.

* * *

At the long breakfast table there were two groups of colleagues and Mort and Charlie took a seat next to the ones who seemed more provincial. It slowly dawned on Charlie that they were a family, although there would be no reason for a family to be in a place like this; there was a man and wife, and a son in his early twenties. Charlie was intrigued. The lady wore a full-length dress that had ruffles around the neck and the ends of the sleeves, as if she had fashioned it out of a tablecloth, doilies and all. Charlie couldn't stop looking at it. It was like staring into the empty eyes of the past. The father wore a beard and had longish hair but did not appear to be a hippie. He wore a red-and-black flannel shirt and suspenders. Charlie had never seen a man like this on Long Island. Could he be a mountain man, perhaps? Frontiersman? The father and son sat close together and conversed in little whispers. Charlie focused on the son for a moment and on his boyish features. He tried to imagine his own father bringing him to a math conference.

Mort immediately started in on the lady. "Hey, baby."

Her face was so rigid that it looked like it was wooden. She didn't respond. Mort turned to the men, who were now paying attention. "What's happening, my brothers?" he asked them. "Do you have any drugs?"

They didn't respond. Mort looked at Charlie and shrugged.

With a few words Mort had quieted their corner of the cafeteria. Another woman from the far end of the table responded to the awkward silence, saying, "Did anyone happen to watch Johnny Carson last night? Did anyone see the little Asian boy do chisanbop?"

"Yeah, it sucked," Mort said. He spoke loud and quickly enough to cut anyone else off. Charlie had seen several people about to say something, but first trying to finish their sip of coffee or taking a half second too long to open their mouth.

The woman looked at Mort with a look of hate.

Charlie hadn't seen anything on TV but did know about chisanbop, or enough to know that it was a Korean form of calculating using a sequence of finger movements. Like eight times six. It was for kids, as far as he knew. Mort said, "Charlie can do it ten times better. I've seen him multiply . . . *four*-digit integers. Using only his fingers."

The lady sized up Charlie. "*You* know chisanbop?" she asked, disbelievingly.

She struck a nerve with Charlie so quickly that something switched on inside him. How dare she speak to him condescendingly? If he had to prove that he was better than all these hack mathematicians by lying, then so be it. "Yeah, I fucking know it."

"Well, enlighten us," someone said. Charlie didn't see who it was. Mort said, "Someone give us an equation."

"Five thousand two hundred and twenty-seven times sixteen thousand eight hundred and five," the lady said.

The mountain man took out a small pad and a pencil out of his flannel shirt. Charlie even noticed out of the corner of his eye that the pencil had been sharpened with a knife. *Fits*, he thought.

With all of the people's eyes on him, Charlie sensed a heightened awareness like right before a fight or a bad argument. He raised a fist in the air and thought to himself that the answer must be around eighty-seven million. He placed his hand back on the table with three of his fingers sticking out. He lifted his fist, made the Spock sign, made the peace sign, then returned his open palm gently to the sticky tabletop. He knew the answer ended with a thirty-five. He raised it again, paused for a second and slammed his fist on the table, hard enough to knock over some of the water glasses. People got out of their chairs to avoid the water that was all over the place. "Eighty-seven million eight hundred and thirty-nine thousand seven hundred and thirty-five."

Mort looked at Charlie in wonder, laughing his ass off. Charlie felt as if he'd been put through the wringer. His hand throbbed and when he looked he thought he was seeing the claw of a boiled lobster. He heard someone say, "He's right," but Charlie was too worried whether he had permanently damaged his hand. The pain made him want to throw up and a cold sweat started on his forehead.

Mort saw him suffering and his face changed quickly. "Come on, Charlie," Mort said. "We should go."

In the hallway, Mort said, "That was funny as hell, Charlie. But you've got something special. I've seen it before. When you're in the right mood, when you're out of your shell, you are quick as hell with those numbers. When it comes to abstract thought, you don't get lost too often, do you?"

Charlie said, "I got lucky."

Charlie smoked three cigarettes outside, and in that period

somewhere, Mort brought him a coffee. Charlie switched hands and smoked with his lobster claw in order to enjoy his cup. Mort had spiked it. Charlie had that awful feeling again, that urgent sense of doing something else entirely. Someone else would not continue to drink. They'd put the coffee down. Maybe they'd even drop everything and take a train back home. But he thought to himself, *Fuck 'em*, and he immediately relaxed and had another sip.

* * *

At lunchtime they had time to drive back to their motel room. Charlie, with a bit of a buzz, ate some of Mort's pot brownies. They made fun of the old-fashioned types and Mort explained that there was a rumor going around during his morning session that the kid was sort of a mathematical genius. "Kind of like yourself," he commented. Mort made him a rum and Coke from the bottle that he had on him, then Charlie walked to the nearest 7-Eleven. The falling snow was heavy now, and the shoes that he'd brought were not appropriate for the weather. As Charlie trudged, the snow fell harder. It was a snow thicker than he'd ever seen. Flakes fell like wet cotton balls.

He bought a twelve of Miller and at the register struck up a conversation with another man buying a twelve of Bud. He had forgotten about that type of instant camaraderie that comes with alcohol. Outside, as he walked through the parking lot, he saw a boy Richter's age waiting in the passenger's seat of an idling car. He cringed, remembering Richter doing the same and being glad, not too long ago, that he never had to do that again.

In the span of two hours, Charlie drank eight, and Mort had four.

* * *

It was in the afternoon session, where Charlie bumped into the woodsman's son, that the day went to rot.

"I know that wasn't chisanbop," the boy said to Charlie.

"I bet you know a lot of stuff," Charlie said sarcastically, provoked by the alcohol in his system.

"I know your type, as well."

"My type?"

"You're bad."

"That's what type I am?" Charlie was able to see that there was something blank in the young man's eyes. "I thought you were going to say 'ruminative underachiever,' or 'perceptive rationalizer' or something a little more complicated. But just 'bad'?"

"You're being bad in a place that is . . . we're supposed to be doing math, not tricks. You're taking away from everyone else."

Although he didn't want to admit it, Charlie knew this kid wasn't far off. He was oversimplifying the entire struggle, but you couldn't say he was wrong. Charlie thought of his job, which he didn't take seriously, his soon-to-be ex, whom he still clinged to emotionally, his kid the artist, whom he didn't really know. He thought of himself, drunk and stoned at a community college outside of Albany.

The boy examined Charlie deep in his eyes. "You're high on something." He sniffed the air in front of Charlie. "You smell like a wino."

The boy stood there, lanky, poorly dressed, like a malnourished genius. Could it be true?

Charlie tested Mort's compliment on the boy. "They say you don't get lost too often in abstract thought."

"You don't make any sense," the boy said. "You should just go home. You don't belong here."

Why was the boy coming out of his shell to mock Charlie?

"If you're so sure it wasn't chisanbop, then don't you want to know how I did it?"

"I know how you did it. You did a half-assed calculation and guessed on the rest. If you'd gotten it wrong, people still might have been impressed with how close you came, or impressed by how you could even remember two large numbers. If that didn't work, you could have just laughed it off as the time you got everyone wet at the math conference."

"What's your name?" Charlie asked.

"None of your business," the boy said, and walked away.

Charlie followed him. "What do you mean that I'm bad?"

The boy turned around. "You're following me," he said.

"You can't just go around accusing everyone of something," Charlie said. His hands were shaking a little.

The boy picked up the pace and Charlie kept up with him.

"Get away from me!" the boy shouted. "Go home!"

"I am not bothering you!" Charlie shouted back. He grabbed him by his shirt and threw him up against the wall. Just as quickly he let him go and the boy ran away down the hall. Presenters from inside different rooms stopped for a second, others who were in the hallway turned around. They had pretended not to notice after their initial reaction, but Charlie knew they had. Had they noticed that he was drunk?

He went down the long hall, peeking into each room. Little by little the rooms got emptier and emptier. He reached a section around a corner that had the lights turned off. While it wasn't completely dark, it was harder to see and obvious that this wing was not part of the convention. Charlie, by habit, entered one of the rooms and opened up the drawers in the metal desk, looking for things that he could take if he wanted to. He was a teacher and this was a teacher's desk, he told himself. It was when he opened the last drawer on the bottom, revealing a box of colored chalk, that he heard the son's voice. "Go ahead, steal it." Charlie startled and saw that he had missed the black shadow in the back of the room. Sensing a force greater than himself guide him, he walked slowly between the uneven rows of desks toward the boy, bumping into a few and knocking away others, and when he was right above him punched him in the left cheek, then, with the heel of his boot, kicked the kid in the chest, forcing out a deep groan. Charlie fell back and ended up on the ground. It was a racket. The boy was heaving, bent over the desk. Charlie left him like that, figuring that he probably had not hurt him so bad that he needed medical attention.

He left the building hastily through a nearby staircase, tripping, and ended up on the top portion of a snow-covered slope that gleamed eerily in the early-winter night with the glow of an orange security light on a shed fifty meters downslope. It occurred to him that he was very buzzed and that his heart raced from the irrational brutality that he'd put himself through. He hadn't hit someone in twenty years, he thought, and here he was kicking a hopeless sap while he was trapped in a seat. He lit a cigarette. Everything was so present. He felt as if the entire day went by without any reflection. It was exhausting. He decided to go inside and finish the day's schedule.

He sat through half a presentation, closing one eye to focus before realizing that it was best that he left. He wandered in and out of a half dozen other presentations.

At one point he was confronted by the hillbilly father and the home-on-the-prairie mother. The beaten son hid behind them. His cheek was swollen. "What you are," the founding father said, "is a sick man. I'm not going to call the police or inform the college, but we are going to pray for you because that is what you need more than anything else."

Charlie thought, *Anyone less than a saint for these guys they probably consider a sicko.*

But the man went on. "We came here for techniques to reach the younger generation of future mathematicians, but God put you in our lives for a more important reason and we will not turn a fearful eye on what is presented to us. A sick man should be treated as a sick man. Our son is sick, but in a different way. Anyone can see clearly that he is not capable of interacting like a mature adult. We know that he most likely instigated the entire thing, but still, you are an adult with full capacity of mind, and I might add an unusual talent for calculating, from what I witnessed this morning. We find it curious why this gift has not been a blessing for you as it would be for countless others. We want to say that we are grateful that you entered our lives so that we can have the opportunity to pray for you and your God-given talents."

Charlie listened to the entire spiel, at first hoping that the man would shed light on his troubles, but ended up doubting that they understood any of his problems. Talents are not blessings, they're burdens, Charlie wanted to explain to them, but he knew that they wouldn't get it. They'd just insist that prayer was still the answer. But praying for something that you don't understand is the same as talking to yourself in the dark. And if you're in the habit of praying for what you don't understand, your relationship with God is not what you think it is. Charlie felt a balance return as he discovered their essential flaw. He took one last glance at the righteous couple, the hillbilly preacher, the woman of wood, and their battered boy, a sense of pride now seeping into his feelings of remorse.

Back at the motel, Charlie told Mort about the son, the kicking, and the old-fashioned religious types and their speech. It was like a confession. Then they both drank as much as they could. They finished off the brownies and Charlie got caught up in a porno movie that was on the televsion. One of the female actors resembled Madelaine. The bronze skin, the long legs, the wavy, dark hair. The last he remembered before passing out was Mort telling him to turn that shit off.

* * *

The next day was a half day at the conference, but Mort and Charlie agreed that they should leave early.

On the drive home, Charlie milked a six-pack of Genesee Cream Ale, with Mort's permission. Charlie had a massive hangover and a guilty conscious. Mort spoke. "I'm glad you got over that high-and-mighty no-drinking bullshit. People drink. It's okay to go on a bender every once in a while. It's what men do. That's what my father said. And when I'd come home from a few-days binge, he'd say, 'Now you're set for a while. You don't have to drink.'"

You don't have to drink.

The phrase echoed in Charlie's mind. Mort didn't understand. Now he *did* have to drink.

At a Hess station, Charlie picked up a twelve of Hamm's for the rest of the trip.

* * *

Back home, Charlie opened the door to an empty house. Under one arm he carried the remainder of the twelve-pack and in the other hand he clasped the box of colored chalk that he had stolen.

The chalk was to be a gift for Richter, the artist. He left it on the plastic table where he'd watched him drawing the other day. He had a great idea to open the box and have one piece of chalk sticking out like an offered cigarette from a soft pack. Opening the box, he noticed that they were all broken, every one of them, into little pieces. His disappointment hit him hard before he was able to safely tuck it away inside. He tossed the box on Richter's table and told himself that maybe his son would prefer them that way.

He got a beer and had a smoke on the front stoop again and waited.

He had no idea if she was dropping him off this evening or before school the next day. A car here and there passed down the street, the headlights threatening Charlie for a moment before leaving him alone again in the darkness. A quiet thought passed through his mind. *You can't do this.*

Charlie brushed it away quickly, but there was a lingering quality to a thought like that in a time like this. The next car that passed turned into the driveway. Richter got out, as did Maddy. Charlie tossed the beer can behind the bush and got ready for what he knew was coming. ■

THE DISSONANCE OF A TASER IN A DINING ROOM

Barbara Haas

On Saturday afternoon the apiary vandalism had not yet happened—I stood there, leaning against my car on one of the mildest of late winter days, idly gazing at our six beehives. Snowy clumps and slushy clods still surrounded them at that point—a typical look for late February. I focused especially on the several inches or so of space right above the top covers of the hives, where it was often possible on a blastingly bright day like this to see a small darting cloud of looping activity—bees taking their cleansing flight. The sun had strengthened to such an extent that a vapor appeared to lift off the ever-present snow still mantling the bluffs just beyond the hives. The vapor colored the air and wavered somewhat, the way heat shimmers seem to rise above hot pavement, an ephemeral trompe l'oeil of ice crystals refracting the sunlight.

Cerulean? I wondered, scrutinizing the hue and radiance. *Azure?* It was what skiers in Colorado meant when they said "bluebird."

Snowshoeing here last week, I'd floated atop fresh powder, an unexpected five inches from a storm squall. Central Iowa rarely resembled a Colorado backcountry, but it did that day—another trick of the eye. Drifts caked the slopes, and snow-laden spruce boughs draped low, framing the subtle white-on-white contours of the trail. The creek was an ice highway, solid and silent. Its surface bore hieroglyphs of the wildlife that had trekked through—the bobcats, coyotes, deer, beavers, muskrats, foxes, and wild turkeys.

But last week's powder had slumped down into crusty piles—unrewarding for any kind of snowshoe trek now—and the only resemblance this place had to Colorado arched above me in the cloudless sky. The creek ice had already fractured, too—a sure sign of a season on the verge. A gush of new water babbled across stone riffles.

Our nature refuge, a woodland acreage nestled into an undeveloped wilderness site, was land the university kept for research purposes. A grad student was meeting me here for help with his barn owl project. Enjoying the sun, enjoying this Saturday afternoon, I directed my attention to the apiary again, visoring my hand above my eyes for tighter focus. Gyring over the row of hives was that telltale looping spiral—the cleansing flight-swarm. The motion, hypnotic and acrobatic, could relieve the housebound, claustrophobic symptoms of late February and salve anybody's tendencies toward stir-craziness. Unlike the ice crystals wavering above the bluffs, reliant on vapor or optical illusions, this was not an ephemeral deception. It represented tangible visual evidence of how well the colonies had survived winter.

Six hives, each housing 20,000 bees—a population of 120,000 altogether. The air was aswirl with darting swoops. Zero activity on a sunny day like this could mean the colonies had perished.

My grad student pulled in soon after, along with his wife and their puppy, and we headed off down the woodland trail to scout out a site for the barn owl nesting box he planned to build. Sometimes tromping through snowbanks, other times navigating gumbo-slick switchbacks where deer tracks had left gouge marks, we surveyed several trees for suitability, and then parted ways for the day.

Driving westward in central Iowa was like driving right into the sky, and I dipped my head from time to time to get the color right. Was it cerulean? Was it azure? There was nothing more complicated on an uncomplicated Saturday than indulging a game like that.

Thirty minutes later, I received a call from Dave, my rural fixer. He was the neighbor who mowed for us at the nature refuge during the summer, removed snow from the driveway during the winter, and provided maintenance. When the wind tore the door off the shed, Dave repaired it. When hail damaged the shed's roof, Dave patched it. When rodents ate the shed's insulation, Dave replaced it. The shed, a frequent target of nature's wrath, maxed out the ordinary handiness any given middlingly competent academic like me was likely to possess. This shed, the only structure at the nature refuge, wore a colossal bull's-eye. However, not even this shed and its repetitive crises could max out Dave's skill set. He'd grown up on a farm nearby and had an excavating business just down the road. He was steeped in the customs, habits, and social mores of the county, one of those people who walk to the barn to do *one* thing but end up doing *five* things on their way. We paid him in honey, which he swore by as a winter tonic. Vitamin H, he called it.

Ag crops bordered our woodland tract, and the straggling remnants of barbed wire loosely demarcated property lines—rusted relics from a time when cattle grazed through the woods. The county had a strong ethic of stewardship—and other landowners respected fencing and boundaries. Everyone who worked the land in central Iowa, which was unquestionably a major venue for working the land, had to trust that mischief-makers or worse—criminals—wouldn't mess up their work. Crop production covered more than 60 percent of the state. In order to turn a profit, one had to operate under the assumption that one's work out there would actually bear fruit, unperturbed. Iowa was spacious, so spacious that it was not possible to know every blessed thing there was to know about every little square foot of anything that might go on in those vast open spaces. One had to trust.

This kind of trust was endemic to unincorporated townships where farming dominated, a guiding principle and pervasive creed. Every tight-knit community had a code, something that delineated it from the codes of other places. The degree to which the ag industry demanded work and commerce in wide-open areas and untended acreages governed the stringency of the code. The code and the degree of trust that twinned along with it fit hand in glove. Those who violated the code violated the trust. They did not get second chances.

Although the nature refuge was a university acquisition, a land gift from a rural donor, and it wasn't open to the public on account of the need to safeguard academic projects there, it fit obliquely in with the prevailing code. Private Property signs stood in key spots. The only trespassing our nature refuge had ever experienced came in the form of high school kids having a beer party one night back in 2013. Even then it wasn't some random act, unconnected to us: one of the boys was the son of our tenant farmer. Nearly every week since then I walked the land, and I never found anything amiss, outside of nature occasionally venting its wrath on our poor dilapidated shed. Plus Dave kept an eye on things for us. He ran his Labradors off leash at the refuge each evening.

Dave, my fixer.

"Where are you?" Dave asked me over the phone.

"What do you mean? I'm at home." My gumbo-laden boots stood in the breezeway, and I was holding the phone with one hand and examining the tread with the other.

"I wasn't sure if you were still here," Dave said. "There's a car like yours in the parking lot. I'm debating whether to run the dogs."

I thought back to my grad student's small SUV. He and his wife had been loading their pup into the back of it as I drove out. Maybe they had returned?

I told Dave it was probably my grad student's vehicle, that he and I had been there working earlier, that the Labs should be okay off leash. "A blue SUV, right? With a roof rack?"

"It's tan," Dave said. "I'm looking at it right now. One of those hybrids." Faintly over the line I could hear a dog whining, and I figured Dave had a Labrador on his lap. "It's like yours," he said.

I had left the nature refuge at 4:00 p.m. and gotten home around 4:30. It was 4:45 when I took Dave's call. My grad student had left in his blue SUV soon after I had, wife and pup onboard. And now Dave was in the parking lot. Plus another car.

The car Dave was looking at was tan, and it had pulled in after I left.

I tilted my head, still examining the tread on my gumbo-heavy boots. For a place that had mainly slumbered through the dormant season, that had been left unattended, all by its lonesome really, unvisited except by Dave and his dogs and sometimes me with my snowshoes, the nature refuge had suddenly seen an uncommon amount of activity in a short window of time for one February day. Other grad students of course tended projects out there: the applied mycology team and its mushroom inoculations, our shitake, oyster, and chanterelle initiatives. Also the Poetry Trail people. Everyone who worked there was someone I knew.

I set my boots back down in the breezeway, and some of the caked mud crumbled onto the tiles. "Well, use your judgment about the dogs," I told Dave. "If you think it's okay to let them out, go for it." I knew how habitual dogs were, expecting their walks at certain hours of the day, almost as if they could smell what time it was, or maybe they relied on a certain angle of the sun. Once Dave got his Labs into the truck, they already knew where they were headed, because they did this every afternoon. I smiled, imagining how they might be panting and slobbering and hassling Dave right now, still seated beside him in the truck—or climbing all over him?—impatient for him to get off the phone and give them their run. It was smell o'clock already—!

Thus the sun set for me on an uncomplicated Saturday.

On Sunday my bee geek, Zack, found the apiary vandalism—all our honeybees dead. Every bee that had reveled in its cleansing flight the day before, basking in that bluebird light, was now gone.

Between my visit to the refuge and Zack's—in those eighteen hours—someone had removed the top covers from each of the hives, exposing the colonies to below-freezing temperatures through the night. Zack sent me the photos. Six hives stood in the still-receding snow, just as I had seen them the day before—but unlike what I had seen when I'd idly gazed upon the apiary, waiting for my student, the hives in these photos were now open and uncapped, each of the top covers leaning against its matching hive body. The vandal's actions seemed orderly and unhurried, even methodical. I looked at the covers, angled against the boxes. I blinked. Operating hive by hive, removing *this* lid, leaning it against *this* box and then proceeding to the next, the vandal had acted in a rational, leisurely fashion.

Taking care, I thought.

Our apiary sustained losses every winter. For a harsh climate like central Iowa's, a 50 percent die-off was not uncommon—so we just had to brace for it. If we fostered bees at the refuge and provided them with a habitat like this, it was on us to do all we could to see to their survival, even knowing how soberingly high the losses would be. So of course we winterized the hives with loose sleeves of black tar paper, good for holding every Kelvin of warmth from even a weak winter's sun. Naturally, we stacked alfalfa bales on the apiary's north side, as a wind break. A fully winter-tested queen was worth the risk of beekeeping in central Iowa, worth the hardships and hazards, worth the investment. She laid the kind of eggs that produced tough bees the following season, and they gathered nectar prodigiously. The ability to survive, now coded into the queen's DNA, built-in, as it were, and programmed into her habits—not to mention into the eggs she laid—got turbocharged when touched by winter. Last season our honey harvest had topped 360 pounds, a personal best.

I studied the photos my bee geek had sent. I stared at the vandal's modus operandi. A single gesture, repeated six times, had wiped all that out. Seasonal losses due to long nights of bitter cold and strafing winds were random, incremental, and varied. Not even winter was this systematic. Never was winter 100 percent.

Farmers whose hard work and labor lay open in the fields, unguarded, had to trust that no one would plow into the rows of newly planted corn, for instance, with their pick-up truck and start doing donuts, ripping through the soil. Farmers whose work lay open in unprotected acres had to trust that only floods could swamp and destroy their fieldwork in one fell swoop—or wind storms, like the rare derecho that rampaged through.

But nothing in nature would take it all.

A week or so after our losses, a colleague in my department asked me if maybe a critter at the nature refuge, a wilderness inhabitant, might have inadvertently knocked the covers off the hives—like a deer herd crashing through the apiary, bumping up against the boxes. It was a reasonable question for someone who had not seen the photos of the vandalism. A herd's actions would have had a scattershot quality, a willy-nilly come-what-may aspect, leaving tousled and tumbled boxes in its wake, all the inner frames and comb lying askew in the snow. I recalled the disposition of the lids. I recalled how they leaned against the hives. Nothing in nature behaved with such intent.

Another colleague wondered if maybe the colonies had already died off earlier in the winter—another reasonable supposition for someone who had not seen the bees in flight the day before. Unlike other insects, bees did not hibernate once their nectar sources faded and the days grew cold, but they gathered tightly around their queen, creating a densely shivering and wing-flapping mass that could insulate her—known as the winter cluster. The bees on the outer cusp of the cluster rotated that duty with those near the core, each individual getting a chance to stay warm and not tire out from the constant wing action. This kind of behavior on the part of bees caused us as a species to laud them and shower them with wistful admiration. We longed to work as cooperatively and collaboratively as they did. We longed to take a lesson from the honeybees' playbook.

The apiary at the nature refuge faced south, which meant that the hives received full winter sun most of the day, and that was key. Even during ultra-cold snaps, that touch of convection and light could make or break a colony's ability to survive. Insulated with propolis, a kind of bee-produced glue, the interior became a weathertight, cold-resistant, windproof habitat in which the colony could hunker down with its food source: frames heavy with honey. Prior to that, during the foraging season, some worker bees had brought nectar and pollen back to their hive from flowers, others had brought resin and sap back from the trunks of poplars and red cedar. They'd mixed the sap and resin with their own saliva and a small amount of wax to create propolis. Pliable above sixty-eight degrees, the propolis grew rigid below those temperatures. Resin was a natural protectant for trees—a wound sealer on damaged bark. As much as the bees used propolis as an insulation, they used it also to protect the colony against mites and fungi. Propolis served an antibacterial purpose throughout the hive. All that had been happening in our apiary— vital, vibrant, and alive. Now: gone.

On that Sunday, still reeling somewhat from my bee geek's bad news, I spoke with the county sheriff, who filed a report, and then I sat down with the university's detective, who planned an investigation. She came to my house that very afternoon, leaving her squad car parked not in my driveway but on the street. Sitting across from me at the dining table, she wore her full police uniform and had all her body equipment on her, including a Taser clipped to a belt loop on her left hip, her nondominant side, and a holstered pistol secured at her right hip. Hers was the look of supreme polish and proficiency. *Stract*—the military term for it. She flipped her notepad open and began jotting a few things down with the nub of a pencil. These analogue old-school gumshoe accoutrements were at odds with the Taser.

My dining room was at odds with the Taser.

A Taser was the norm for the halls she frequented at the university, however, the halls that connected the campus police department's offices. Like all tight-knit communities that shared a code and a purpose and a mindset, ours had its customs, its social mores, its equipment and manner of dress.

Only when her world came into contact with mine did a dissonance occur, the dissonance of a Taser in a dining room, for instance. Her world came into contact with mine only on account of a crime. Otherwise, the detective and I were unlikely ever to sit down like this.

I was aware of her scrutiny. When I made a minor correction to the Saturday timeline, she flipped back through her notepad and jotted a symmetrical correction there. And then her gaze fell on me again, evaluative. She was deciding whether to believe me or not. She was deciding whether to conclude that I had vandalized the apiary. Naturally, suspicion could fall on any of us; there were no sacred cows when it came to investigating a crime, nor should there be. This did not bother me. The university's problems ran the gamut from sexual harassment cases to embezzlement of funds, so any detective assigned to any case had to be nimble, keen, unbiased, observant. I was glad for her healthy skepticism—which is to say, the *professional* level of her skepticism—and I was glad that she was being thorough.

Our case number was 020-000-178. The year was young, but the university's detectives had already opened 177 cases before this one. The 000 indicated how high the numbers eventually would climb in the coming months, with plenty of room for more.

Of course, the detective interviewed my bee geek, Zack, too.

Of course, she interviewed the grad student who was planning the barn owl project.

Of course, we learned who owned the tan hybrid Dave had

seen in the parking lot. It was another grad student, a fellow who occasionally hiked at the nature refuge.

When the detective contacted him and described the apiary vandalism, he confirmed that he had been there the day before. He said he had never had anything to do with the bees out there, however, or with the honey production—and he declined to sit for an interview.

The detective told me later that she thought he was not being truthful. Obviously there was some *tell*, some quirk or instance of inconsistency, a trick of the trade that she had come to trust and to look for, maybe the timbre of his voice over the phone, a revealing hesitation, something that clued her in, as reliable and as sure as a Taser on the left, a pistol on the right.

Even so, the trail went cold.

Playing a *cerulean or azure?* kind of game in my mind, I assumed the grad student with the tan hybrid had indeed vandalized the apiary—but my assumption didn't result in any kind of hope for resolution, restitution, or closure. It didn't move anything forward: sometimes cerulean looked like azure or azure looked like cerulean. But blue was always blue, and you had to live with it.

The bees were gone.

We had no proof of culpability.

No leads to follow, no clues.

Barring an eleventh-hour confession, there wasn't more to do.

My bee geek cleaned the hives, we replaced all the colonies with purchases from a local provider—and we introduced new queens in May. "Agriculture is a gamble," he told me. "It's a risk."

I installed an infrared game camera within sixty feet of the apiary, the kind hunters use, "to capture prey on the move," as the packaging said. Dave showed me how to hide it in the crook of a tree, an unblinking eye that would surveil our hives 24/7. It wouldn't stop vandalism, but it boosted our ability to nail a culprit. Motion triggered the camera's shutter, which fired at a laser-fast four-per-second clip. It featured arm/disarm modes.

When I mentioned this last to the university detective, I sensed her quiet satisfaction. ∎

WHAT FRANNIE LEARNED
Michelle Massie

When Frannie was born there was no indication that anything in her life would prove particularly extraordinary. She was the third child in a family of five, not exactly planned but not unplanned either. She would not suffer from the overattentiveness that comes with being the firstborn, nor would she be placed on a pedestal and every flaw overlooked, as often happens with the last. Frannie was square in the middle. Neither flawed nor perfect, she thrived in a milieu of mostly benign neglect.

As a newborn Frannie seemed to accept her position without question. Her mother's labor was short; she nursed without fuss, gained weight and met milestones without a hitch. One might suggest that she benefited from the siblings that came before, but it was also true that this seemed to just be her nature; she did not need drama to find her place in the world.

* * *

When Frannie was three she learned to read on her own, or at least that is what her parents believed. She sat for hours staring at the books piled on the bookshelf in the corner of the family room. *Tikki Tikki Tembo, Lyle, Lyle, Crocodile, Where the Wild Things Are*, she could read them all. But in fact what she had done was learn them by heart, having heard them recited countless times to and by her older siblings. Frannie thought she *was* reading until the day she started school. Her mother bragged to Miss Hill that Frannie was smart beyond her years, but when Miss Hill placed a book in front of her that Frannie had never seen, Frannie just stared, unable to make any sound whatsoever. Her mother blushed and explained to Miss Hill that Frannie must be nervous—it was the first day, after all. When Frannie got home that afternoon, her mother scolded her. Why had she pretended she couldn't read? Her mother had demanded to know.

What Frannie learned about her world that day was that embarrassing her mother was about the worst crime she could commit. What she also recognized much later in life was that this was the day she learned that love can become conditional, easily overshadowed by one's own insecurities.

* * *

The summer Frannie turned nine she was sent to Girl Scout camp. The day before camp she had cut her left index finger with a kitchen knife and had to have it bandaged by Dr. Hansen at the corner clinic. He placed special tape over the cut to keep it closed and told Frannie it could not get wet for two weeks. This meant that Frannie would not be swimming in Blue Lake, nor would she be making clay pots in craft class, playing with water balloons, or jetting down the Slip 'n Slide set up on Bear Mountain. (It was really more of a steep hill.) Frannie would spend many hours at camp reading, walking alone in the woods, and sketching in her new sketchbook the flowers she came across on her hikes. Frannie didn't mind solitude, in fact she learned to favor it. She watched from the sidelines as the other girls squabbled and the counselors gossiped.

What Frannie learned at camp was not how to tread water in the deep end or sing camp songs in a round, but how the power of observation was something that she could fold up, keep in her back pocket, and pull out when everything else seemed at odds.

* * *

When Frannie was thirteen she got her period. Her mother had not told her anything about what would be happening, but what Frannie surmised was that her mother was more embarrassed than forgetful. Frannie could have talked to her older sister, Larabee, but Larabee was the kind of sister who would use any information against you. When Frannie lost her first tooth, Larabee told her it was because she had eaten too much sugar and she was rotting from the inside out. When she developed an itchy rash, Larabee claimed it was because she was allergic to certain TV shows, especially *Captain Kangaroo*, which happened to be Frannie's favorite at the time. When chicken pox went around the family, Larabee had claimed the mailman had brought it. It wasn't so much that Frannie believed her older sister, she was wiser than that, it was just she didn't want to give her another opportunity to feel superior.

So Frannie said nothing. But she did go to the library. Miss Beecher, the librarian, was accustomed to seeing Frannie and when she understood what Frannie was up to, she quietly left a copy of *Are You There God? It's Me, Margaret.* where she knew Frannie would see it.

What Frannie learned that day was that there are hidden angels in the universe whose presence you know by how careful they are to remain invisible.

* * *

At the age of sixteen Frannie fell in love with her high school math teacher, and even though he couldn't show it in any conventional way, Frannie was sure he loved her back. Mr. Stewart had singled her out as a "gifted" student although really what Frannie was, was committed. She would do anything for Mr. Stewart. Mr. Stewart was thrilled to have such a devoted math student, especially a girl. He invited her in for special tutoring and helped prepare her for the advanced exams. The more he took his role as mentor seriously, the more Frannie was sure he loved her. During the advanced exam, though, Frannie had to run to the bathroom and began vomiting violently. She was unable to complete the exam and although she had done quite well on the portion she had completed, she received a barely passing mark. Mr. Stewart tried to reassure her that everyone got nerves now and then, but this only served to mortify Frannie. She had not had nerves. She had been ill.

What Frannie learned that day was that people make up stories to fit their own narrative. Frannie would have to be careful in the future not to become a wearisome plot element is someone's badly researched story line.

* * *

When Frannie was twenty-two she slept with Brett Bartle. It was a badly construed evening in which they were meant to be listening to Professor Longhair but ended up in a bathtub full of lukewarm water. The sleeping came later, exhausted and fitful.

What Frannie learned was that love and sex are not the same thing, but both have utility.

* * *

When Frannie met Fergie, Frannie worried she only wanted to marry him because she liked the sound of their names together, Frannie and Fergie—like one of the books she had memorized as a child. But Fergie turned out to be a good man. He did the dishes and the laundry just because they needed to be done. He brought her small gifts, not expensive, but gifts that indicated he could see inside her—like the time he brought her a used copy of *A Wrinkle in Time*. If he bought flowers, they were the kind *Frannie* liked, wild and colorful, not the white roses that he himself preferred. And he was a good lover, Frannie thought.

What she learned from Fergie was that goodness comes from somewhere down deep inside when you don't expect it. Goodness is like a clear mountain lake, deep and inviting, boundless and nourishing.

* * *

It was 1:07 a.m. when Frannie's water broke. The sheets of rain pounding on the roof punctuated by cracks of lightening heralded the arrival of Tara and Kip. Yes, they knew they were carrying twins. No, they didn't know they would come five weeks early. But as her own birth had predicted, Frannie proceeded to deliver the twins without drama, one right after the other, and if one could say there was any drama at all, it would have to be that each twin weighed in at seven pounds, three ounces precisely. The doctors and nurses were so astounded they did not believe the numbers at first. They weighed the infants several times that first hour and each time there were hoots and hollers at the unlikely coincidence. By the next day though, Kip weighed two ounces less and Tara one ounce more, as each one tried desperately to claim their right to inhabit her breasts.

What Frannie would learn from that day was that people will find meaning in almost any useless detail, and that life is made up of a series of these events.

* * *

It was when Kip and Tara started first grade that Frannie decided to finish her dissertation. Rather than attend parent-teacher meetings or field trips to the pumpkin patch, Frannie preferred to cloister herself in the library researching the aspects of identity and social class as they related to Henry James and H. G. Wells. The children didn't miss their mother so much as they minded that at times she would dash off in the middle of a conversation and bolt to her writing study, where she could be found frantically writing down the latest morsel of insight. These unpredictable moments when their mother disappeared both physically and emotionally went on to shape their expectations about how human interactions can be fickle and unpredictable. But they also offered the insight that mothers are just people, flawed and imperfect, despite what we are led to believe. Frannie believed it was advantageous to learn this information sooner rather than later, if later meant it would coincide with many of life's other disappointments.

* * *

When Tara started her period and Kip began spending countless hours in the bathroom with the shower running and the radio blasting Creedence Clearwater, Frannie remembered to tell Kip how much she loved that band. To Tara she carefully wrapped a copy of *Our Bodies, Ourselves* in paper covered in pink roses. Fergie wondered if they should do more to educate their children, but Frannie insisted that life taught its own lessons, and experience was the best teacher. What Frannie really thought though was that bringing up these topics made everyone involved uncomfortable so her actions really just revealed her need to keep everyone in their comfort zone. Frannie understood better how her own mother might have felt—and what she learned was that eventually one day you become your mother, or at least some facsimile of her, and many of the mysteries you experienced as a child and adolescent are revealed.

* * *

Frannie drove to the top of Mount Tamalpais the day she dropped Kip and Tara at college, and she cried. She cried and she cried, not because she defined herself as a mother but because she understood that her children had their future in front of them and hers was behind her. She grieved for the loss of possibility. When she stopped crying, she drove home, made a dinner of chicken kabobs and brown rice, watched *The Great Escape* with Fergie, and went to bed. That night she had a dream she was trapped in a car floating down a raging river. She was trying desperately to roll down the windows when the alarm went off, announcing it was already seventy-two degrees outside. It would be a hot one today. Frannie got out of bed, took a shower, and prepared to take Luca for a walk before the heat became unbearable.

What Frannie learned that day was that it is not good to walk a dog in the heat of the day or to discount your future in the heat of your sadness.

* * *

When Frannie fell in love with Victor it was not because she didn't love Fergie; she loved him very much. But Fergie was like her favorite pair of warm socks and Victor like a waterfall crashing down on her. She needed them both. When Fergie found out that Thursday-night dancing class was in fact Frannie and Victor in each other's arms, he wasn't angry. He wasn't angry because he was quite sure that he and Frannie loved one another. Frannie explained to Fergie what he already knew—that love is not a pie, finite and to be divided up. Fergie was the air she breathed, Victor the comma in the middle of an elaborate sentence. She needed them both, and one did not take away from the other but only added goodness to the world. Truly because Fergie was a good man, he understood this.

What Frannie learned was not that the capacity for love and forgiveness is boundless, but that the capacity for true understanding is always there, waiting at the door.

* * *

When Ella was born with a chromosome deficiency while Tara was finishing her medical residency, Fergie and Frannie packed up their house and moved in to take care of the child. They loved her every move even if it didn't fit the image of a perfect grandchild. They also grieved for Tara and Lincoln. They knew everything they would be missing. But they stored their grief up high and out of the way and set about creating a new family, one that carried an extra change of clothes when they made a trip out, one that invited only close friends over, one that celebrated long meals together and cheerful music. What Frannie learned, and Fergie too, was that the future doesn't belong to anyone. Stories write themselves and you don't get to choose the ending.

* * *

When Frannie found a painless lump in her groin, she ignored it for several weeks. She ignored it until Fergie noticed she looked pale. That next week the doctor diagnosed stage 4 pancreatic cancer. Fergie scaled back on his consulting, and between the chemotherapy and radiation appointments, they spent time together reading to one another and watching old movies. Fergie found opportunities to rub Frannie's feet and massage her shoulders. He even was attentive to removing the small hairs that appeared on her chin when she could no longer see clearly: he learned to carry himself softly so that his lumbering around the house did not wake her. They were holding hands when Frannie took her last deep sigh.

When Victor came to the funeral, Fergie gave him a big hug and the two men sat quietly drinking a scotch together on the front porch. Moths that had gathered by the porch light repeatedly collided with the screen door and fell to the floor at their feet. Fergie got up, flicked off the light, and he and Victor sat in the dark listening to the soft chatter of voices in the next room. That evening he realized what Frannie had taught him was that grief can destroy you if all you see is emptiness, but it will also heal you if you manage to embrace the deep gratitude for a life well lived. ∎

THE LAST TIME I SAW HER
John Robinson

My first date with Peggy Hincks was the night of August 28, 1963. It was the summer before my senior year of high school. Jack Kennedy was president. It also was a historic day, though we had no idea how famous it would become. It was the day of the March on Washington and Martin Luther King Jr.'s powerful "I Have a Dream" speech.

I parked my father's Pontiac Bonneville on a small street beside the planetarium, and we strolled along Chicago's lakefront on a beautiful summer's night, walking all the way across Grant Park into downtown, known as the Loop. Our destination was the Chicago Theatre, which was featuring a movie starring Doris Day and James Garner, *The Thrill of It All*. I don't recall our conversation that night. I only remember she wore a wraparound skirt that she awkwardly tugged at the entire journey. It was the beginning of a relationship that would last for an intense nine months. We ran into each other off and on for a couple of years after our break-up, and the last time I saw her was in late December 1966. I never discovered, after that final goodbye, what happened to her.

* * *

My early dating life with her began with a series of verbal skirmishes. And this struggle began over something rarely occurring in today's nascent courtships: books. Though at seventeen I was starting to entertain some vague notion of becoming a writer, I had no clear direction on how I might become one. Up to that point in my young life, I had read very little and had no discussions about books with my peers or elders. The idea of becoming a writer seemed like another adolescent daydream that would soon fade with time, only to be replaced by a new one. Despite this, my interest in reading was beginning to stir.

Back in those days, most everyone with whom I attended high school knew the names of great authors and books, even if they hadn't read them. To have read the "classics" carried prestige; it was regarded by my peers as a badge of honor. And even those who did not try to read the sacred volumes of world literature secretly admired (though they would never admit it) those who had.

Peggy clearly belonged to the admired group. But, for her, it wasn't enough that she silently educated herself with the canon of quality lit. She felt compelled to let others in the world know, with more than a little needling, what she had accomplished. I was a frequent target of that needling.

She would never fail to taunt me about her reading exploits whenever she could. I recall arriving at her house one fall night in 1963 and seeing that self-satisfied grin she wore whenever she possessed something—a joke, a trip to England, a freshly baked chocolate chip cookie—that she instinctively knew I wanted. That night, on our third date, she announced as she opened the front door the lines: "I just finished *Anna Karenina*. It was *won*derful."

"Oh yeah," I said. "Well, I read Dostoevsky's *Crime and Punishment*." It was true I had read the book. But it was two years earlier, and I'd found it tedious.

"I've already read that," she said. "Three years ago. And who cares about that book? Everyone has read it, but no one likes it." When she was on the attack, she employed a smile that was both mischievous and seductive. It was a smile that had first attracted me only a few months earlier at a Saint Sabina social.

I wanted to argue, but I knew she was right. And this vexed me even more, though I dared not show it.

Two weeks later, I arrived at her house, and the same front door opened to reveal her holding a large book in one hand with that same mischievous and seductive smile.

"Hi," I said. "How are you?" I spoke first, feebly attempting to steer the conversation someplace other than where it was inevitably headed. Along with a somber expression, I wore my athletic letter jacket, bearing a winged foot. My words and my attire made me feel like a dumb jock on the dead run from anything intelligent that might transpire between us.

"I just finished *Pride and Prejudice*," she gleefully declared. "I feel *soooo* wonderful. So liberated! Jane Austen is intelligent. So witty and ironic! Not like your dour Dostoevsky. What a sourpuss! And kind of stupid, too. He's the Grape Imposter."

In the early sixties, there was a popular and flippant practice among youth to change every title containing the word "great" to "grape." Peggy gravitated toward this frivolous irreverence. Perhaps because she disliked solemnity of any sort, she delighted in these quirky put-downs to grand titles. For instance, the second movie we saw together, *The Great Escape*, became the Grape Escape. And soon after there was the Grape Gatsby, the Grape Society, the Grape Barrier Reef, the Grape Depression, the Grape White Hope, the Grape Wall of China, the Grape Pretender, and the Grape Train Robbery.

"He's not an imposter, and he's not stupid," I said without conviction. He might not have been stupid, but at that moment I felt stupid defending him.

"Oh, yes he is," she said, cooing. "And you think so too."

"No, I don't," I said. "He doesn't need me to defend him."

"I think he does," she said. "He really does. And who knows: you might just be the only one left of his devoted readers to do it. Certainly, nobody else is going to." She got down on one knee before me and extended her hands together as if in prayer. "Please defend him, kind sir! For 'he knoweth not what he hath done!'"

A fortnight later, the same scene was replicated. This time the book was *Madame Bovary*.

I couldn't challenge her with my reading. It was enough for me to keep pace with the truly awful reading assignments at my all-male Catholic high school, most of which bored and frustrated me. By contrast, at the Catholic girls' institution she attended, better books were given to read. That in itself was enough to ignite my envy, but then there was also the fact of her being class valedictorian and a year younger than I to add sustenance to my inadequacy. And if that wasn't enough, she also held the lead role in the school play. I couldn't imagine how she managed to accomplish all these things. Some of the novels she'd been reading hadn't even been assigned. She correctly sensed I was jealous of her achievements, and this perception only fueled her delight and taunting. I should have despised her arrogance. But I didn't. I found it irresistible.

Things seemed destined to continue this way until one Saturday night when we went to a showing of the movie *Lord Jim*.

I should mention quickly that, among our peers, along with a respect for good books, there was an equal and requisite respect for good movies, especially those based on literary masterpieces. Since "the teenage movie" was just emerging as a phenomenon, it was an odd place in time, and as a result, youth often watched the same adult movies as their parents.

The great Irish actor Peter O'Toole starred in the film adaptation of Joseph Conrad's classic novel on heroism and cowardice. O'Toole was the reason we chose the film, and therefore—because of his superlative performance—the movie adaptation of the novel lived up to our expectations.

Something unique happened that night.

As we quietly exited the theater, Peggy said, "Oh now, I just have to read the novel." I seconded that resolve as we began our walk back to the car. From that moment to the end of the night, we discussed the film's theme and its implications. At age seventeen, I had never spoken to a young woman in this manner. Though a little clumsy at times, it was thrilling.

As for Peggy, there was no trace of her supercilious manner. She seemed genuinely intrigued by my thoughts on the film. Understanding this, I carefully steered my words. More than that, she made me value my thoughts in a way to which I was not accustomed. And I tried to reciprocate.

After that night, our relationship changed. We selected movies of quality, skipping the popular rom-com movies of the day. Instead of seeing another saccharine romance starring James Garner as we had on our first date, we instead chose to see him in an intriguing film on war, irony, and courage called *The Americanization of Emily*. I didn't know it at the time, but my high school dates with Peggy were preparing me for participation in great dialogues that were to come in both the classroom and, later, in print.

* * *

This should be the place in the story where the serious development of a lasting relationship begins. Though we were officially going "steady" by the time we attended *Lord Jim*—and she wore my class ring on a chain around her neck as was the fashion—things had slowly, almost imperceptibly, begun to slide. What started out as a small fissure between us soon became, with time, a yawning chasm. It was created out of something as simple and intense as a teenage interest in other teenagers of the opposite sex. By going out exclusively, we began to yearn for the company—and touch—of others we denied ourselves. It was only a matter of time before one of us broke our unspoken vow of fidelity.

That time occurred on a spring weekend when I had an obligation that prevented me from joining her on our usual Saturday-night date. On the Sunday afternoon of that fateful weekend, as I was striding past an outdoor phone booth, I suddenly, on a whim, phoned Peggy and inquired about how her free Saturday went away from me. Since at that moment everything I was doing was spontaneous and frivolous, I decided to call and jokingly ask, "How did your date go?" I was walking on a street in my old neighborhood on the South Side of Chicago with my childhood buddy, John Schmitz, when I got the inspiration to make this prank call. And I was looking out the glass window of the phone booth at him when I heard her say, in a distressed voice, "How did you *know*?" I signaled to my friend the shocking news, and his face contorted in disbelief.

I told her I was leaving right then to see her and got into my car and swiftly drove to her house on the other side of town. We met, but she didn't speak at first. Later, she asked for my forgiveness. Secretly I felt ashamed. In my heart, I'd been tempted to do the same thing, and I might have if she hadn't beat me to it. But I did not tell her that. Instead, we "made up," and then returned to being the couple we'd been before the indiscretion. I never told her there had been no informant. I thought it gave me some advantage.

But, of course, things were never the same. Six weeks later we got another Saturday free of each other, and I phoned again with the same inquiry (from the same phone booth) and received the same instant confession. The only thing different this time was her inquiry, "Who told you?" And I honestly replied, "Nobody," but I could tell she didn't believe me.

After the second incident, we broke up for good. And although I wrote to her from college (she was a year behind me and still in high school), we were never the same again. During the summer after my sophomore year, we dated sporadically, and things began to rekindle, but by the winter of 1966, our relationship had deteriorated again, and Peggy was already seeing another beau. Still, we had one last date into the city to see a musical, and that was that.

Or: it should have been over. But it was not. For reasons I couldn't comprehend at the time, I continued to carry the torch for her. And the fact that she had no interest in resuscitating our relationship only made the idea of our reunion all the more appealing to me. I did not understand this appeal, and I did not understand myself.

* * *

Though I began reading some pretty challenging texts while I dated Peggy, it would be another ten years before I read Marcel Proust. As a teenager, I had never heard of him. This was an omission with psychological repercussions. It wasn't until I was twenty-eight and living in Spain that I discovered my relationship with Peggy vividly portrayed in the characters of Charles Swann and Odette de Crécy from *Swann's Way*, the first volume of Proust's masterpiece *In Search of Lost Time* (*À la recherche du temps perdu*).

In the novel, an upper-class gentleman, Charles Swann, falls in love with Odette, a courtesan, who does not hold him in similar regard. Instead of gradually losing interest in her, he does the opposite: the more she ignores him, the more he becomes enamored of her and foolishly intensifies his efforts to gain her love when there is little chance of success. His rational mind knows this. And yet he vainly pursues her, frantically hunting for her one night (in one of the most spectacular and hallucinatory scenes in the first volume) on the grand Parisian boulevards, searching for his "lost Eurydice." Nothing curbs his resolve. The more futile the effort, the more he escalates his pursuit. To visually emphasize this futility, Proust employs the metaphor of a great ship leaving port with Swann racing along the dock trying to catch it.

When Swann is away from Odette, her importance swells to Brobdingnagian size, as she rises to Olympian heights in his head. But later, when he is finally alone in her presence, he cannot believe this very ordinary person is the same one for whom he had been so desperately pining. In his mind, he remarks incredulously, "This is she?" Proust's poignant, powerful, and accurate portrayal of unrequited love is considered one of the finest in world literature. Reading it a full decade after my romance with Peggy, I felt as if I were viewing the antics of my own soul. And had I read it at that time, I often believed, it might have saved me considerable grief. Or perhaps I was just deluding myself as Swann had done.

Proust believed that there was no worse agony than desiring something unattainable when, at the same time, believing it was attainable. The essence of the attraction lies in its being unfulfilled. And therefore it's that aspect that must be ignored to receive the full heartbreaking measure required for unrequited love. It's not unlike the indispensable lure of drugs, alcohol, and gambling: the promise that you'll achieve an orgasmic high by dint of sheer desperation to achieve it. Odds are ignored; pain endured. Despite abysmal failure, the addict keeps repeating the same mistake.

Because of Peggy, all the stories I'd heard of lovers hanging themselves or jumping off bridges suddenly made sense. After her, I was wary of ever trusting unrestrained attraction. Instead, I believed that to survive the swiftly approaching adult world, I needed to practice restraint in matters of the heart.

In *Swann's Way*, Charles Swann finally marries Odette, only to lament at the end of his life living with a woman to whom he was ill-suited: "To think that I've wasted years of my life, that I've longed to die, that I've experienced my greatest love, for a woman who didn't appeal to me, who wasn't even my type."

* * *

After my last and uneventful date with my Odette, Peggy, I felt despair. We said our final goodbyes, and I didn't hang myself.

Though suffering, I used restraint and waited a whole fortnight before attempting to see her again. It was a crazy Charles Swann thing to do, but I couldn't help myself. Then, on a warm winter's night, driven by unreciprocated love, I drove my father's new Bonneville to her house with some vague plan to take her for a romantic evening drive. I had no thought as to the foolishness of this enterprise, or what I would even say to her. I didn't even know if she was home.

As my car reached its destination, I quickly spotted her walking away from her house holding a leash with her dog, Farley, attached to it.

I slowed my speed and rolled down my window as if I was about to speak, but suddenly, just as the car drew even with her, I was struck by, at long last, a searing sense of humiliation. Instead of shouting out the window, I stared straight ahead, accelerated past her, and avoided looking back.

I never found out if Peggy saw me that winter night. And I never found out what happened to her. If she is still alive and was asked about me, I assume she would respond the same way I would: though no longer attracted to her old suitor, she now saw our relationship as significant, and the Grape Love of her lost youth. ∎

THREE SCENES
Yoram Naslavsky

Desert

We have recently witnessed irregularities in the geographic space to which we have been accustomed since childhood. If we enter a big department store from the busy city street, we don't know if we'll find our way out into the street again or whether the store will spit us out into a desert in Yemen. I particularly remember the first time we experienced a transition of this sort, for we found ourselves witnessing a great happening. A stage was standing in the sand in the heart of the wilderness, and around it wooden chairs were arranged in rows and circles as far as the eye could see, as if awaiting an audience, but we were the only audience. Several men were standing on the stage, their bodies painted white from the waist up, and also their heads and faces, except for lips as black as blood. They looked at us with curiosity. One of them addressed me and asked for a volunteer from the audience. The volunteering spirit pulsed in me and I went up onto the stage. They gathered round me, poked me with extended fingers, felt me, and it was as if to say that we, the department store people, owed them something, that we were not meeting our obligations, that our apologies had become a nuisance. They signaled me to the microphone. I didn't know where to start, so I started right at the beginning in the hope, perhaps, that they would tire and I'd be released from justifications. I told them about the beginning of time, the stories of the patriarchs, the bondage, the Exodus. You see, I told them, we too had nothing but the desert. They consulted and eventually asked me to continue, but in their language it sounded as if they said, No. By the time I got to the story of the atom bomb dropped on Hiroshima, the sun was going down. They collected the boards of the stage, piled them in a big pyre, and set fire to them. At the other side of the department store the neon signs were aflame: an advertisement showing palms and a well.

In Class

In class the teacher ordered me to solve the exercise. I stood at the blackboard, my thoughts pulling me outside through the window. From their seats the other pupils laughed, then dozed off, and alternately laughed and dozed off, and their wide shirts billowed like a wave with every movement of their body as they lay their heads on the desk, and the rhythm of the movements increased so much until it swept everything up, and for a moment the whole classroom floated in the air. The teacher stared at me with sweat-moistened eyes. His mustache tickled my face and ears, and the more I hoped to evade it, the more it wound itself around me, enveloping my neck with thick, prickly scarves of bristles. He ordered me to solve the exercise, and the blackboard was filled with numerals and tubes and nails and metal parts, and the eraser was swept away on the big gust, and I clutched at the mustache scarf and pulled until it came away in my hand, long and fibrous as a rope. The blackboard was actually clean, and the wind had stopped, and the rope was in my hand, and the teacher's face was visible, the face of scandal, and the tip of his mustache was in my mouth, and I cleared my throat and swallowed, and my throat was scratched. So I turned to run, and I ran down the corridor and up the stairs and down them, and my throat scratched, and the mustache was half inside me, not going and not coming, drooping and hanging from my mouth and trailing behind me. And I was pulling one way and my insides the other in a paroxysm of swallowing, and the scouring mustache was like a pipe cleaner in my windpipe, poking around in my esophagus and palate walls. The windpipe is finally clean. With an effort I remove the pipe cleaner, and now my throat's clean, I start talking. First about something on the similarity between Man and a brush, I say, both are long with bristles at their ends. The pupils have finally dozed off, heads on desks. The teacher's eyes are moist, and with his hands he examines his now smooth face, and I say to rend, to slash, to foam, to peel, to carve, to crush, and to blight, and my voice thunders and is hoarse, and they are sleeping and he, the teacher, ordered me to solve the exercise, and the blackboard is empty, and the class is laughing, and in the middle is me, and I have no solution, and my soul wanders out through the window.

Body

My left shoulder broke. I splinted it to my thigh but that was my undoing: now my whole torso was inclined to the left. My spine was bent into a curve and I found my chin was banging against my knee. I took a cane in my healthy hand, the living one, to steady and balance my posture, but the effort was so great that it tore my wrist ligaments. I sat down to revive myself in the eating house renowned for its resuscitative powers. My neck ached from the effort of looking straight ahead. In a series of assertive movements, the waitress, fluttering her eyes and pursing her lips, dropped some patently sexual hints. She was a delicate creature, her gathered hair cradling a long, soft neck. With great patience and infinite understanding, she led me to her room behind the counter. It was a small staff room, its walls peeled of paint, bare. Groaning and moaning with pain, I managed to throw the weight of my body onto the bed, a narrow single bed, covered with a dusty blanket. The dizziness I felt from the arduous journey caused my head to drop heavily. The iron corner of the bed hit my eye and a stain of blood and mist shrouded its vision. The waitress, who was busy peeling off her many layers of clothing, lost all ability to detect anything of my distress. The wonderful attentiveness that had earlier suited her so perfectly was now replaced by a purposeful, sick, and malignant indifference: at first she cut my fingernails and toenails while strictly observing the rules of an ancient ritual. Then she removed the hair from my body and head while softly growling, a growling that echoed the squeaking of the scissors. She rubbed my skin with a knobbly rolling pin, and when it was sufficiently transparent, she whipped it off in a skillful movement. I remained supine on the mildewed bed, a scrap of physicality with multiple immobile limbs. The limits of my possibilities were reduced to a shining point in an imagined firmament, and I strained to look at it, alternately grasping and releasing. Then it too waned, and I remained a silent body in a weightless space. ∎

-translated from the Hebrew by Anthony Berris

THE GHOST TIGER
Francis Walsh

When Lucy said, "California," I pictured a hazy sidewalk lined with palm trees where sun-bronzed men and women wore short shorts and tank tops and roller-skated while carrying boom boxes. In my head, the California sidewalk floated in space, detached from the Earth—I could see the borders of the cement and nothing beyond but spirals of purple and black, like an artist's rendering of the galaxy in a textbook.

Our second-grade teacher, Mrs. Litchfield, had divided the class into pods, which meant she had arranged four desks into a square where two sets of students faced each other. Mrs. Litchfield introduced Lucy to the class. I sat across from Lucy. I don't recall who sat beside me. In my memory, I have identikit classmates with interchangeable haircuts and outfits, like a suite of dolls.

The first thing Lucy said to me was, "A pod is a family of whales."

She wasn't looking at me when she debuted this fact; she busied herself peeling the rind from an orange into a single ribbon. She had dark, glossy hair that fell across her face as she worked the orange, and her comment about whales filled in the wilderness beyond my image of California. Now an ocean of whales lapped at the sidewalk. The palm trees quivered with the wavering notes of a whale song while the legs of the skaters scissored up and down the promenade. The sun was always shining in my image of California. I still haven't been to California.

I went home that afternoon and opened my notebook to a fresh page and wrote the following heading: "Lucy—November 1993."

And beneath that I wrote: "A pod is a family of whales."

* * *

How I began compiling information in a notebook, I do not know, but my mother approved of my habit. After school, I lay on the carpeted floor while she sat on the couch, a cup of coffee perched on her knee, and watched a talk show—gasps often emitted from the television, or claps, or hoots, while a man with glasses waved a microphone through the air like a nervous bank robber with a gun—

and during commercial breaks, she would tap my butt with her foot and ask, "Whatcha writing?"

I shrugged at her question. But I often recorded quotes from my mother and father and acquaintances. Some of them were stock phrases, colloquialisms ("Hard telling not knowing"), most from my father, who, when he spoke at all, tended to speak in such phrases and remained as remote as the ocean upon which he labored, God rest his soul. These days, the pages contain technical jargon from coworkers in the real estate office where I now answer the phones ("Comparable market analysis") and unattributed phrases overheard from strangers in restaurants ("It's like he expects me to play Abe Lincoln every year").

I never recorded significant personal events from my day—no references to birthdays or lost teeth—as if the empty space around the sparse portraits of others could define me. And while I do not recall where the first notebook came from, I know my mother delivered all the others and still reliably purchased me one on birthdays and major holidays. I suspect she marked her calendar.

* * *

In my notebook, animal facts comprised the first few entries of Lucy. Later, when I revisited the words, I relocated to the moment; I heard Lucy's voice and pictured Lucy's face and her chubby limbs. Lucy did most of the talking when we first met. Eventually she moved beyond animal facts. Lucy and her family had moved from California to Maine. Lucy's mom was Korean, and her dad was white, so Lucy was half-Korean. Her father worked for the US Air Force. The family moved often. When Lucy spoke, I noted how her shirt was stretched taut across her belly.

One morning in school we were standing with our hands over our chest and reciting the Pledge of Allegiance. The American flag drooped from a corner of the classroom. A banner poster of the alphabet ran around the ceiling trim. After the word "God," a chorus of squeaking chair legs filled the classroom, and everyone sat down, and Lucy, breathless, leaned forward and said, "Bald eagles have a seven-foot wingspan."

She flung her arms wide and wriggled her fingers as if to stretch to the length of a bald eagle. She glanced back and forth between her hands, and then tucked them beneath her armpits and bowed her head. Her face pinked. She roosted.

I labored over my writing later that day, approaching each letter with a slow, deliberate pace, as if coaxing the words from the world of my memory and onto the page, where they still exist today, available to me in case I ever forget the wingspan of the American bald eagle.

* * *

My friendship with Lucy blossomed when I began practicing how to draw tigers. In class, Lucy displayed an enviable memory, reciting a variety of facts both directly and obliquely related to the teacher's daily lesson, such as announcing the Alabama state bird ("Northern flicker") during a unit on the civil rights movement and Rosa Parks. Often, Mrs. Litchfield gently thanked Lucy while reminding her to stay on topic. Lucy always smiled. Sometime during her third week, she paused from coloring the Pacific Ocean with a purple crayon and addressed me.

"My family has a cat named Waffles. My dad says we're a cat family, but my mom wants a dog. But it's easier to move with a cat."

And I mirrored her statement.

"I have a dog named Shadow, but my dad's friend David has tons of cats and he let me name one. So Sheba is sort of my cat, but she doesn't live at my house."

Lucy nodded and resumed slashing the ocean with purple.

And so later, I thought about cats when I recorded what Lucy had said, and that thought led me to a book on my shelf: *How to Draw Animals.* The book featured step-by-step instructions. There were no instructions on how to draw a house cat, but there were instructions for a tiger. The tiger page was divided into eight panels, and the first panel featured disembodied circles floating on the blank white space of the page, one each for the head, the shoulders, and the haunches. From there, one of the circles grew triangles for ears and a mouth, and tendrils extended from the head circle to the shoulder circle to the haunch circle, as if the animal were willing itself into existence. I practiced. I inked the stripes on the tiger. My circles were often poorly sized in relation to each other, so I produced an ambush of tigers with impoverished skulls and overgrown haunches. But they did, in their own way, replicate the animal, and I memorized the pattern and began drawing tigers at the header of all my school assignments, placing the animal on the line after my name, and while my drawing skills improved over time, my slow pace resulted in hastily summed numbers and red marks that cut across my worksheets. For a week or two, my mother frowned.

Eventually Lucy noticed my tigers and said, "A tiger's roar can be heard from three miles away."

At first, that was all she said, but she continued to stare at my page. She propped her elbows on her desk and rested her chin on her fists while Mrs. Litchfield circulated through the classroom, pausing occasionally to lean forward and inspect a student's work. I worried for a moment Lucy and I might get in trouble.

"Where do you live?" Lucy asked.

"Archibald Lane."

"I live on Deering."

Lucy continued to stare at my tiger.

"Is that nearby?" she asked.

And so we discovered that our homes were on parallel streets, a fact that compelled Lucy to say, "That's good, because I have an idea."

* * *

Looking back on that moment when I first spoke to Lucy, and, in fact, the first days of my friendship with her, I always wonder what led me there. What compelled me? Lucy was a strange child. Before she addressed me, she had only spoken in my vicinity. At lunch, she sipped milk with every mouthful of food, gasping after each swallow as if it were a battle. She smelled green and bland, like an anonymous houseplant. Chlorophyll. She grasped her pencil with her fist, without refinement, and swiped at her worksheets. Despite her roughshod penmanship, the answers were always correct. Mrs. Litchfield frequently nodded in Lucy's direction. Did I like these things about her, or did I simply notice them? Her nearness played a role, but there were other children around me. In the end, whenever I wonder what urged me forward to speak, I always accept that my notebook showcases no other six-year-olds besides Lucy Buckley, whatever that means.

* * *

Our town was a small town, and children roamed free. After school, Lucy accompanied me to my yard, where we both sat down and reviewed the plan while plucking fistfuls of grass from the earth. I listened to Lucy as she pointed to her house, and our homes were almost exactly parallel, or at least half of each house was (they were offset slightly) with only one shared neighbor—a large gabled house with a wraparound porch and a split-rail fence—separating the two. The neighboring home, a seasonal residence, remained unoccupied during the school year.

"So I'll go over the fence and through the yard, and when I'm home I'll watch the clock and try to get Waffles to meow. And you watch the clock too and see if you hear anything. And take notes."

I nodded and cast a clump of grass into the air. The blades scattered, landed, and disappeared into greenery.

"How far is it between our houses?" I asked.

Lucy stood up and tugged at her shirt. She set her hands on her hips and squinted into the distance.

"Probably a mile. But that's okay because cats have smaller meows than tigers," she said.

Lucy promised to come back after, and I walked toward my front door while craning my neck to watch her scooch between the rails of the neighbor's fence and jog across the yard. With my hand on the doorknob, I waited for Lucy to bound up the steps and reach her own door, and once there, she turned and waved before disappearing.

Inside, I sat on my bedroom floor with my notebook and quickly scribbled a measure of time in fifteen-minute increments—2:45, 3:00, 3:15, 3:30. I stared at a clock, but I don't remember what the clock looked like. And I waited. But aside from a question mark beside 3:15, the chart remained blank. And of course, now I wonder what I thought of while Lucy tried to make Waffles meow. Perhaps I strained my ear. Perhaps I tried to block the sound of the talk show host that slipped from the television and drifted upward through the floorboards of my room. Looking back, the moment held a strange allure: Lucy and I working in tandem in separate locations while time and a cat's meow tethered us together.

* * *

When Lucy returned, we compared notes, although she hadn't written any. She trusted her memory.

"Waffles meowed at 2:55. So right there." Lucy stabbed a finger at the page, scratching her fingernail across the slim space between 2:45 and 3:00.

"I didn't hear anything," I said.

"Did you watch the clock? I watched the clock. Also, he growled at 3:20. Did you hear that?"

"I don't know. Maybe."

Lucy shrugged.

"Well, he meowed. You believe me, right?"

We stared at each other. Lucy blinked. Her eyes appeared watery, expectant, and I felt I had to nod and say, yes, I believe you, and then I asked, "Do you want me to show you how to draw a tiger?"

I opened my notebook to a fresh page and demonstrated my tiger-drawing method to Lucy. Then I passed the notebook to her and spoke the instructions aloud while pointing to different locations on the paper where the head circle, shoulder circle, and haunch circle should go. She followed along, breathing through her mouth, and soon two tigers prowled the page together, and though they struck the same pose, they were not identical, merely mimics. The sunlight had begun to dim and so Lucy thanked me and ran home, but I remained in the grass and traced my finger over the shape of the tigers until my mother opened the front door and called to me. Lucy had pressed so hard with the tip of the pencil that she had indented the paper, and when I turned to a fresh sheet, I found a ghost tiger etched into the blank page. Nowadays I am less enamored with the ghost tiger, but for a long while the ghost tiger stalked through my mind. The notebooks were a timeline, and Lucy had created something in one space of time that extended into the future. Or a possibility of a future tiger. The outline was there, and we could fill in the lines if we wanted, or else draw something new over the faint shape of the tiger.

At least, that was how I felt when I was young.

* * *

After the experiment with Waffles, I continued to spend time with Lucy: she taught me how to peel an orange over a year of school lunches, and I learned about all of the states that she had lived in ("California, Alaska, Alabama, and now Maine"), and I made her a heart-shaped Valentine's Day card when for all my other classmates I had purchased a sheet of flimsy cards separated by a perforated edge. On Saturday mornings, I would lean against my neighbor's fence and call to Lucy, waiting until she appeared on her porch. On Sunday mornings, she would holler across space to reach me. Always, we went to Lucy's house, and I would say hello to Mrs. Buckley, often as she lugged a vacuum cleaner into the back of a car before heading to one of her part-time house-cleaning jobs. In my mind, she always wore yellow rubber gloves. Mr. Buckley lingered in the background. Lucy's home held the faint scent of garlic, and on the wall in the entryway hung a framed holographic image of Jesus—if I tilted my head left to right, Jesus knocked on a door, although no one ever answered, and Lucy laughed the first time I saw the image and stood and tottered in place. We attempted the Waffles experiment again, with little success. We practiced drawing tigers together, and then graduated to other animals—elephants, deer, rabbits, and an eagle. Each day, we walked home from school together, and my mom noticed enough to ask questions about Lucy and her family, and Mom would smile and say, "That's good, sweetie. That's good you're making friends."

But one Saturday I found myself waiting longer than usual. So, I wandered over and knocked on Lucy's door. Waffles meowed from somewhere inside, and after a moment, Mr. Buckley opened the door. He was like a lot of fathers. He kept his hair trim, and he smelled spicy, and he tended to make jokes that plied on my unknowingness and disbelief, as if it were funny to fool a child into believing cats could walk on their hind legs. But he was kind in his own way and offered me sodas and snacks whenever I visited. That day he did something unexpected: he hitched his pant legs up and crouched until he was eye level with me and he shared a secret.

"Lucy is a bit upset today. She's in her room. You can run on up if you want, but you should know—we're going to be moving at the end of the summer."

I nodded and he rustled my hair. I don't know what I thought of his news, but I headed to Lucy's room and found her cross-legged on her bed as she read a book. Her room was full of books, but I hadn't quite noticed before because I had never seen her read one. Inactive, the books became wallpaper, but now I noted them—books on animals and books on birds and books on different states. She must have noticed me staring because she said, "My daddy gives them to me. If we run errands together, he always lets me buy a book. And he gives me a new state book whenever we move," she said, and held up the book so I could read the cover—*Ohio: What's So Great About This State?*

And then I learned that the cardinal was the Ohio state bird.

* * *

For a while, Lucy and I kept in touch, mailing each other letters and calling on the phone. At first, the novelty brought excitement, but when the newness of placing a stamp on an envelope wore away, the distance between us became more noticeable. Where she had once been my neighbor, Lucy now existed somewhere in the obscure Ohio of my mind, a state of buckeyes, Thomas Edison, and a song my father hummed while I sat beside him in the cab of his pickup. My attention drifted, and the responsibility of friendship became a burden, until, after about a year, the letters and calls dwindled to cards on holidays and birthdays before ceasing altogether.

I heard from Lucy one more time, in high school. She had found my phone number tucked away in a box while packing to move.

"I mean, I figured it was you," she said. "The area code."

We talked for a while. She was headed to Texas. Waffles, miraculously, still lived, and she held the phone to his belly so I could hear him purr. We said goodbye. She never called again, but I see photos of her online sometimes when I'm bored at work and clicking through the internet. She went to Dartmouth, where she joined the ROTC. She travels extensively.

But I remember, on that day when she called before moving to Texas, that I went to my room to read through my notebook entries, and I found the ghost tiger prowling. ∎

FROM: 340 RIVERSIDE DR
Ann Pedone

March 7th, 2018

Woke up late. Vertigo. Happens
every time I sleep on my right side.
I pick up my phone and see that
his ex-wife called me again last night.

March 12th

Spent twenty minutes in the doctor's office
with my feet in the stirrups waiting for the nurse.
At one point I reached into my bag for something to read.
Anne Carson's *Helen of Troy* and Kafka's letters to Felice.

March 13th

Out for coffee. Going through the missed calls
trying to figure out which number is his ex-wife.
When she first called me two months ago, I thought
about saving the number, but panicked. I remember
there are three five's in it.

April 1st

At a reading at the department. They put too many chairs
in the room, and only half of them are full. Hard to breathe.
Luckily there's no one here I know. I sit through it all
imagining the fawning that will take place during the
wine and cheese. I've never thought much of his work
even though he won that thing last year. I tell myself that
it's not bitterness, that his stuff is just genuinely not good.
But what does that even mean? I check to make sure
no one is looking, and slip a finger up under my panties.

April 12th

In bed all day. I pick up the phone and stare at what I've
determined must be his ex-wife's number. I don't want to dial it.
I want to eat it. Not whole. Just nibble at it.

April 15th

A friend of mine from grad school texted
last night and has offered to read what I have
so far. Told her to give me a couple of days
to get it into shape, and then I'll email it to her.
I think I should explain to her that I'm
trying to write about myself without the book
really being about myself. I could mention
something about Philip Roth, but that's
probably just asking for trouble. I think
Sontag would say that we create the self
by writing about the self. Fuck. Maybe
what I really want is just to be someone else.
I open my laptop and type in Philip Roth and Sontag.
Want to see if they ever fucked.

April 20th

Had lunch with a writer friend of mine. We hadn't
seen each other in over a year. I spent the whole time
debating whether to tell her about the phone calls.
I don't want her to say I'm obsessing. Which I'm now
thinking is something women are accused of doing
more than men. We say good-
bye and I fall asleep in the car from the wine.
Woke up an hour later when an older man
knocked on my window and asked
if I was alright. I waved him off and when
I went to put my seatbelt on, could feel
that my panties were soaked through.

From Susan Sontag's Journal
October 1959 [otherwise undated]

I'm not pious, but co-pious

HOW I FREED THE HORSES
Sheldon Costa

I t was in the house. The kitchen, in fact. They could hear it smashing plates. One at a time, like it was taking a long look at each one before tossing it to the ground.

"Those belonged to my grandmother," Mora said. "She brought them over from Europe."

The china was the only thing of value the withered old woman owned at the end of her life. She'd given them to Mora on her wedding day, wrapped in thin pink paper—a reminder, she said, of all their family had survived to bring them to that special event. They were the sort of frighteningly delicate things whose fragility seemed the only proof of their value, and Mora had been planning on getting them appraised sometime soon, curious just how much her lineage, with all its war-torn corridors of grief, was worth. No chance of that now.

Her husband, Earnest, shook his head. "Disgusting," he said. "No sense of history. No appreciation for culture."

Renee, their daughter, stared at the door to the kitchen. On the other side, it began to screech—a sound not unlike a very large lobster being dipped into a pot of boiling water.

"Are you sure it's locked?" Renee said.

"Of course it's locked," Earnest said. He was busy pulling shelves out of the wooden cabinet under the TV and flinging cushions off the couch. Scouring the room for a weapon.

The door to the kitchen opened. It was standing there, broken plates scattered at its feet. When it roared, Mora could see row after row of crooked fangs webbed with thick saliva in its mouth. Strands of fur and meat—its previous meal—were wedged in the crevices of its scalloped pink gums.

"Oh," Earnest said. "Guess I forgot."

They ran upstairs to the study. It followed behind them, panting. It was huge, and terrifying, but slow. They could easily outrun it—even Earnest, who'd been having some problems with his heart lately. The doctor had advised him to stay away from beer and red meat, but Earnest wasn't big on surrender. He ate steak every other night, no matter how many heads of broccoli and bags of spinach Mora bought on her way home from the office.

In the study, Renee made sure to lock the door. She pushed the room's heavy mahogany desk against the entrance. She glared at her father.

"You said it was locked."

Earnest shrugged. "My mind was elsewhere. I was focused on protecting my family."

He stared at each of them, as if the simple act of holding his wife and daughter in view was enough to keep them safe. Mora caught faint traces of Earnest as a younger man in the look—the soldier she'd met all those years ago at a bowling alley in Santa Cruz. He was wearing his uniform when Mora first spotted him, even though he'd been home for weeks. In the tan fatigues, he looked dangerous and handsome, like a knife in a jeweled leather sheath. Only later did Mora learn that he'd been wearing the outfit because he'd spent what little money he had upon his return to the states on a beat-up Camaro, forgetting to set some cash aside for new civilian clothes.

"We need a gun," he said. "We need to fight."

"A gun won't work," Renee said. "We should jump out the window. We can outrun it."

"I will not leave my house," Earnest said. "This is my property."

"Please don't fight," Mora said. They'd been arguing so much lately. Renee had taken to calling her father a *war criminal*—an unfair indictment, Mora thought, given that he'd never even seen combat during his time in the service. Earnest was just as antagonistic, though: he liked to sit close to Renee at the kitchen table, chewing his steak loudly in her ear and asking if she'd like a piece, knowing full well she was a vegetarian. It had been a tough year for all of them; after yet another disagreement with his manager at the furniture store, Earnest had been let go, and his continued failure to find new work had left him as coiled and tense as a mousetrap, ready to snap at any sign of conflict.

She thought they both had a point. If they jumped from the window and ran for the car, it would never reach them in time. But it would be a shame to leave the house behind. They'd only bought it last summer—a beautiful white Victorian with a blue trim that ran around the building like a velvety ribbon. Every time Mora opened the front door, she felt like she was unwrapping a gift. It was the kind of home she'd dreamed of living in since she was young, a far cry from the dingy motel rooms and boarding houses her mother had ferried her through growing up.

It was at the door now, pounding its fists against the wood. The frame cracked and splintered, hinges creaking with every blow.

Gradually, it developed a rhythm, heaving itself against the door a dozen or so times, and then moaning and pacing for a few moments, only to begin again once it caught its breath.

Hoping to create a barricade, Mora helped her family pile every object in the study on top of the desk: lamps and chairs, Earnest's heavy biographies of the founding fathers, the giant gray desktop computer where Mora, three months earlier, had discovered an email her daughter had sent to a friend in France, in which she called her mother a *deluded housewife*, an odd accusation given that Mora was an accountant and had always made more money than Earnest, even before he'd lost his job.

Mora's mother had been a real housewife, the sort of high-strung woman who'd buckled completely when Mora's father left, her despair vaporized into a poisonous cloud Mora spent her teenage years carefully navigating around. She'd watched her mother cycle through increasingly volatile men—each one more ruddy faced and cruel than the last—in a hopeless attempt to reclaim a marital bliss Mora knew, even at that age, didn't exist. She considered it a valuable lesson in tempering one's expectations in a spouse. Reliability, she'd learned, was a key trait. As was sobriety. Earnest, she'd been glad to discover early on in their courtship, possessed both.

Mora often wondered if Renee had intentionally left the email on display to punish her for not agreeing to help pay for the gap year she wanted to take in India before college. Her daughter was clever that way. Once, when she was fifteen, she'd donated all but one of Mora's suits to a local Goodwill, telling Mora that other people needed them more than her mother. The act produced a perplexing dilemma: How to punish your daughter for caring about the poor? How to teach her that momentary wealth was no proof of future safety, that one needed to save and protect what they had, should things one day unravel?

The blockade gave way with a crash. One of its scaled hands bashed through, sending splinters flying in all directions. The hand clutched the edge of the desk, talons digging into the wood, and pushed it out of the way so easily that the motion looked almost gentle. Its massive body followed soon after, tearing off chunks of the wall as it heaved itself into the room, cluttering the air with clouds of plaster dust.

"Shit," Renee said, and they retreated through the double doors to the master bedroom.

"The bed," Earnest said. "Let's use the bed."

They each grabbed a corner of the king-sized mattress and leaned it against the door.

While Renee and Mora carried the dressers to block off the other entrance, Earnest went straight for the safe in the closet, where he kept his gun.

It was nice, Mora thought, to have them all working together again.

When was the last time they'd gotten along so well? Maybe that trip to the Monterey Bay Aquarium three years ago. Earnest making funny faces at the sunfish while Renee snapped photos of him, rolling her eyes in a way that meant she was still having a good time. Those kinds of days seemed almost impossible now.

Back in the study, they could hear it wrecking what they'd left behind, shattering any bits of glass it could find and diligently tearing the pages out of every book.

"Maybe we should call the police," she said.

"We are perfectly capable of protecting ourselves," Earnest said. He'd found his gun and was loading it with the sort of concentration and care Mora wished he'd given to searching for jobs these last few months. How many nights had she returned home to find him slumped on the couch, muttering his private grievances against a world that refused to waltz through the door and lay employment at his feet?

Renee scoffed. "The police are too busy harassing poor people. They wouldn't make it in time. I'm telling you: we need to go out the window."

She pointed outside, where Earnest's truck was sitting in the driveway beneath an elm tree.

"We're only two stories up," she said. "We can reach it if we leave now."

"But the house," Mora said.

"Fuck the house."

"Watch your language," Earnest said. He waved the gun in the air so frantically that Mora unconsciously raised her hands. "We will not surrender this house."

It bellowed from the study and hurled itself against the door. The bed budged but held. Mora heard it clicking its claws around the frame, trying to find a place to grip. She could smell it now, a rotten, amphibian stench that reminded her of pond scum.

"I'm getting out of here," Renee said, and started to tug at the window.

"Please listen to your father," Mora said. "Whatever we do, we should do it together."

"We're not the kind of family that runs away from our problems," Earnest said.

The sentiment made Mora smile. Though Earnest's methods were often theatrical—he'd buried Renee's CD collection in the backyard two weeks ago because he was sure it was the root cause of her various rebellions: the nose piercings and the student protests and the boy with dreadlocks he'd once caught her kissing in the driveway—she knew he always had his daughter's best interests in mind. When Renee was a baby, he was so terrified of her little body that he carried her around at arm's length, as if she were a bomb that might explode at any moment. Yet at night he let her fall asleep curled beneath one of his biceps, clinging to the appendage like it was a bit of driftwood in a shipwreck. She loved watching them, this hulking man balancing on the edge of the bed so their baby had ample room to roll and wiggle, his carefulness proof of some inner tenderness that lay unwavering within him.

There was a roar, and its upper body abruptly broke through the wall and into the room.

The mattress was still in the way, so its torso was stuck halfway in the frame, like a cougar trapped in a doggy door. It swung its claws out and tried to grab them, but its arms were still too short to reach. Earnest fired his gun, and the bullets disappeared between the scales covering its muscled flank, drawing no blood.

"The attic," Earnest said breathlessly. There was an entrance overhead, and he climbed onto one of the dressers to pull the chain that brought down the retractable stairs. "We need the high ground."

"Renee, come on," Mora said, her ears ringing from the gunshots. But her daughter was still struggling with the window. They were caked with years of paint and tended to stick. Mora began to move towards her, but Earnest grabbed her shoulder.

"Get over here," he shouted at Renee. They couldn't hear what their daughter shouted back, because the bed finally gave way, and the rest of its body avalanched into the room, a roiling wave of gnashing teeth. Earnest yanked Mora up into the attic, pulling the string behind him as he went, raising the stairs and sealing them inside.

"Earnest," Mora shouted. "Renee is still down there."

"There was no time," he said, frowning. Below, they heard Renee begin to shriek. For a moment, Mora hoped her daughter, always so fierce, would be able to fight it off, but her shouts were quickly silenced by a single crunch, followed by a slow, methodical slurping. Mora wasn't sure, but she thought she heard it moaning in pleasure as it ate.

"Our daughter sacrificed herself for us," Earnest said. Tears ran silvery rivers down his wrinkled cheeks. "I'm so proud of her. She died for something bigger than herself."

"What are you talking about?" Mora said. Earnest shushed her and pointed at the floor with his gun. They could hear it down below, crawling around the master bedroom, swiping furniture out of its way as it moved. It stopped right below them, and Mora imagined it standing up on its haunches, leaving a serpentine trail of slime on the ceiling with its tongue as it searched for its prey.

"See if you can find something to fight it with," Earnest whispered, gesturing to the other side of the attic, where stacks of cardboard boxes waited in the shadows. "We'll make our stand here." Mora noticed an edge of excitement in his voice. Her husband was enjoying himself. In fact, it was the happiest he'd sounded in months. He wasn't smiling, but there was satisfaction in the fierce determination with which he stared at the attic's entrance. It was the same face he made when they had sex, an expression that said: I know my purpose here, and I am glad.

Mora walked to the back of the attic and began to push the cardboard boxes aside. She sifted through Christmas decorations and old photo albums. She averted her eyes from the one she knew contained Renee's childhood mementos—the soccer trophies and the crayon drawings and the book she wrote in third grade, a ten-page pamphlet titled *How I Freed the Horses*.

The closest thing she found to a weapon was a broken garden hose stuffed in a crawl space behind the boxes. She held it above her head, swinging it like a lasso.

Below, it began to press up into the ceiling, the house's timber frame groaning. Mora imagined trying to wrap the rubber hose around its throat. Vengeance, for Renee. But its neck, she knew, was too large. She dropped the hose.

"How's it going back there?" Earnest said.

Like a whale breaking the surface of the sea, its head slowly ruptured through the floorboards, the heavy planks bending outward as easily as if they were made of rubber. All of its eyes, glittering in the darkness like dark red rubies, fixed on Earnest.

"It's time," he shouted. He fired the gun. It unhinged its jaw and received the bullets like a child catching raindrops on their tongue. "We can do this. We can win."

Even now, with its drooling lips parting to receive him, Earnest seemed so sure of himself. He'd sounded the same way on their wedding day, when he stood up from their table and gave a twenty-minute speech about how *marriage, like our country, is a nation forever in need of defense.* She'd known, even then, how embarrassing he looked, sweating in his rented suit, quoting *The Federalist Papers* and unironically reading phrases like *the sparkling republic of holy matrimony* from the speech he'd written on a crinkled sheet of notebook paper.

But he'd looked determined, too. Solid. The kind of man she could depend upon to hurl himself at any and all oncoming dangers. At the time, it seemed like enough, that kind of stupid certainty. As she watched him speak, one hand slicing the air as the other held a glass of cranberry juice aloft, she'd thought of her grandmother and her sad collection of plates—all the things life could take away from you if you weren't careful, if you didn't protect yourself accordingly. What was marriage, after all, but a kind of fortress? A concrete box to huddle within when the bombs finally fell, a bit of barbed wire and steel to withstand the endless barrage of the world outside?

While it closed its mouth around Earnest, she backed up into the crawl space. Her hand slipped against something soft—rat shit, she thought—but she just rubbed it off on her jeans. The gun continued to fire, until suddenly it didn't. There was a noise like someone crushing a bag of glass. The coppery scent of blood filled the attic.

Mora squeezed herself further back into the darkness and shut her eyes. She was certain, even as she heard it shambling towards her hiding place, that if she only made herself small enough, it would never find her. ■

READY FOR SERVICE
William Crawford & Charlie Hahn

DOUBLES
William Crawford & Charlie Hahn

BACKSIDE
William Crawford & Charlie Hahn

THE MULBERRY TREE
Kristine Thatcher

My grandmother had a passion for gardening, which she passed on to me. She was a wizard who could grow anything, and her eye for design was unique. She wasn't one for tidy rows or formal beds. There were cabbages among the daisies, green carrot tops feathering around yellow zinnias. Giant blue delphiniums towered over red bee balm and white baby's breath. The effect was dazzling, like walking straight into a painting by Monet.

She was a patient teacher, too, who showed me how to weed and lift and divide, how and when to prune a rose, and how to pick out the miniature armadillos called iris borers from an iris bulb. Together we watched the progress of each living thing.

And after a day of hard work, she would give me a cold glass of root beer Fizzies, and we'd sit together in the warmth of the fading sun and talk things over. Those were the finest days of my childhood. Even now, certain smells remind me of those times: newly mown grass, lilacs, and cow manure. Among the various things I wanted when I grew up was to be a gardener just like my grandmother and to provide the delights of her cottage garden for my own children.

That wasn't to happen until I was well into my thirties. I spent my twenties on the road as a regional theater actress, playing in venues from Seattle to New York City, moving from one small apartment to another. But finally I met the man of my dreams and settled down in one city at last.

My new husband, David, was the proud owner of a lovely three-story Victorian home in the Rogers Park neighborhood on Chicago's North Side. There was a huge backyard with this tree in the middle of it, and nothing else—no grass, and no plants—just this huge spreading mulberry tree, whose multiple trunks could be encircled by four adults holding hands. Its canopy stood in towering roundness, one story taller than our home. It sent out massive branches in such long and graceful sprays that the drip line encircled our entire yard and a bit of our next door neighbors'. I moved into the house in the late fall, when there were no leaves on the thing, and wondered just what kind of shade the tree might cast come spring, if it would present a problem for the kind of garden I had in mind. In my optimism, I pictured dappled shadows here and there, and, armed with my Burpee seed catalogues and my graph paper, I set to work planning my own personal tribute to Monet. One of the first things I wanted to do was to put down my bulbs for the spring. That's when I started learning about that mulberry tree. I found an underground root system as vast and as complicated as the Roman catacombs, so that no matter where in the yard I put my shovel, I hit wood. But I persisted and finally found the places between the roots to put my bulbs.

The result, the following spring, when the iris and the tulips came up, was a crazy patchwork design, so haphazard that my neighbor, Mr. Katz, asked me if I had been drinking that day last fall when he'd seen me planting them. I explained to him that what he saw before him was a method known as "naturalizing."

"Oh," he said. "You mean it's the way God would have done it if he'd been drinking."

Mr. Katz was a friendly fellow, around seventy years old, I would guess. He was the kind of neighbor that stops by just to tell you you're using the wrong tool for whatever job you happen to be doing. He always has the right tool and would be happy to lend it to you if he could just figure out where the heck he put it. He was an amusing sight on hot summer days as he stood there looking at me from behind his Coke-bottle glasses, with his spiky white crew cut, his crazy Bermuda shorts, and his knobby little knees sticking out. He had just retired when we met and his life now had one purpose, which was to rid himself of the root fungus that had attacked his perfectly manicured lawn. I could have grown extremely fond of him except for his absurd love for our mulberry tree. He said he wished he had one like it in his yard. Whenever he came across the back alley to talk, he'd look up at that tree and lean in confidentially, "Great climber," he'd say. "You've got yourself a great climber there."

"Yeah," I'd say. "Too bad I gave up climbing twenty years ago. Nothing grows back here, have you noticed? I'm not so fond of that tree myself."

"Try a ground cover," he advised. "Just cover the ground with kudzu or some damn thing and forget about it. You don't want grass. Grass is trouble. Grass can mean the heartbreak of root fungus."

I planted many kinds of flowers that first year, completely ignoring the catalogue recommendations for light requirements. I'd always wanted foxglove, so I put in foxglove. I wanted roses, so I put in roses, and on and on. When the leaves appeared on the mulberry in late spring, the yard turned gloomy and cavernous. Not a bit of sunlight came through. My poor plants either withered away immediately from its lack or put out a tremendous display of leaves and no blooms whatsoever. As I cursed the tree, Mr. Katz merely pitied me.

"You ought to put a hammock in the tree and take a load off," he said. "That's what I would do if it were mine."

"Then grab your shovel and get over here," I told him. "I'll make you a gift of it."

In June, the mulberry came into fruition, which is to say that it rained down sloppy red berries for days, staining the new patio, and my clothing if I happened to be under it, and to be anywhere in the backyard *was* to be under it. We couldn't take a step without squishing red berries underfoot. We had to wash our shoes or take a footbath before we could come into the house.

In late July, the tree gave birth, putting out little fuzzy brown seedcases by the thousands. They carpeted the still-bare ground and got tracked into the house, ending up in our food, our bathtub, and even in my underwear drawer. Mr. Katz surveyed the mess sympathetically, "Look on the bright side. At least you can't tell there's no grass under there anymore."

Then he waxed philosophical, "That's the price you pay," he said, "to have a great climber like that mulberry." I uttered a silent prayer that his lawn fungus would spread to *his* underwear drawer.

In September, the seedlings sprouted and took hold, so David and I moved along for hours on our hands and knees pulling out little five-inch trees. The plants wouldn't grow. The grass wouldn't grow, but these little trees grew with a vengeance and flourished. At the end of the first year, I tallied up the garden account book and realized we had spent several hundred dollars in quest of my grandmother's garden, and it had all come to nothing. Mr. Katz merely told me I should have listened to him because he'd told me so. "Next year, do the hammock thing we talked about."

But in the scheme of things, this proved to be the least of our concerns regarding the mulberry, for in late November, it began to deliver fat, shivering squirrels to our roof. It was a veritable Interstate 90 to any rodent looking for a warm place to spend the winter. The animals chewed through the siding and the shingles to gain entrance to the attic. My original distaste for the tree turned to hatred. At night, we would lie in bed and listen to incessant scampering. Each morning we discovered more damage. We patched the holes we could find and took to setting live traps. But no matter how many squirrels we caught and let loose in a nearby park, when we got home, there was that same dreaded scurrying sound overhead.

Mr. Katz listened to the latest diatribe against the mulberry, leaning thoughtfully on the handle of his snow shovel. "I think drastic measures are called for here," he said.

"Well, yes, that's what I was thinking, too," I replied, hoping against hope that Mr. Katz, the mulberry groupie, would actually say it first.

"It'll cost some money," he said.

"How much, do you think?"

"A bundle," he replied. "First you have to peel off the shingles, line the roof with metal, and then re-shingle. And, of course, you need aluminum siding. I think we're talking about thousands of dollars here."

"Mr. Katz." I surprised him by putting my hand on his shoulder. "Can't you think of one other solution to this problem?"

He looked up at the house and the old mulberry, and then he nodded his head slowly. At last he spoke. "You could move."

The last straw came early one icy January morning. A squirrel managed to chew through some wiring in the attic and set the house on fire. It was a magnificent blaze that required three hook-and-ladder trucks. It was also quite difficult to put out, for the firemen had trouble gaining access to the back of the house, due to the position of the mulberry, and it cost us the top third of our dwelling. The smoke and water damage to the downstairs quarters was total. When the firemen and the board-up people and the insurance adjusters left, it was only David and me standing in our pajamas and overcoats on a patch of ice where the bedroom closet used to be. David said rather helplessly, "Well, what do you think we should do first?"

I looked straight up through the black hole at the mulberry and said, "The first thing we're gonna do is cut down that goddamned tree."

So I called the man from Bartlett Tree Experts, and it turned out I had to wait until spring to have the work done. On the appointed morning, I was outside under that tree focusing hard. "You're out of here, sucker," I said. "Your stump will be an excellent sitting place from which I can view my rodent-free, beautiful summer garden."

At that moment, Mr. Katz wandered over, "Are you back in the house?" he called out cheerfully.

"A couple of more weeks," I said.

"It'll be great to have you back home again." He was warm and welcoming.

Just then, the side gate opened and a man in green work clothes came around the side of the house. He introduced himself as Todd the Tree Man. I smiled at the alliteration. It was not lost on Mr. Katz either, who said as how he'd once known a family named Tree, who'd called their three kids Jack Pine, Douglas Fir, and Merry Christmas. We all had a good chuckle over that one.

"Is this the patient?" Todd looked up at the tree and whistled in admiration.

"Great climber," Mr. Katz beamed.

"Now, what can I do for you?" Todd asked.

I wandered deliberately toward the tree and away from the fence and Mr. Katz, mumbling to Todd the Tree Man. "How much to cut it down?" I tried to speak in a quiet voice, but Mr. Katz heard, because with my peripheral vision I saw his hands fly to his chest like maybe he was going to have a heart attack.

Todd didn't think he'd heard right. He still smiled at me, but he looked baffled. "Cut it down? Cut what down? The tree?"

"Yes, the tree. You are Todd the Tree Man, aren't you?" I asked, hoping he wouldn't make me say it again.

A look of alarm spread across his face. "You're joking!"

"I want a garden," I said. "Nothing grows back here."

"Well," he chortled. "This old mulberry tree seems to be doing all right."

"Let's just cut it down, okay? Squirrels came into our home and started a fire. This tree helped cause a major fire. I want it down." I stole a glance at Mr. Katz, who looked fragile suddenly.

"So, Todd," I said, wrenching my eyes from the fence, "What do you think?"

Todd the Tree Man looked at me the way my mother had looked at me fifteen years before when I'd told her I was leaving the church. Not friendly. "What do I *think*?" he said. "I think we should give this mulberry a good feeding, cable the limbs to keep her strong, and prune some of those branches back."

"That's not really what I asked, Todd." I suddenly felt sheepish. Mr. Katz was moving a little to the side so he could see Todd's face.

"You asked me what I think," Todd said. "I'm giving you my professional opinion. I don't think you really want to cut down this old tree. Why she's been here for a few generations."

She?

"She stood here giving food and shelter to birds and animals before you were born. Before your grandmother was born!" I found it curious that he had brought my grandmother into the conversation because I felt certain she would be on my side for this one.

"There's not a thing you could plant in your garden that would be more beautiful or life-giving than this old mulberry. And there's nothing you could plant that would last nearly so long. Do you realize she's a cousin to the olive tree and the rubber tree? I don't suppose you've ever used the fruit in a pie or to make jam."

"You would be correct," I replied.

"It's edible, you know!" He was practically shouting now. "Tastes like you're eating fireworks! Delicious! You'll want children someday, and she's a—"

"Don't tell me, Todd. I know! She's a great climber!"

But he continued, "This tree will entertain your children and your children's children. She's a miracle is what she is. And every tree on this planet is crucial to our survival. I'm talking about you and me. This tree is a source of oxygen, and it plays a very important part in keeping down the level of carbon dioxide in the atmosphere. You know, that stuff that causes the greenhouse effect?"

"Yes," I said, "I've heard about that."

But Todd wasn't finished with me yet. "Why, if you lived in Korea, this tree would be a great status symbol. Only the rich can afford to have the luxury of sitting under a shade tree like this. You'd take your meals here. Your neighbors would covet your good fortune."

To drive the point home, Mr. Katz let out an envious little sigh.

"The new roof they're putting on should take care of the squirrel problem," Todd said. "You might try aluminum siding if it doesn't. Anyway, if a squirrel wants to get in, it doesn't need a tree to gain entrance. It can just climb straight up the outside wall. So come on, lady. Why don't we just feed her, cable her, and prune her up real good. What do you say?"

There was a moment of profound silence. Todd the Tree Man. They didn't call him that for nothing. I looked at Mr. Katz, who was wringing his hands and managing an encouraging smile. I cleared my throat and peered up through the branches of the mulberry. The sun appeared to be winking at me.

"Yeah, Todd, you got it. Go ahead. Feed and cable her, and prune her to within an inch of her life." I didn't want to look, but I got the impression Mr. Katz was doing some sort of little hop step in the alley.

Todd smiled. "I'll write you out my estimate, and I'll send a crew out tomorrow," he said. "You've made a wise decision."

I didn't fall in love with the mulberry immediately after that. It took some time, and a lot of experimenting with plants that loved her, too. This spring I stand in my backyard and realize it isn't the yard I planned for myself as a little girl growing up in my grandmother's sunny garden. I will never see that dazzling array of color, or grow a vegetable, or feel the sun on my face the way I used to at Grandma's. What I have in its place are cool, mossy greens, feathering ferns. I have sought out strange plants with even stranger names: jack-in-the-pulpits, Jacob's ladders, forget-me-nots, and lilies of the valley. And over it all, there is the splendid leafy canopy of the mulberry tree. This garden will be a dark and mysterious planet for my brand-new little daughter. I know just where I'm going to build her playhouse: in the back corner surrounded by yellow forsythia.

I pat the old mulberry and lean up against her, congratulating myself. The mulberry spits its red gooshy fruit at me. It could tell stories about close shaves and survivor's guilt.

This year, a robin is building a nest in its branches. This nest is made of toilet paper and Christmas tinsel. In the first heavy rain, it totally dissolves. Immediately the bird returns with dirty paper towels and a gum wrapper. I marvel at the screwed-up creativity of city birds and wonder, as the second nest disintegrates, if it will come back and try again. It returns with a shredded potato chip bag. Well, it's chosen a great spot in the mulberry, where the branches come together to form a small bowl. Maybe that, and a few more gum wrappers, will be enough. ∎

WEIGHT
Gary Houston

Theresa — you are an enlightened angel. Gary

I t was July slipping into August. At 9:00 a.m. Jim waved to Gail in the driveway. With the Bonneville gassed up the night before, he had showered, shaved, patted his cheeks with Old Spice and was now headed out of Canton for Philadelphia, suitcase in the trunk, a bag of quarters for the tolls, coffee thermos by his side, which he would empty before the state line. He wore pleated slacks, navy canvas shoes and a plaid blue-on-white cotton shirt, short-sleeved. He figured a seven-hour trip, looking so forward to New England clam chowder in one of the Howard Johnson's on the Pennsylvania Turnpike he might not have left home otherwise. But he had hopes Henry would be at the conference. Henry's wrestling team was a powerhouse. It had won a district championship in north New Jersey and soon come out on top in the state finals.

Powerhouse. Not my guys, that's for sure. The worst bunch I've ever coached. He wished he could blame injuries or expulsions, but injuries were negligible, expulsions none. They were just a sorry crop. *They mean well, but what does that mean, mean well?* He hoped they didn't mean to lose over and over again. He kept seeing Glen Morris, his heavyweight, 243 pounds at the weigh-ins but 243 pounds of pale flab that hung from his body like soggy bread. He wished just once Glen had faced an opponent with the same pitiful build, at least then he might have waged a winnable battle. *People in the stands would see we were trying.* But unbelievably every high school team they met had a heavyweight built like a bull. Glen rarely reached a minute. Look away from the two boys on the mat for an instant, then look back and already Jim would see a blob of lard quivering beneath a slab of granite. The hard hand of the ref would slam the mat next to Glen's ear, deafening it with a stupendous cry of "FALL!" The opposing crowd would not even cheer. They were too occupied in laughter. Glen would be helped up by his opponent, they would perform the obligatory handshaking, and even then the victor just had to rub it in, gripping Glen's hand like a vise before he flung it away, immediately turning to the howls of his teammates. It was a mercy, Jim thought, that so often a match had already been lost several weight classes before Glen's. *Sure, because if Glen lost the* deciding *bout, boy oh boy, who knows how it would scar his life?* Jim guffawed then felt childish and told himself to stop it. *Even lesser things can scar a kid's life.*

He took the entrance to the Ohio Turnpike, wondering why they didn't fire him. *Because I've had better seasons? I guess. I suppose. I don't know.*

He proceeded southeasterly on the turnpike glad for a break from the sun that had dogged him since Canton. By the time the road went due east again, he would be on Pennsylvania's turnpike, the sun well over his head. *Over my head.* The conference check-in at the hotel was 6:00 p.m. He had plenty of time. He'd check in, look up Henry and they'd get a drink. They did that when they could get together. *Over my head.* They did not talk of the war, never, but always, underneath, they knew they both were thinking of the time their friendship was sealed. German tanks had taken their splintered unit by complete surprise in overwhelming numbers. In their ditch, hardly a trench, they looked at each other and said exactly the same thing: "Well, brother, this is it." That should have made them smile. Instead they invested the moment waiting to die. Nothing to it. They sure had seen others die. A world of mud descended upon them, blacking out everything. They heard the tanks ramping in ascent over their heads. But next the tanks reversed, turned and went left somewhere. Clearing their eyes, they never knew what had saved them.

While cars passed Jim he watched distance markers pass him the other way. He enjoyed the child's illusion of the ones ahead in hot pursuit of those that already had gone by. *Yep, there they go.* There was also the idle fancy in which the sign you pass (or that passes you) eventually disappears in the rearview so it must no longer exist— unless you cheat and drive back to find it is still there and still of this world. Silly stuff. The GI Bill had put him in touch with epistemology but produced little beyond a mind that wandered while driving. It could be everyone did that on the highway, but as a side thought he considered that a wandering mind accounted for his willingness to let himself be passed, which in turn made him question his competitiveness in other aspects of his life, notably his coaching. *It's not the kids, Jim, it's you. You don't have the fire in the belly.*

Then he recovered his train of thought. Some time ago he'd started likening a marker gone from view yet not from this world to the past and to the men he knew in combat. You knew their faces, their attitudes and gestures as they did their jobs, as they gathered in bull sessions. You had names for them. This somehow told Jim that if you could still see them in the mind's eye, then the dead ones still existed on some plane, that they still—not figuratively but really—had existence, still lived, still did what he remembered them doing. *That's right. Yes, I really do believe that.* He had brought this up when he last saw Henry, but Henry said, "Jim, have you gone all *Twilight Zone* on me?" Henry laughed, and Jim, conceding the undeniable vagueness of it all, crimped his eyes and grinned his silent acquiescent laugh.

Howard Johnson's beckoned before he reached the Alleghenies. *The tunnels.* As he spooned the white chunky soup into his mouth, he commanded himself not to spoil it thinking about the seven tunnels now not so far ahead. He was glad that three were earmarked that year for bypass, but this trip he still faced all seven. They were harrowing despite electric lights overhead and you had to go in a single lane, which in his experience did not at all cause drivers to slow down after entering, neither those ahead of you nor those impatient, apt to honk, drivers behind you, so you didn't either. *It's the weight, too.* The tremendous weight of a mountain, held up by the scorching toil of men thirty years ago, many surely young enough to be in the war to come, most probably dead now. *What if it gave way?* He couldn't put it aside. It didn't matter how often he'd heard of its impossibility. The thought was frightening, the chowder disappointing.

What would people think of a wrestling coach with such fears? Would he dare share them, even with Henry, especially with Henry? Gail? He grabbed quarters and went to the pay phone.

"Well, hello, stranger! Where are you?"

"About halfway. No, a little farther."

"I just walked Clarice and scraped the palm of my hand." His wife often sounded amused reporting Clarice adventures.

"How did you manage that?"

"She saw a squirrel and bolted for it. It was my fault. I wasn't holding the leash by the handle, so it zipped through."

"Ouch. Time for 'ssss goes the Bactine / ssss goes the Bactine / down goes the mean old germ.'"

"Already done."

"But it's not bad, is it?"

"It hurt like the dickens when it happened. But it's all right now, just a bitty little scrape. There's a Band-Aid on it. And, Jim, she's so cute. She knew she'd been bad, and you know how cute she is when she looks guilty."

I know. "I'll give it a kiss when I get home."

"Clarice beat you to it."

Jim chuckled. He knew those smelly frantic Bedlington terrier kisses.

"How's Julie?"

"Jim, you just left."

"I feel days away."

"She's playing tennis with Richard May."

"I don't like that kid."

"Oh, Jim, I think he's okay, just a little talkative."

"He doesn't know when to shut up."

"Well, apparently she likes to listen."

"Yeah."

Glad we had a girl. He didn't like the thought of a son going through the school where he coached. *Awkward. But why? Why awkward?* Gail was still talking.

". . . no but listen, Jim, you've been gone just a few hours but your girls already miss you—Julie misses you, Clarice misses you and I miss you. You know why?"

"Why?"

"Because we need a big strong man to unclog the bathroom sink."

"Jesus H. Christ, when did that happen?"

"Just after you left. I think it's from Julie's hair. She's always washing it."

"That's the second time this month. Did you try Drano?"

"But Jim—yes I did. It didn't work. But Jim—"

"We have to call in a real plumber."

"But, Jim, the real reason your three girls miss you?"

He paused.

"Yes, the real reason?"

She paused.

"Is that they love you."

"I'll call you after I check in, all right?"

"Drive safely."

"I love you too."

"I should hope so. Bye."

The waitress was clearing his booth.

"Did you like the chowder?"

"You bet, I always do."

"You must in this heat."

"It's good stuff all right."

"You can pay at the register."

Four longhairs sauntered past.

"Just sit anywhere you like, gentlemen," she called to their backs. She lowered her voice to Jim. "You know, we like people to stop at the front and wait for us to tell them that, but these . . ." She gestured their way.

"Do many of them come here?"

"You mean these, what do you call them, hippies?"

"Uh-huh."

"Oh Lord, yes. But, you know, I have a friend who waits over there"—she pointed to the restaurant's twin on the other side of the turnpike—"and she says they've taken the place over. She's never seen so many—just in the last two weeks. I'm glad I don't work over there."

"Does she say where they're going?"

"She says she always hears them talking about Chicago. Well, you know . . ."

"Oh sure. Well, I guess that's a big deal." Jim handed her a dollar.

"Thank you, sir. You come back now."

Back on the road he reconsidered his team. He had thought there was nothing more to its poor showing that year than lack of talent. But maybe he was wrong. Every year seniors showed symptoms of distraction, no longer wrestling to win, no longer craving glory and prestige in a school they could only look forward to leaving behind. No longer really caring. They called it senioritis. But this year every kid on the team regardless of grade had come down with it. While you could say no one exactly tried to lose, you could only be sure of a few, like Knobloch and Greiner, who wrestled to win. It was weird. It was like most of them had come to the conclusion that signing up had been an awful mistake and they should have been doing something besides wrestling. *A little late to realize that, boys.*

But what was it? The assassinations? A sign overhead announced the approach of Laurel Hill, the first tunnel. *Ignoramus, they got King when the season was well over, they got Kennedy after school was out.* It awaited Jim like a Cyclops. It ran, like all the tunnels, straight through the mountain, a black hole surrounding a wee white spot of sunlight at the distant east end.

But still, a good coach would know how to motivate them. Henry would. At the cookouts Jim and Gail threw, Jim liked to tell the neighbors about Henry, the middle linebacker at Rutgers who'd racked up a record number of sacks before enlisting. When they first conversed as buck privates, Henry stood up straight, planted his feet and dared Jim to come at him from a lineman's crouch and try to knock him over. *I gave it all I had and I tell you this guy didn't budge. No kidding, he was an ook. I might've dislocated a shoulder—not his, mine.*

As he entered Laurel Hill, he slowed down and immediately a black Ford behind him commenced honking. Jim ignored it.

After the war they got into wrestling more or less the same way. Henry joined the Pascack Valley (NJ) High faculty thinking he'd coach football, but once there, he was told they didn't need football coaches, they needed a coach for the recently installed and underfunded sport of wrestling. Henry being Henry was game. He had losing teams up to the mid-1950s. "I think I finally got the hang of it," he then wrote Jim. From that point on his teams almost always made it to the state finals, a few times to the regionals and only six years ago, his 1962 boys came in third at the national.

Jim pretended those victories had been his as he took on Allegheny Mountain, Rays Hill, Sideling Hill, Tuscarora Mountain, Kittatinny Mountain, Blue Mountain. In this state of Gettysburg they did sound like battle engagements. He wished he could see the face of whoever drove the Ford as he slowed down going through them and sped up on the stretches between them. After Blue Mountain he heard the angry accelerant roar of the Ford, which now he allowed to pass. It featured a slightly peeling Expo '67 bumper sticker, so he was able to identify it an hour later when he saw with some guilty satisfaction that a state trooper had pulled it over. As he passed he sang the jingle he'd heard televised a million times the previous summer: "Come one, come all / Come one, come all / To Expo '67 Montreal." He didn't think he'd remembered it right but he smiled. Last summer they thought of going, but Gail and Julie couldn't bear to leave Clarice behind. *Well, neither could I.* They had to figure something out, though. They were long overdue for a trip.

He switched on the radio searching for music, tuning through many gaps of static. Johnny Cash and June Carter, "Jackson" . . . some group singing, "Take a load off, Fanny / Take a load for free—" . . . the Beatles, whom even he could recognize, singing "While My Guitar Gently Weeps" . . . a crackling voice talking about Tet, the Battle of Hue, the Viet Cong—well, he had enough of that stuff at home on the six o'clock news . . . a Phillies game—no, sports on the radio frustrated the bejesus out of him . . . some screaming about Jumping . . . Jack . . . Flash? . . . then at last something that simply hit the spot—Sinatra. Even better—a medley of Frank, Bing and old Dino, who came more or less from his own part of Ohio. *Where's*

Sammy? He sang along with them the rest of the turnpike.

He called Gail as soon as he was in his room on the fourth floor. He hadn't expected anything plush yet he felt let down that his room seemed utilitarian. Even so he could not say what would have made him a happier guest. They told him in the lobby the hotel was unusually full.

Julie picked up his call.

"Hi, Dad! We thought you'd call sooner. Where are you?"

"I'm in my hotel room, sweetie. I called as soon as I got in."

"Is it a cool room?"

"Oh, it's just fine. How was tennis?"

"Richard May is a jerk."

"What happened?"

"I don't want to talk about it now, Dad."

That meant they'd never talk about it, but maybe it was just as well.

"Is your mom there?"

"MOM!"

Gail took the phone.

"Hi, handsome."

"Well, I got here in one piece. It was an okay drive."

Jim heard yelling from the street and the long cord of the phone allowed him to carry it to his window. It was dusk. To his left he saw that his street had a slight bend to it that was almost charming. He could not see where the voices came from.

"Jim, Henry called. He wanted to be sure you'd be there."

"I'll see if he checked in. Maybe we can get a drink. How did he sound?"

"He's a lot of fun on the phone. He told me a joke he heard on *Jackie Gleason.*"

"Don't tell it to me. I'll get him to do it."

"If you don't call me later I'll know you enjoyed yourselves."

"Love you."

"Love you."

As he showered his phone rang. He ran dripping and picked up. It was Henry in good spirits. "Ditch the broad and have a snort," he said. They agreed to meet at the bar in a few minutes. When Jim arrived he saw Henry had taken a table.

The first thing they noticed about each other, as they caught wafts from other tables, was that they had quit smoking. "Hardest thing I ever had to do," said Henry. "Same here," said Jim. They ordered steak sandwiches, onion rings and beer. Henry ordered his fully: "Hamm's, 'from the land of sky-blue waters.'"

The waitress walked away laughing: "You sound just like the commercial."

"Honey," said Henry, "that's just who I am. You want my autograph?"

"When I bring you the check."

Henry turned back to Jim. "God, I tell you, I just love 'em, love 'em all. Jim, tell me this. Why do we have to grow old? That must be the most frequently asked question in human history and yet I never hear any good answers. Do you?"

"Not lately, Henry."

"And lately is when it counts. How's Gail and the kids?"

"She's great, Henry, she says hi. And we only have one kid, our daughter Julie. I don't think you met her."

"No, I don't think so either. Does she look like you?"

"No, more like Gail."

"Well, then she has good taste."

Henry had a long fleshy face that might belong to an overweight man with heart problems, but below his neck was the same hard-muscled, mesomorphic build he'd always had. Jim the coach could perceive such things. Henry's handshake was as merciless as ever. Like Jim he sported a military haircut in allegiance to the service— the phrase *semper fidelis* ran through Jim's mind—but equally it was a badge of the coaching profession.

They talked about coaches who were listed as attending the conference, some of them mutual acquaintances but most known only by Henry. After the beers arrived Henry recounted a match he'd had against one of the conferees.

"We get to the one forty five class, and I think his boy is going to win, good as our kid is, but this guy is yelling positively the dumbest instructions from the other side." Henry snorted in reflection. "You know, Jim, from day one we teach them don't do a half nelson when your guy is on all fours because he can bring his arm down into the inside of your elbow and flip you. Right?" Jim nodded. "But that only makes sense when they're fresh! These kids are in the last period, they're completely exhausted, at this point both are just trying to keep from making a mental mistake and being pinned. My boy is in the down position, his boy is in the up position, they're at the edge of the mat and on the OTHER side of the edge, I mean the ref just lets him crawl right up to it, is this . . . asshole," he spoke the word in a whisper, "now SCREAMING at his kid because he's put a half nelson on my kid. 'DON'T DO THAT! REMEMBER WHAT I TOLD YOU? DON'T USE THE HALF NELSON, TONY!!'" Jim and Henry laughed. "Excuse me, ladies," Henry said to two women staring from one table over. "My guys start laughing at the coach. I try to shush them—disrespectful, you know. Then I see HIS guys laughing at him. At their own coach! So I can't help it, Jim, I crack up!"

"I would too!" Jim joined in the laughter. Eventually: "So who won?"

"Oh, who cares?" They laughed again and drank, Jim realizing he had developed a big thirst over the course of the day. After some moments savoring Henry's story, Jim felt he should ask after Carol, Henry's wife, but Henry spoke first.

"Are you happy, Jim?"

It was a question that took Jim by surprise. Henry had always been direct, but it was the directness of one colleague to another even if the other was an old war buddy.

"Happy? Well, if you followed the last season you can see I'm not happy about that."

"Oh, hell, you do what you can do with high school kids. I know you're a good coach, you know you're a good coach."

"No, I'm not so sure."

"Come on, Jim."

"Henry, you wouldn't believe what a miserable season I had."

"Okay, lecture time." Henry set his beer down. "It wasn't just your season, Jim, it was your boys' season too. And don't forget your team doesn't just crop up. You brought them up from ninth grade, most of them. Some waited years before you thought they were good enough to be varsity. But they hung in there, you could say they made a sacrifice. You know and I know that sports takes you away from the books. We're not supposed to say that, but it's true. So, Jim, whatever you're doing you're doing a good job, and I say screw the season outcome because you have boys who stuck with you all the way to the end of their senior year. So cut it out, don't be so hard on yourself. There are good years and bad. I remember your boys in '61. They were animals. I'm glad we didn't have to wrestle them."

"Sixty-one goes back a ways, Henry."

"Aw hell, let's order another round." Henry saw the waitress and circled his forefinger. "Jim, do you trust me?"

"Absolutely."

"Then trust me when I say you're a damn fine coach and that's an end to it." He stared at Jim, forcing him to nod.

Henry took a long swallow of Hamm's.

"All right, let's try something else. Say you teach them the fundamentals—all the moves, things to watch out for on the mat from their opponent. Say you taught them everything you know."

"All right."

"Say you hold a scrimmage, internally or you get on a bus and scrimmage with another team."

"Yeah."

"Well, do you see those teachings of yours reflected when they're actually wrestling?"

Jim got the point quickly, too quickly for his peace of mind. He could see one of his boys, Kevin in the 145 class, built solidly, worked with a barbell at home. And smart, one of the school's best students—Jim called him "the professor," and it caught on with the team. But he could not see the need to put his mind to work when he wrestled. He tried to rely on his power and bull his way around, and if he was up against an opponent who wrestled intelligently, Kevin suddenly found himself out of gas and was either outpointed or pinned, frequently pinned. Now that was the worst case, but Jim could see the same tendency in at least half the others.

"No I don't," he said, and he told Henry about Kevin and the rest.

"Smart kids are like that, Jim. They separate their mind from their body. It's like their mind stays on the bench, having wished the body good luck as it walks to the mat."

"What do I do about it?"

"Simple, tell them to take their minds with them when they wrestle. What I mean is, Jim, tell them and then tell them again until it sinks in. Getting it to sink in is the key. Nothing to it, except maybe a sore throat."

They laughed.

"No, Jim, but what I meant before was, are you happy in your life? Your . . ."

"Oh, well sure, Henry. I love what I'm doing, I love my wife, my daughter. I love my dog. I wish I could say I love my salary, but maybe one day I'll love that too. Of course that's a big maybe."

"I hear you." Henry paused. "But are you happy?" Henry must have read confusion on Jim's face. "No, the reason I ask is sometimes I get this sensation that everything isn't all right."

"With me?"

"No. With me."

The food arrived with the refills. They tested the sandwiches in silence. *What's going on here?* Henry looked at the onion rings.

"Hand me the Heinz, will you?"

Jim passed him the ketchup. After Henry slathered it over the onion rings, he began to stab at them with his fork.

"Sometimes," he said, "sometimes I just feel out of whack." Jim waited. "Sometimes," Henry began again, "the world catches up." He looked at Jim waiting for a response. Jim nodded, but it was only by way of telling Henry to go on. Henry smiled.

"You know that Mr. Chips story? Guy teaches all his adult life. He can always tell the boys apart, always knows their names." He quit the fork, picked up an onion ring and bit off half, chewing while talking. "But over the long term they all kind of flow together like the sky-blue waters. Sorry about that, the joke just came up like a belch, speaking of which . . ." Henry belched. "No, but, they all kind of blend together, and they are his life, too, a river of his life, Jim, and while he watches it go by, the river, he feels as alive as he did the first day he started teaching, and he loves his life because of that feeling."

Henry laughed at himself, or seemed to. Jim looked at him not knowing how to respond but decided saying anything would be an interruption even though Henry had fallen silent again.

"Well, anyway," Henry said at last, "that would be me."

"Henry, I've always wished I could put my life and work together like you have."

Henry hadn't heard it.

"But that's not really me anymore, Jim. I came—" He reached for his beer, changed his mind and took a sip of water. "I hit a wall."

"Now it's my turn, Henry. Come on, your team this year did great!"

Henry flared. "I'm not talking about the damned team!" Some heads turned from the bar. "I'm talking about no longer being able to see the point of it all because it's stopped being something that matters and I'm not young and grow up, Jim, neither are you."

"Oh sure, I know that all right, Henry, at least about me." *But I wish I knew what's up with you.*

Whatever it was subsided, but now they both ate too fast and without enjoyment.

"Do you want another round, Jim?"

"No, I don't think so. We have to be up early for the opening whatever you call it."

"Yep, let's settle here." He motioned for the waitress. "Sorry I snapped there, Jim. I guess I was being dramatic." He laughed his old laugh. "Hey, maybe I'm teaching the wrong thing! Can you see me putting on a play?"

Back in his room Jim called Gail and said he was turning in. It had been a long day. He slept, dreaming hazy dreams of driving. In one segment, for they came and went segmented, he was carrying his car, which had become a satchel, and was following a group of distance markers walking into a gym. He was in the stands and saw a vast red wrestling mat, and soon he realized he was a coach of one of the teams. He urged the markers who sat on the bench to go out there and do their best. They nodded as if they understood, but in the first period of the very first bout, the two opponents circled three times before clasping marker versions of hands and thumbs. The thumbs commenced their own wrestling match. The ref thundered, "FALL!" with a great slap of the mat and the defeated thumb of the losing marker pointed at him and the marker laughed; its teammates turned around and pointed at him with their thumbs and also laughed. Then the whole gym laughed.

He didn't see Henry at breakfast. The registration line moved fast. As Jim chatted with some coaches he remembered from the last such affair, he thought he spotted Henry far to the back in animated conversation. The banquet room for the initial proceedings held possibly fifty coaches now wearing name tags on the lapels of their sports jackets. Jim wore a navy one over a white polo shirt, and he wore tan pants and black loafers. These had been carefully packed as his conference wardrobe, supplemented by a light-blue polo shirt either for later in the day or the following morning when things would be wrapped up. The air above harmonized Old Spice, English Leather and witch hazel.

The coaches were greeted by a man who introduced himself as Stan Kish, president of the National High School Wrestling Coaches Association. Looking about thirty-five, Kish did not seem the type who had ever wrestled or coached but might have been a promising statistician. After words of greeting he introduced the guest speaker, "noted" author George Plimpton. The coaches, some of whom had heard of Plimpton, clapped deferentially. Plimpton explained that after his forays into baseball and football he thought he'd try wrestling. "But I couldn't determine whether wrestling meant the sport you fellows coach or the real thing—you know, with Haystacks

Calhoun." As his audience laughed Plimpton scanned the room. "Hey, has he retired?" Someone shouted, "No such luck!" Plimpton shaded his eyes with his hand. "Is that you, Haystacks?" He was very funny and kept the men entertained a half hour before turning serious.

"You know, I don't have to tell you we're living through a turbulent time. But eventually we are going to live to see a better day, the proverbial light at the end of the tunnel. And that will be due in no small measure to the development of character. I mean the character of the students coming up, those whom you are coaching in high school—or will be when school starts again. And don't forget they are also the ones you are *teaching*. For that essentially is what you do, teach. You teach courage, you teach resilience, you teach a virtue of something we don't hear about much anymore—you teach grace, inner grace. Strength comes from that kind of grace. Kipling wrote about it in his poem 'If.' I know you know it, the poem about keeping your head when all about you are losing theirs. Well, that's where you come in. We'll have a better country, my friends, because of what you do." A noise intruded from outside. Loud voices from the lobby. As if cued, Plimpton went on. "Remember, despite all the tumult out there today, the clamor of voices pulling them in all directions, the boys still listen to you. Think about that. They still put a value on what you say. And, gentlemen, if you say it well, if you say it and you mean it, they'll continue to put a value on it for the rest of their lives." He thanked everyone, received a warm hand and took his seat.

Kish thanked the author and told the coaches to take schedules from a table in the hall. He said one of the slots was allotted for an exhibition bout between two boys whose coaches, Todd Byrnes of York and Gil Wiley of Lancaster, were recent district winners. "It's been a while since the season ended," Kish said smiling, "but Todd and Gil assure me the boys are still in shape." He then listed a few other topics on the agenda. "The schedule will tell you the rest. Thanks, one and all." The coaches began to rise from their chairs when Kish remembered something and raised his voice. "I'm sorry, I almost forgot. It's not on the schedule but half an hour or so after dinner, around seven thirty, we'll gather in the hotel vestibule for a chartered bus because we have been invited to a special screening, just for us, of a new Hollywood movie called . . ." He took a piece of paper from his inner jacket pocket. "It says here it's called *Chitty Chitty Bang Bang* starring Dick Van Dyke. And I hear it has nothing to do with wrestling whatsoever."

"That'll be a relief!" shouted someone, eliciting a few chortles.

The coaches could choose when two sessions were held simultaneously. Jim nodded through the one on extra funding for high school athletic programs with, as Kish said, "a particular focus on wrestling." Kish himself did not attend. Only two others did, but they at least had questions to ask. Jim hadn't followed enough of the discussion to ask anything. After it ended he learned he hadn't read the schedule with much care: he'd missed the matchup between Coach Byrnes's boy from York and Coach Wiley's boy from Lancaster, held in a lounge cleared for half of a regulation-sized mat. As quickly as Henry appeared in the lobby—"You missed a good one, Jim! I saw some new moves, too."—he rushed off calling back, "We'll catch up later."

But through the sessions of the rest of the morning, then the afternoon, he did not see Henry. Nor did he see him at dinner, held in a banquet hall on the mezzanine, and he looked around for him as he waited inside the hotel's front entrance for the movie bus. Through the glass doors he saw it was still light out. *Well, of course it is.* About twenty-five coaches showed up to watch Dick Van Dyke. As they stood looking for the bus, it crossed Jim's mind that the remainder would hardly be content to stay holed up in their rooms. In fact, he did see a number of them leave the banquet hall before the apple pie was served. *But that's their business.* Gail would be mildly pleased to hear he had a nice night out with fellow coaches watching—what had Kish called it?—a "screening."

Suddenly he was aware of a new group of people, young people, gathering in the vestibule. He had heard there was another conference in the hotel, some college event—editors of college newspapers?—who, by and large, when Jim would see them in the lobby, seemed to be a well-groomed bunch. But along with them he started noticing a scruffier crowd, some with hair that came down to their shoulders "like girls," as one of his colleagues remarked with undisguised contempt, some whose hair curled or kinked and whose heads reminded him of dandelions when they were just bubbles of seeds. There were not many women, yet quite a few of both genders wore army jackets with peace symbols stitched on. Many wore dungarees, many wore sandals.

They did not talk boisterously, but they did talk volubly, and all about Jim was a din he was not used to. "There is something about the suavity of your manner . . ." he heard a voice behind him. He turned and saw a slender man in his late twenties wearing John

Lennon glasses, his hair long in the back while thinning in front. ". . . something that leads me to believe that you do not actually care whether reports of the atrocities are true or not." He was addressing an older man in a suit writing on a pad of paper. Jim could not see his face but heard him say that Viet Cong aggression was "well-documented." A second longhair, younger than the first, protested. "What about the thousands of peasants, men, women, children, who've been run over, slaughtered, by U.S. troops? What about the napalm? What about Agent Orange? Every day people are dying, man.You talk about documentation? What about what we're doing there?" The one with glasses, who all the while had been studying the man taking notes, jumped in. "How dare you smirk when he says that. How dare you make light of what he just said."

"I am not making light of it," said the older man. "I'm just making light of him."

"Well then all I have to say, if you'll pardon me, is interview over and go fuck yourself." The man shrugged and disappeared in the crowd.

Jim did not know who these people were, but more and more of them accumulated. And with their discovery that they had inadvertently merged with high school athletic coaches, types they viewed as their diametric opposites in worldview and personality, one was heard saying, "Perfect!" Another, "Man, how out of it can you get?" Another, "How ironic." Jim could not fathom the snickering. But others could. It was over the coaches' short, "masculine" haircuts, the smell of their aftershave, their very calling. For not long ago these kids had attended public school, where in junior high they'd endured mandatory gym, from which point on they had memories of coaches and the mentality of coaches. And this brought to mind other authorities whose mentality reminded them of coaches.

Above the noise Jim heard a shout.

"I CAN'T STAND IT! I CAN'T STAND IT! YOU . . . BABIES . . . WE FOUGHT A WAR FOR YOU. MY FRIENDS DIED FOR YOU." He spoke names. "MURPHY. TABORELLI. RICHARDS. BUKOWSKI. MCGUINNESS. HANDLER. DELGADO. DEAD! BLOWN APART!" It was Henry. His face was red and glistened with tears Jim could not see streaming down because Henry's hair and all of his face were moist with perspiration. "YOU WEREN'T EVEN BORN, BUT WE WERE THINKING OF YOU, WAITING FOR YOU. WE WERE MAKING A NEW WORLD FOR YOU, ALL FOR YOU! AND

LOOK AT YOU!"

"Back to the drawing board," retorted someone. "Okay, man, don't get a heart attack," said another. Other taunts followed. The longhairs, versed in guerrilla theater and earlier in that very hotel having been given a sample of it by a group called the yippies, could not at first interpret this spectacle but rapidly overcame its ambiguity by choosing to view Henry as someone out of central casting. Henry did not hear them. Towering over most of the heads around him, brandishing his huge red hands in fury, he continued his rant that again and again would come back to the list of the dead. Murphy. Taborelli. Richards. Bukowski. McGuinness. Handler. Delgado.

Jim could not move. He could not guess what had gone wrong. The other coaches were equally helpless, but Jim above all bore the weight of duty toward his friend. Yet still he could not move. He saw that from the back of the crowd a large young man had emerged wearing an army jacket and an earring. He had dark brown hair curled into ringlets and a bushy beard. He was tall and burly. Jim could not, despite the chaos, avoid extraneous thought. *Give him a shave and he might make a good heavyweight.* The boy, sporting a grin that might have been mocking or beatific, Jim couldn't tell, began to advance on Henry as though he were either the angel of mercy or the angel of destruction. Henry, sobbing and screaming, repeating the names, began stepping back, not exactly seeing the kid, more just sensing someone's approach.

Then Kish appeared. "All right, that's enough," he said. The big boy held on to his knowing smile. "No, really," said Kish, now speaking to all the young people, "this is serious. Please leave him be. He's sick. He's a sick man." The big boy knew nothing about the howling older man other than he was a coach, all the more "ironic" a high school coach; he did know he liked the precocious triumph he believed wore well on his face and did not want to give it up. But soon he realized his cohort in the hall was losing interest and thinning, that the smile then was fast becoming devoid of purpose. He laughed it all off and sought his friends who had wandered to the street.

Henry had quieted down.

"Can some of you help here?" Kish asked the stunned coaches. "Can you help this gentleman to his room?"

Jim and two others led Henry to the elevator. Jim asked them to hold the door a minute and hurried back to Kish.

"His name is Mullen. Henry Mullen. He's in room 302."

"I know Henry," said Kish. "Everybody knows Henry. You said

302? I'll ask if any doctors are staying here."

He moved for the desk, but Jim grabbed his forearm.

"What did you mean, by that—sick?"

"What?"

"You said he's sick. What did you mean by that?"

Kish looked as though he thought Jim was sick, too.

"Excuse me," he said.

Jim released his arm.

Henry remained silent as the men eased him into his bed. Finally: "Thanks, fellas. You can go now. I want to talk to Jim here."

Jim thanked the coaches and saw them out. Henry breathed heavily. "Well," he said. "That was really something, wasn't it?"

"What happened, Henry?"

"I was hoping someone could tell me. First thing, I'm just standing there, looking at the carnival, listening. Then I'm—you know that expression, 'have you flipped your lid'? Well, now I know we really do have lids. And, brother, I sure flipped mine."

"Henry . . ." Jim hesitated. "It looked like something just snapped."

"You know what I think? It was just a damned big bubble that came up to the surface." He chuckled. "Like a belch."

He felt his face.

"Christ, I'm wet all over. Hand me a towel, Jim, will you?"

As Jim gave him a hand towel, Henry studied his friend.

"Where were you?"

Jim knew what that meant. He'd dreaded the possibility that Henry would ask. He sighed and shook his head.

"I let you down, Henry. I was there, and I just stood there, I just . . . I was just useless . . . I don't know, I guess I was afraid, Henry . . . I'm sorry."

"Afraid, Jim? What were you afraid of?"

"I don't know."

"Well, I hope it wasn't—I hope it's not me."

"Oh no."

"Are you still afraid? Are you afraid of me now?"

"No, no."

"Because I don't think I could take that. You're my pal, Jim, that's all there is to it."

Jim couldn't help it. He welled up, looking down at Henry.

"Do you want me to call Carol at home?"

Henry clamped his lips together for a moment.

"She's not there, Jim."

"Well, then—"

"Neither of us is."

Nothing was added for several seconds. Henry for an instant was like a chastened toddler. His blue eyes roamed in worry. There was guilt in the worry but also some innocent incomprehension. At last he spoke. "I did something stupid. I don't know where she is."

There was a knock at the door. Jim let the doctor in. The doctor and Henry talked quietly for a few moments, then the doctor asked Jim if he wouldn't mind seeing Henry later.

"Of course," said Jim. "Henry, I'll call you first thing in the morning." Henry kept his eyes on Jim, nodding slowly. They waved to each other and Jim returned to his room. He called Gail and described the day except for Henry's explosion. He wanted to wait until he was back home.

He might say, "He flipped his lid. He said it himself."

She might say, "It must have been a long time coming. It must have been a heavy lid."

The next morning he called Henry's room, but no one was there. He called the desk. "He checked out early, sir, about an hour ago." *Where would Henry go?* Jim had no idea, but now he knew he was not cut out for conferences. He decided to check out as well. There was only a half day left of the thing, which now struck him as incompetent planning.

He drove westward on the turnpike, once more set in the right lane, slower than most cars on the road. He scarcely noticed his passage through the seven tunnels. Of course while it was nice that the sun was behind him in east Pennsylvania, hours later it could be in his eyes, so he counted on the northwesterly stretch in west Pennsylvania that would take him into Ohio. The sun would be less direct.

Occasionally he abandoned his mental games with the passing road signage to his right to look to his left. He wondered how many young people were en route to Chicago. He thought he saw a few likely ones behind the wheel.

As for me . . .

As for Jim, he went no further than Canton. ∎

COTTONMOUTH
Jane Morton

When the dog comes home
snakebit, soaked through the coat

with bad water, my mother knows
we'll find the snake

flung limp in the dirt, holes
bright in the belly.

Some say the flesh of the snake
will cure its bite. We think

we know better. Know to bite harder
than you're bit, and then let go.

Once the swelling goes down,
the dog's teeth are soon to fall out.

When they do, we'll pour
a little milk in her bowl.

SOLSTICE
Jane Morton

How long until the fruit begins to rot?
The parts we've wasted lie
around the kitchen—over-soft
strawberries, pomegranate seeds we forgot
to eat, tomatoes wet and veined as hearts
quartered on the counter, a fly in your hair.
My mouth is full of red.
The walls are full of flies you'd only know
if you listened right.

The heat never breaks this time
of year but we don't know that yet.
We sit out on the front steps
and watch the sky burn to soot,
sweat beading my forehead
a crown. We wait for a sign
we should or shouldn't quit; a sparrow
or a crow, something feathered
unfettered or fallen.

When the light goes,
all we have to watch are flies,
unafraid or careless, hardly
moving. We could go on
forever like this. Our lives unspooling
before us. We won't die
all at once, but piece by piece—an ache
creeps in marrow-deep.
It takes a while even to notice.
The night almost at the end of its rope.

GOOD DOG
Malcolm Rothman

Tell me what you eat; I'll tell you what you are.
—Anthelme Brillat-Savarin

It was another brutally hot day in our district village of Phuc My, Republic of Vietnam: a great place to be from. The two adorable three-month-old puppies born to our pet bitch, Nuoc Mam, had disappeared. They had become the favorites of all the American advisors in my team. It wasn't until we had searched for a half hour through the garbage heaps, slit trenches and mud barricades that made up our compound that anyone noticed that their mother, Nuoc Mam (named for the stinky fish sauce found everywhere in Vietnam), was also nowhere to be found. She was the most dependable of dogs, and in spite of her powerful, rank smell, a well-loved pet. The fact that she was also missing added to the sense of dread that had been my second skin for the past eight months.

"Sin fuckin' loy!" said Spec 4 Isaiah Manton, the team radioman. "So sorry. Too bad, so sad." He shrugged. Isaiah was from rural Mississippi and was normally impervious to hot, humid weather. He was genuinely one tough customer, but Nuoc Mam and her pups had brought out a gentle streak in him that none of us had ever suspected. We were all well aware that where we lived also lived many creatures that could put you in a world of hurt: cobras and other snakes, rats, centipedes (one had gotten under my mosquito net two weeks earlier and bit the shit out of my upper lip, swelling it to grotesque proportions), spiders the size of softballs, feral cats . . . any one of them could have done the puppies in, let alone their mom. Life had made the already hypervigilant Isaiah a realist, and for the past fifteen minutes he had been hinting to me   that we should give up the search. I was too depressed to reply. I had lost my dogs, it was ninety-five degrees at 0900 hours and it was Christmas Eve.

I had been in Phuc My District for six months as a navy hospital corpsman assigned to an American advisory team stationed in Nhut Sac Province, tucked away in one of the more relatively peaceful areas in the Mekong Delta. Assigned to a district MACV advisory team, my job was to assist the district health worker holding regular sick calls in the more remote hamlets in our district for people who had never had access to Western medicine. Also, and off the official books, I performed the duties of field medic during combat missions throughout the district. These operations were always held with the Ruff Puffs—the regional force cadres with whom we lived.

Our advisory team leader, Captain "Ranger" Joe Lupaletti, was a graduate of Fordham University on his third tour in Vietnam. He was a passionate anti-Communist and was committed to the preservation of the South Vietnamese government with an intensity that puzzled the Vietnamese. Nevertheless, he was a good officer, so no one much minded his occasional political pep talks. He took no unnecessary chances, was very good with the local civilians and militia and treated everyone like human beings regardless of nationality or rank. Together with First Sergeant Ripley, a lifer's lifer, we made up the local team of advisors.

Isaiah started back to our hooch, and I tried to work up the energy to follow. A voice called out, "Good morning, Bac Si!"

It was Captain Thanh, the cheerful commander of the Vietnamese irregulars that we allegedly advised. He was five foot five and a proud 160 pounds—massive weight by Vietnamese standards. When not obliged to lead his troops into the field, Captain Thanh made his living operating brothels popular with the American chopper crews based in Nhut Sac, the province capital, and, of course, dealing in black-market medical supplies and USAID building materials. He was especially cheerful this morning. "Christmas pah-ty, tonight," he chirped. "Joyeux Noël! You bring cognac, yes? Hennessy? Reh-mee Mah-tan? Très bon! Numbah one!!"

Captain Thanh was a northerner and a Francophile. He missed the French so profoundly that he would sometimes speak to us in that language in the hope that we would abandon our charade as Americans and reveal our true identities. But mostly, his speaking French instead of English tended to put us off balance, which was really why he enjoyed doing it. My raggedy high school French was just barely adequate to the task of responding coherently.

"Apportez, s'il vous plaît, de Mumm's Cordon Rouge." His thick, well-formed lips surrounded the words lovingly. Captain Thanh was familiar with all the brands of liquor available to us at the chopper base PX. They were his chief pleasure and a valuable currency on the local black market. That night, we would drink the cognac and leave the champagne for the captain's discretionary use.

Isaiah was starting to look pissed off, as he often did when it got this hot this early in the day. Isaiah disliked Thanh, with his effete manners and high spirits. He had once overheard Thanh compare American Blacks to Cambodians, and it was said that the Vietnamese despised the dark-skinned Cambodians, whom they considered barbarians. Then, of course, there was the night raid two months earlier that had gotten two Ruff Puffs killed by friendly artillery fire. As the architect of that fiasco, it was Thahn who had called in the coordinates. That he had gone without punishment or even reprimand deepened Isaiah's resentment.

He walked up beside me. "What the fuck's he talkin' about?" Isaiah muttered. "Why don't he speak English?"

"He's just telling me what he wants for Christmas."

"Dai Wee," he addressed the Captain by his Vietnamese rank, "you seen our puppies? Puppies?"

Thanh looked puzzled. "Qu'est-ce que c'est, pop-eez? What is pop-eez?"

"Baby dogs, sir. Baby dogs. Little cuddly motherfuckers. Like this." Isaiah tilted his head to one side and let his eyes grow big and sad, like a waif in a Charles Kean painting, and started moving with the mincing steps of a circus poodle. The puppy impression was obscenely unconvincing.

Thanh let his hand drop casually to the grip of his chrome-plated .45. Not taking his eyes off Isaiah, he said to me apologetically, "Sorry, Bac Si. Je ne comprend pas, pop-peez."

I quickly scanned my brain for the French necessary to get the idea across before the tension escalated any further.

"Uhm . . . Un jeune chien, mon capitaine." A long second passed. "B-Bébé chien," I stammered.

His eyes suddenly lit up. "Ah, un chiot!" he cried. "J'aime beaucoup les chiots!" And, as if nothing had just happened, he began a rapid-fire discourse in Franco-Anglo-Vietnamese patois far beyond my ability to understand even a single word.

Isaiah relaxed and turned away, glad himself for the break in tension. After a few minutes of my pretended interest, the captain wrapped up his lecture and we stood there smiling stupidly at each other, long past anything else to say.

Thanh manufactured an enormous stage yawn and said, "Time for asleep, Bac Si," and flashed a gold-studded smile. As he turned to go he shouted, "Joyeux Noël. Do not forget, ce soir a dix-neuf heures," and grandly waving his right arm, he waddled back to his quarters across the compound.

Stunned, I watched him disappear through the door. Isaiah let out a quick breath and said, "Next show at seven." He read my mind. "Hey, cheer up. I wasn't gonna do nothing. Just havin' some fun, that's all. Tell you what, though, I heard that the dai wee puts out quite a feed. I don't mind sitting down to a big Christmas dinner, if it's done right. Which reminds me, Doc. I don't suppose I could get you to stop this bullshit and come inside now."

"What about Nuoc Mam and the pups?" I asked miserably. Through the morning's search I'd kept imagining life without the diversion of our pets.

He put his hand on my shoulder, looked me in the eye and said, "Doc, they're gone. I feel bad about it too but they're gone, you understand? It don't mean shit. Now c'mon, let's go see if there's any coffee left. If you want, we can look again later."

I turned away and looked past the mud ramparts, useless against anything but the smallest of small-arms fire. Past the concertina wire festooned with old C ration cans and Claymore mines, out over the broad expanse of rice paddies that surrounded us to the far horizon. Numberless filaments of young rice stalks stretched from the sea of oily brown water. Miles away and barely visible, the closest tree line was a heat-warped smudge of green. As I stood staring, I knew with hopeless certainty that the puppies and Nuoc Mam were lost forever.

Isaiah had reached the end of his patience. "Yo, Doc! Come in, Doctor Dinky-Dow!" He waved his hand up and down in front of my eyes. "Bye-bye, Nuoc Mam. Bye-bye, puppies."

"Just like that?" I asked. " Aren't you worried about them? I mean, I thought you were crazy about them."

He shot me an angry look.

"Yeah, I was. But there's only one thing I'm really worried about and that's getting my short-timer ass back to the world in one piece. With any luck I might be able to get on with my life and forget about this shithole and everything in it." His glance got harder. "No, I take that back. I'm worried about you, too. Your mind's not on the job, boy. Lately, your head's up your ass, fooling around with the dogs and shit, going into town and daydreaming and generally fucking up. You're not careful, you're gonna get somebody killed, and I mean me, and that would be one helluva fuckin' shame, you understand what I'm sayin'? Now, you wanna go look some more, you look yourself, okay? I'm outta here!"

He turned on his heel and briskly walked back to the advisor's hooch. After a long moment, I followed.

* * *

By evening the temperature had fallen to just plain hot. It being Christmas cease-fire season, we had relatively little to do throughout the day. At four, clothed in our undershorts, the team bathed under the rainspout of our building during the daily thundershower. It was one of the few local customs we enthusiastically embraced. We finished our afternoon busywork, napped and assembled for dinner with Captain Thanh and company. Heavily laden with bottles of PX cognac and two cases of Mumm Cordon Rouge, we crossed the compound to the captain's quarters. It was a comfortable bungalow that contrasted starkly with the squalid mud, thatch and corrugated metal shacks of the cadres and their families.

We were greeted by four of the captain's female employees, who quickly relieved us of our burden and led us in. They welcomed us with smiles and seasonal good wishes in Vietnamese and English. They had, at one time or another, had all of us as customers. I was a special favorite because, in addition to my loyal patronage, I provided them with large doses of antibiotics on demand and was less stingy and more friendly than the Baptist I had replaced. One girl, Ha Mui, a playful and shapely farmer's daughter, fancied herself my number-one girlfriend. Looking into my eyes, she took my hand and gave me a small kiss on the cheek, causing the others to laugh and tease her. The music of their laughter accompanied us to the large table that dominated the main room.

Ranger Joe said, "Behave yourselves. That is, until the Vietnamese start dancing on the table. Then you can go nuts." Already seated and half in the bag were Thanh, his second-in-command and his noncoms. Ordinarily quiet and businesslike, they were chatting noisily. They were smoking cigarettes taken from a display of American cigarette cartons, which served as a festive centerpiece, and drinking a clear spirit out of an unmarked bottle called Ba See Day, which was said to mean "vomit and fall down." They greeted us with lavish goodwill and bade us sit in the chairs at the captain's end of the table—the places of honor.

We helped ourselves to Salems and Marlboros and watched as the rice whiskey was pushed aside and replaced by the Remy Martin VSOP and iced Budweisers. Over the next half hour we toasted the captain's health and our own, the United States, the Republic of Vietnam, the defeat of international Communism, the amazing world-champion New York Mets, Elvis, the Pope, the Pips, and the four fetching young women who were presently serving hors d'oeuvres—a mountain of crispy shrimp crackers and some scary little canapés of raw garlic, fresh bird peppers and what looked like and could very well have been ground Spam.

As the liquor took hold, a feeling of well-being passed over me. Isaiah, Ranger Joe and Top Ripley were amusing the others by eating the macho garlic-pepper treats greedily, crying copiously from the incendiary peppers and clutching their throats in mock strangulation. We were in the first wave of intoxication, euphoric and full of goodwill. I looked around me and loved everyone I saw. Captain Thanh and his juniors were flushed and jolly, radiating the camaraderie that we were presumably there to create. The months of my tour in the 'Nam now seemed, for the tiniest instant, to be bearable and worthwhile.

My reverie was interrupted by the girls reentering the room. Ha Mui carried a platter at arm's length; the others flanked her. The effect was like the presentation of a birthday cake. All were smiling, and when the Vietnamese soldiers saw what was on the platter, they too grinned and began a staccato chatter among themselves, all the while focusing on the four Americans.

Clearly, something was up.

Captain Thanh said, "Ah, Bac Si, you try, you eat. Les oeufs de canard!" The platter was placed on the table before me. In it were a dozen or more gray eggs resting in a bed of aromatic greens and surrounded by small bowls of dipping sauce. I looked to the others. Ranger Joe, who had been to one of the captain's parties before, tried to shake his head without being obvious. Everyone saw and began to hoot and point.

"Duck egg numbah one, Bac Si. The best!" He smacked his lips wetly to let me know that I was in for the treat of my life. "Le meilleur! I show you." He picked up the egg with one chubby hand, and in the other, a teaspoon appeared. Holding it over a small bowl, he gently tapped the narrow end of the egg, peeled away the shell to reveal a fully formed fetal duck molded into the egg shape it was cooked in. He wrapped it in a couple of the leafy greens and dipped it in some fish sauce and, in one motion, he brought the egg to his lips and sucked the contents into his mouth. A round of applause came from the Vietnamese. I had never seen them all look so happy. Captain Thanh chewed contentedly and handed me his spoon. As I took it, I noticed that the Vietnamese were now leaning forward on the table, waiting for the real show to begin. The girls were behind me, giggling and whispering. *Fuck it*, I thought. *What's the big deal? Anything these folks can eat, I can eat too.*

I picked up an egg. The room fell silent with anticipation.

At arm's length, I tapped open the narrow end and daintily removed each piece of shell to the tablecloth. After wrapping the egg with the leaves as the captain had done, I dipped it into the bowl of sauce. I raised the egg to my lips. I took a whiff.

Its smell brought to mind the kind of hard-boiled eggs my germaphobe mother used to cook for forty minutes in order to kill all the bacteria she imagined they contained. It was not exactly a stench, but sulphurous and far from a savory aroma. But far worse than the smell was the anatomical completeness of the moist fetal duck embryo I held in my hand: head, eyes, beak, feathers, feet, innards, the works.

A small groan of pleasure went up from my Vietnamese audience. Their expressions made it clear that they either expected me to chicken out or, better yet, to eat it and react like I'd swallowed a turd. I realized then that I was the evening's headliner. I heard Ha Mui unsuccessfully stifle the smallest of laughs behind me. There was no way out: I would have to eat the damned egg or go completely without face for the rest of my time in Phuc My. *Oh well*, I thought to myself, *no guts, no glory*. I held the egg to my lips and shoved its contents into my mouth.

The smell, strange as it had been, had not been ample warning. The egg had the flavor of yesterday's scrambled eggs awash in a bath of regret. But that was not the worst of it. This was an actual, fully formed fetal duck, covered in a fine fetal down and cold, wet, fetal skin. It covered the length of my tongue. With growing panic, I realized that it would have to be chewed in order to be safely swallowed. But there was absolutely no way I could spit it out and still retain my manhood. I saw that all eyes were on me. The Vietnamese were in a state of rapture. Of the Americans, only Isaiah, now fully aware of what was happening, looked concerned—could these eggs cause permanent damage? I wondered myself. I reckoned that five or six chews would do the job. After the tenth, eleventh and twelfth, the ghastly duckling seemed, paradoxically, to grow in size. Chewing revealed new horrors. Inside the duck were tiny gelatinous bones, soft enough to chew but unspeakably unpleasant. And, of course, there were the innards. Feeling myself grow faint, I chewed faster until finally, with one mighty effort, I swallowed it all. A huge cheer went up from all present. Hands slapped my back and a large glass of Ba See Day was placed in front of me. I drank it in one gulp. And then I drank another. When I was at last able to open my eyes, I was surprised to see happy approval flooding the room. A blue gecko, now visible on the window screen in front of me, bobbed its head spasmodically in appreciation.

I tried to appear nonchalant, snapped my fingers and croaked in a high raspy voice, "Number one." Captain Thanh picked up another egg and offered it to me; I took the egg and passed it to Isaiah. "Thank you and fuck you!" he shouted in genuine terror. But it seemed that only one of us would be subjected to this test tonight. I had saved face for us all. The egg was passed to Ranger Joe, who simply held up his hands in polite refusal and said, "No thanks. I'd rather die."

Waves of fresh merriment filled the air as one by one, the Vietnamese took and blissfully ate the remaining eggs. There was much lip smacking and extravagant yummy sounds to let us foreigners know just how much we had to learn about good eating.

I was, by now, ravenously hungry and quite drunk. Fresh plates of exotic-looking foods came to the table: crunchy grated papaya salad and two gigantic platters of artistically arranged charcoal-grilled meat. Both looked delicious and were quickly attacked with chopsticks. A thick, unctuous stew was eaten with mounds of fragrant rice. Three massive whole fried fish appeared in a nest of fried rice noodles. The papaya was sweet and spicy, flavored with hot pepper, peanuts, lime and fish sauce. The charcoal-grilled meat was savory and tender. The stew and fish delectable. I fought my way to large portions of all and ate with gusto.

Between mouthfuls, I leaned to the captain and asked, "This is all delicious, Dai Wee." I pointed to the grilled meat. "What are we eating? Comment viande mangeons-nous?"

I saw his eyes move over the room. After a long pause, he licked his lips and said, "The stew is pig. The other I do not know word in English," he said. Another pause. "En français, on dit 'le chiot.'"

And I thought, *Where have I just heard that word? Just recently, I . . .* And then it hit me. *Chiot! The captain beaucoup loves chiot. Puppy. Holy shit, we're eating puppies! WE'RE EATING THE PUPPIES!* I couldn't believe it. Six months in this place had acquainted me with more confusion than the rest of my life put together, but this took the cake. Whatever expression crossed my face at that moment, it was observed by enough people to drastically bring down the level of mirth at the table. Although puppy meat was looked on as a treat by many Vietnamese (or, at very least a protein of convenience), they knew that Americans regarded dogs and cats with childlike sentimentality and found it puzzling that we weren't also emotionally attached to pigs or cattle. Captain Thanh smiled and looked at me expectantly. "Dog is very good, no?"

I then understood that this, not the egg, was to be the real test. I thought of Nuoc Mam and the pups and realized that they had just become martyrs to the cause of US-Vietnamese solidarity, sacrificed on the altar of intercultural goodwill. These people were, after all, our allies. Our host's intentions were good, and there was nothing to be done now but move along and not let this evening and other times to come be ruined by a lack of grace on my part. Two days from now, a dangerous operation was scheduled to commence, and all of us at this table, Vietnamese and Americans both, would be involved. We needed, as always, to depend on each other for our very lives. This was not a good time for hard feelings. And besides, to my surprise, I found that I couldn't help admitting to myself that when all was said and done, Nuoc Mam and her puppies had, indeed, been awfully tasty.

I looked at the Captain, belched and said, "Dog good? Hell no. Delicious dog. Best goddamn dog I ever had!" I poured some Hennessy into my glass and raised it high. A cadre sergeant at the other end of the table did the same. Isaiah, Ranger Joe and Top joined in with an explosion of laughter. Soon, the whole crowd was toasting to us, we to them and all of us to the glory of Christmas.

Dog bless us, everyone! ∎

BISCUITS FOR PREVENTING SADNESS
Ulrica Hume

I was overdressed, but so be it. I had thought Hildegard's was a five-star German restaurant, not a trendy vegan café that was staffed by the formerly homeless. The black dress would have made more sense there, here it just seemed pretentious. A waitress, slim and haunted, placed on my table a glass of water.

I'm on a blind date, I confessed, gesturing to the empty chair. Saying nothing, she solemnly gave me a menu. As if she doled out second chances and this would turn back time, life viewed again through rose-colored glasses. I sipped the water, aware that I had no appetite.

Man after man came in through the door, but not one was Edgar the economist.

You'll really like him, my friend had said. He's nice.

But I don't like nice, I said. I like men who are wild, risk-takers.

Like your ex-husband, she said.

So he had gambled. And on rare occasions struck me. So he had belittled me in front of my aged parents, whose mortified expressions I would never forget. Perhaps I had more in common with the waitress than I knew. I hid my shame, while hers was a small dark cloud that traveled above her.

I looked around the café at the bold mandalas: angels with golden wings. The truth was, I didn't know what or whom I wanted, only that I was sure the world was falling apart, and I along with it. The idea of falling apart with someone new appealed to me though. It hadn't occurred to me that I could ever be happy.

The steamy windows gave the café a sheltered ambiance. Everything felt light and effervescent. I scanned the menu. Wild thyme spelt pancakes. Garbanzo beans drizzled with pumpkin seed oil on a bed of spearmint. Wine was needed.

Meanwhile the café door opened and closed, the rush of cool air from outside causing my mood to rise, before triggering a sense of desperation.

A chef in white jacket and hat could be seen in the open kitchen and I was struck by his slow, methodical style, since most chefs these days seemed to be in a hurry. Now he was dutifully grating something, and now he was feeding a fire.

Chestnut soufflé? Ratatouille? I felt flustered, unsure. My blind date was supposedly a passionate scuba diver. I didn't even swim. I always clung to the side, even in shallows.

After an hour and fifteen minutes, Edgar the economist still hadn't shown. I felt gutted. I instructed the waitress that if a gentleman turned up who looked like Piers Morgan but without the hair, she should tell him I had left and not to call me. The waitress agreed she would do that.

Outside it was chilly. I had dressed with glamour in mind, not practicality. I felt punished, demeaned, as if by a ghost. I tried to walk quickly down the dark lane, toward the mirage of a Tube station.

I was feeling a little sorry for myself when I heard the labored sound of footsteps behind me. Maybe it was Edgar, or maybe it was the notorious Camden stalker, who went after women as if they were prey. My instinct was not to quicken my pace, but to become like a deer whose senses were gathered in alarm, to make myself invisible. Then a hand tapped my shoulder. I turned.

A middle-aged man with intense grey eyes and a complexion like rose petals. Sorry, he said. I was watching you. You seemed rather sad. I thought—

Edgar? I said, recoiling.

No, Hans, he said.

* * *

So here I was, somewhere in North London, wearing my clingy black dress, and here was this pleasant stranger, drawing near. In a precise but understated way, he unfolded a white cloth napkin to show me a dozen or so biscuits, still warm. They reminded me of magical runes.

Because I was both spooked and starved, I gullibly tried one. Then another. In his mellifluous voice he warned me not to eat too many, because the fresh nutmeg had narcotic properties. Loftily he said that its musky aroma made birds of paradise fall from the sky.

I laughed, sure he was joking.

He claimed to have baked the biscuits in his fire stove, following a medieval recipe by Saint Hildegard of Bingen. Did I know her? I did not. I was not even faintly religious, despite the gold cross I wore as a statement accessory. He said he had researched her extensively, had fallen in love with her story. I tried another biscuit and the night seemed to sparkle.

The reason I hadn't recognized him as the chef from Hildegard's was because he was out of his white uniform. But now I was able to superimpose the man before me onto the one wearing a puffy hat in his stainless steel kitchen, and this was a small relief. It started to rain.

Hans had an umbrella, which he wielded like a sword, and like his lady I strolled beside him in my wobbly high heels, wondering how this had happened and where it would go from here, certainly not dreaming that I would marry the chef exactly six months later.

He said he had named his café after Hildegard because he was indebted to the German mystic. Hence the strange elixirs on the menu, his preoccupation with health, for both the body and the soul. Also, he wanted to help people, such as Elly, the Caribbean waitress, whose life had been full of tectonic shifts. Elly became real to me in that moment, and I realized how self-centered I'd been, even down to the five-pound note I'd tucked under the glass, which had been a sort of bribe. And so I was seeing things in a new way, through him, and it was like being ensorcelled. But even fairy tales don't last. They have their sharp and bitter ends, the pierce of goodness, the way the lost damsel finds herself by losing yet more.

Hildegard of Bingen was born in 1098 and died in 1179. Her feast day is September 17. She had extraordinary visions, which she described as "the shades of the living light." These took form as colorful artwork, songs and text, and remedies rooted in a world beyond. She favored certain restorative foods, like sweet chestnuts and fennel, apples and sloeberries. Peaches, plums, and potatoes were the "kitchen poisons." Hers was a palate inspired by the very art of giving, whether it be counsel or biscuits so dense and imponderable that they seemed not like biscuits at all.

Apparently nutmeg opens the heart. I did experience a certain irrepressible gladness, an ethereal warmth rising and spreading through me as I tasted that first biscuit, and listening to Hans go on about the resolution of bitter feelings, my senses felt bright. As I stood there before him in my dripping black dress, he promised that if I ate five biscuits a day they would make my spirit strong. I believed him. He seemed an urban shaman, svelte and full of powers. A modern-day healer. What I didn't know was that he was in the process of healing himself.

It began to rain harder. He suggested that we go back to the café to dry off.

We arrived at Hildegard's just as Elly the waitress was about to turn off the lights. She regarded me with light suspicion, maybe amused that the jilted lady from the table set for two was now with her boss.

* * *

A beeswax candle. Silence. In the flickering darkness we drew closer, in a cone of light of our own making. Crumbs on the table from our decadence, our spiritual gloaming. Remains of a quince parfait made with organic goat's milk. The trick was to follow the crumbs to an imagined beginning, but it was nice being lost, and Hans was good company.

Then he looked at me with those kind grey eyes and said there was something he should tell me. Not I need to tell you, but should. Because stories, especially intimate ones, cannot help but emerge at odd moments, on buses and trains, over a table in a shuttered café, the melancholy Bach-Busoni Chaconne in D Minor playing in the background. The café became like a shrine, the angels alert to mortal causes. He was dying, he said, that was why he had earlier behaved so impulsively, so freely.

* * *

When someone is terminally ill, time changes. Dawn becomes gold. You walk outside holding the hand of a stranger and pink threads of sky seem to protect you. You joke about becoming addicted to biscuits prescribed by a medieval mystic. You feel like the luckiest person, but for shadows cast when you cross the road, there is no way back, not now—his hand is already slipping away.

You try to tell yourself that it is worth it, *worth* being a word that discourages you for its undercurrent of judgment. You tell yourself that all things end, but his voice is an illogical cipher, you cannot let it go, you will let it go, as a white lie of joyful confetti.

He tells you not to think too much of the future, but that is all you can think of.

His café does well, wins awards, he is honored for his humanitarian heart, but even these things feel like slaps, you are ashamed of your own greed and defiant desire. This feeling lessens whenever you eat one of his happiness biscuits.

* * *

Elly the waitress was expecting a baby. She became too cumbersome to fit between tables. I tried to help her. I gave her a small toy, very soft—a yellow lamb.

The baby was born the same day Hans was carried out of his kitchen, and when I looked at the moon that night, and through salted tears I tasted the nutmeg again, and the familiar warmth spread, I knew that it was one thing that still connected us.

His death, though not unexpected, was its own unwelcome surprise. The rapturous hollow, an inversion of feelings, the chart of grief that I was expected to follow.

But first: the rain, his smile, sustenance. Everything slick and glowing. A chance.

Life carried me along. It brought me to the edge of myself, and just when it seemed that I would surely drown, it gave me a nudge.

I learned to bake Hildegard's biscuits for preventing sadness.

In the center of the nutmeg fruit is a red-robed seed, and that is what you grate. Next, you measure a few teaspoons each of cinnamon and cloves. A soft dough is formed of flour, sugar, and water. You carefully roll it out. You cut the dough into circles, scatter crushed almonds. Then you wait. Have patience. These hardtack coins are dry but flavorful. Love is beautifully imperfect, yet it lasts. ■

NOTES ON CONTRIBUTORS

PRAD APHACHAN is the pen name of a writer and poet from Bangkok. He has a degree in Physics from the University of Illinois at Urbana-Champaign and has spent time as an acoustical engineer in Chicago and San Francisco. He is currently back in Thailand, teaching English and writing short stories about ghosts, immortality, and the rain. His stories are a self-exploration of absurdities and uncertainties in both humanity and nature, often through the lens of horror and humor. Though a native Thai, he chooses to write in English. He started writing in college after he discovered the works of Italo Calvino, Jorge Luis Borges, and Yasunari Kawabata. On any given day, you can probably find him walking down a quiet street in downtown Bangkok, meditating on pigeons and contemplating the chalky quality of the sky. His writings have appeared or are forthcoming in *The Chicago Review, Cha: An Asian Literary Journal, Frogpond Journal,* and *Chrysanthemum Haiku,* among others. He is currently working on his MFA application.

ANN VOORHEES BAKER has published two short stories; one in this journal (25th Anniversary Issue, 2019) and one in the *Noyo River Review* (2019). She turned to creative writing only recently after a fledgling attempt at writing during her college years (encouraging rejections from *The New Yorker* and *Ladies' Home Journal,* but, alas, no publications) and a subsequent forty-year writing hiatus during which she pursued various careers and undertakings: enforcement attorney for the United States Environmental Protection Agency, publisher of a regional parenting magazine, communications director for a school district, web designer, ghostwriter, content writer. She has now written several short stories and a first novel, which she is spending an inordinate amount of time editing. Ann lives in Southern California with her husband Brad in a house near the ocean. She takes yoga classes on the beach and ballet classes at the Lauridsen Ballet Centre. Her two adult daughters continually amaze and delight her but live very far away. She hopes they will follow their passions much sooner in life than she did.

A. J. BERMUDEZ is an award-winning writer and director who divides her time between Los Angeles and New York. Her work has been featured at the Yale Center for British Art, the LGBT Toronto Film Festival, Sundance, and in a number of literary journals, including *McSweeney's, Boulevard, The Masters Review, Story, Fiction International, Hobart, Columbia Journal,* and elsewhere. She currently serves as Artistic Director of The American Playbook and Co-Editor of *The Maine Review.* She is a former boxer and EMT, a recipient of the Diverse Voices Award, a *One Story* finalist for the 2021 Adina Talve-Goodman Fellowship, Winner of the 2021 PAGE Award, and Winner of the 2021 Alpine Fellowship Writing Prize. Her first book, *Stories No One Hopes Are About Them,* will be published as winner of the Iowa Short Fiction Award in fall 2022.

ANTHONY BERRIS was born in the United Kingdom and lived in Israel for most of his adult life. He was a translator and editor.

SHELDON COSTA's fiction has appeared in or is forthcoming from *Electric Literature, Michigan Quarterly Review, Conjunctions, The Georgia Review,* and *Crazyhorse,* among others. He is a winner of the AWP Intro Journal Project, the 2018 Helen Earnhart Harley Creative Writing Fellowship Award, and the *Cream City Review's* 2019 Summer Prize in Fiction. His work has been selected as a runner-up in both the Pinch Literary Awards and the *Masters Review's* Short Story Award for New Writers, and nominated for a Pushcart. He received his MFA from The Ohio State University.

WILLIAM C. CRAWFORD (Crawdaddy) is a prolific itinerant street photographer based in Winston-Salem, North Carolina. He got his start in Vietnam as a combat photojournalist. He was then inexperienced but Crawdaddy profited immensely from staunch mentoring from three Pulitzer Prize winners. Much later, he co-developed FORENSIC FORAGING, a throwback, minimalist technique for digital photographers with veteran Sydney lensman, Jim Provencher. Crawdaddy has published four books chronicling his photography adventures. He seeks to elevate the trite, trivial, and mundane of everyday life to pleasing eye candy. He believes that there is hidden visual value almost everywhere, waiting to be uplifted through digital images. See more at -bcraw44 on Instagram.

ALICIA DEROLLO wrote her first "real" poem as a high school junior, a memoir of her six-year-old self. After placing first in her school's "All School Writing Day" for a controversial piece, Alicia went to the east coast, majoring in English and writing her way through the emotional roller coaster of a teenager navigating life while rejecting navigation. The most important role in Alicia's life is being a mother to a blended family of eight and a wife to the most amazing man in the world. Her poems are inspired mostly by his love and her journey through life's disappointments and joys along with her recent struggle with blood cancer. As an elementary school teacher for the past twenty-one years, she has used her love of words to engage students and teach the art of poetry. In usual times Alicia enjoys time under the sea. Scuba diving with her husband is a favorite pastime. The beach has been her home since birth. A perfect day is a morning under water, an afternoon in the sun on the beach with her husband, a bottle of good wine, and the laughter of her children building sandcastles. She holds a bachelor's degree in English from St. Vincent College in Latrobe, Pennsylvania, and a Master's degree from CSU Monterey Bay in Curriculum and Instruction. She served on the California Commission on Teacher Credentialing for ten years and as the single teacher board member for WestEd.

TERRI DRAKE is a graduate of the Iowa Writers' Workshop. Her poetry collection, *At the Seams,* was published by Bear Star Press. Her poems have appeared in *Crab Creek Review, Quarry West, Perihelion, Heartwood Literary Magazine,* and *Open: Journal of Art and Letters,* among others. She is a practicing psychoanalyst living in Santa Cruz, California.

MARK DUNCAN is a family and business law attorney. He attended Louisiana State University for his undergraduate degree and earned his law degree from the University of Arkansas School of Law. After completing his studies, Duncan cut teeth working for Manhattan attorney Aaron Richard Golub, representing various luminaries in the New York entertainment, arts, and business world whose names will remain "un-dropped." A decade later he returned to his New Orleans roots, ultimately starting his solo law practice. His work in the area of family law has given voice to countless battered and abused women and others who sacrificed their best years at the altar of marriage and family. Duncan's literary works have been published in *The American Journal of Poetry* and his maiden voyage as a playwright resulted in an award-winning play performed on stage in a national competition. His practice and writing were featured in *New Orleans Living Magazine*. In his spare time, Duncan coaches boys' basketball at a local high school. He is the father of three beautiful teenagers and resides in Mandeville, Louisiana. This is his first published essay.

BANZELMAN GURET is a writer from the Wiener Lakes Region of Connecticut where he lives with his wife. His fiction has most recently appeared in the *New Orleans Review* and the *Potomac Review*. When he's not writing, he teaches composition classes online.

BARBARA HAAS is a landscape enthusiast who writes from the Idawahio region of the country, a geographical pile-up in a vast sprawling hinterland of states whose three-syllable names might signal forests, might signal prairies, might signal tire factories. She crafts her nonfiction from a place where vowels search for consonants and yearn for clicks and glottal stops, the curved clasp of a claw in the throat, a kck, kck, kck. This sort of writing finds a home in journals like *The North American Review*, the *Virginia Quarterly Review* and *The Hudson Review*, to which Haas is a repeat contributor.

CHARLIE HAHN is a street photographer based in Winston-Salem, North Carolina. His high school photography class project, *Chippewa Street 1975*, launched his career with a portfolio that is now a throwback classic in his hometown of Buffalo. It features a seedy, red light district which has long since been sanitized from the city scene. More recently, his *Beyond the Edge of the Fields* focuses on in situ portraits of the down, out, and marginalized denizens of the street. Hahn befriended and personally helped many of these vulnerable souls. Charlie is also an instructor of photography at the Sawtooth School for the Visual Arts where he met Crawdaddy. See more at hahnphoto.net

STEPHANIE HAYES is a journalist and fiction writer. She is a columnist with the *Tampa Bay Times* and syndicated via Creators Syndicate, which supplies content to publications worldwide. She is the author of the novel *Obitchuary*. Her work has appeared in *McSweeney's Internet Tendency*, *GQ.com* and more. Her short fiction published in this journal, "The Cronuts," is part of a forthcoming collection of connected short stories. She has received writing prizes from the National Headliner Awards, Green Eyeshade, the Society for Features Journalism and the Florida Society of News Editors. She lives in Dunedin, Florida, with her husband, stepdaughter, enormous cat and tiny dog.

GARY HOUSTON is *CQR* managing editor and formerly an editor and writer for Show/Book Week, the Sunday books and arts supplement of the *Chicago Sun-Times*. His stories have appeared in *Catamaran* and this journal. His articles, essays, reviews and interviews have appeared in the *Sun-Times, Chicago Tribune, Chicago Reader, Chicagoland, Christian Science Monitor, New England Review, Michigan Quarterly Review, Los Angeles Free Press, Detroit Free Press* and many others. His interviewees include Joseph Heller, Saul Bellow, Studs Terkel, Eugène Ionesco, Elie Wiesel, Sam Greenlee, Herman Raucher, Maria Irene Fornés, Kenneth Tynan, Murray Schisgal, Peter Bogdanovich, George Cukor, Stuart Gordon, David Mamet, Robert Altman, Walter Matthau, Ginger Rogers, Arthur Penn, Antonio Aguilar, Stacy Keach, Hume Cronyn and Jessica Tandy, and Mr. Frick of Frick and Frack.

ULRICA HUME is the author of *An Uncertain Age*, a spiritual mystery novel, which was longlisted for a Northern California Book Award. Her earlier work, *House of Miracles*, a collection of tales about love, was a finalist for the D.H. Lawrence Fellowship; the title story was selected by PEN and broadcast on NPR. She has written about tearooms, reading rooms, the seven deadly sins, and how 9/11 changed religion in America for the *San Francisco Examiner, Poets & Writers Magazine, The Bloomsbury Review,* and *The Huffington Post,* respectively. Her lyrical flash pieces appear online and/or in print at *Firmament, Litro, Longleaf Review, Lunate, Short Édition, Tiny Molecules,* among others, as spoken word at *The Cincinnati Review* and *Micro* podcast, and in anthologies, such as *Choice Words* (Haymarket Books). She is also the author of *In the Labyrinth* (Blue Circle Press). She agrees with Anton Chekhov that "A writer isn't a confectioner, a cosmetic dealer, or an entertainer, but a person who has signed a contract with their conscience and sense of duty." Find her on Twitter @uhume

AMY KIGER-WILLIAMS has published work in *Yale Review Online, South Carolina Review,* and elsewhere. She earned an MFA from Rutgers University-Newark and a BA from New York University. She is at work on a novel and a short story collection. You can read more of her work at amykigerwilliams.com.

FEDERICO GARCIA LORCA (1898-1936) was a Spanish poet and a member of the *Generation of '27*, especially known for introducing symbolism and surrealism into European literature. Notably, Lorca studied with future Nobel Prize-winner Juan Ramon Jimenez and found companionship with filmmaker Luis Bunuel and artist Salvador Dali. Lorca's "Andalusian Songs," the *canciones* he wrote that intrinsically were instilled with both the sound and the tone of the guitar within them, were imbued also with the spark of the heels of the dance, with the essence of the *flamenco*. Additionally, more so than any other Spanish poet, Lorca cast his poems with the ethos of Spanish folklore, known as *Duende*, whose impish and dark but beautiful qualities also denote the *expression* of passion and inspiration. *Duende* can also intimate tone, color, rhythm, and music. He was murdered in the Spanish Civil War by Nationalist Forces and his body was never found.

MICHELLE MASSIE is a retired family doctor and mother of two grown children living in a multi-generational home in Santa Cruz, California, along with her husband, two dogs, and one grumpy cat. Michelle attended Bowdoin College, the University of Rochester School of Medicine, and the Maine-Dartmouth Family Medicine Residency. While she has always been a writer (she penned a memoir of her family's experience living in London in 2004-2006), only now, having retired from medicine, is she able to pursue the profession seriously. Michelle has studied fiction with Justin Torres (*We The Animals*), Elizabeth McKenzie (*The Portable Veblen*), Pam Houston, and Clifford Mae Henderson, and poetry with Danusha Lameris. Michelle's first novel, *Secrets*, completed during the COVID quarantine, is currently in editing — and a second novel is in the works.

MICHAEL MATTES' fiction has appeared in *Cirque, Santa Monica Review, World Literature Today, West Branch, The Carolina Quarterly, Southwestern American Literature, Northwest Review*, and elsewhere. He resides in Sammamish, Washington, and online at msmattes. wordpress.com.

GEORGE MCDERMOTT has been an English teacher, a speechwriter, a screenwriter, and a poet—roles that aren't actually all that different. His poetry has appeared or is forthcoming in such journals as *Painted Bride Quarterly, Toho Journal, Passengers Journal, Fourth River*, and *Notre Dame Review*, as well as in the *Philadelphia*

Inquirer. His first collection, *Pictures, Some of Them Moving*, was published by Moonstone Press in 2018. He is also co-author— with Roberta Israeloff, who was a student in one of his high school English classes—of the nonfiction book *What Went Right* (Rowman & Littlefield, 2017), a conversation about the successes and missteps of public education in the United States.

SAM MEEKINGS is a British novelist and poet. He is the author of *Under Fishbone Clouds* (called "a poetic evocation of the country and its people" by *The New York Times*) and *The Book of Crows*. He has also been featured on the BBC website, in *The Independent*, on Arena on Radio 1, and in *National Geographic*. He recently received an award from the Society of Authors, and has been published in a number of international magazines and academic journals. He has spent the last few years living and working in China and the Middle East. He balances his time between teaching, raising two kids as a single father, and drinking copious cups of tea.

JANE MORTON is a poet based in Tuscaloosa, Alabama, where they recently received their MFA from the University of Alabama. Their poems are published or forthcoming in *Boulevard, Passages North, Poetry Northwest, The Offing, BOOTH, Muzzle Magazine, Redivider, Yemassee,* and *The Rupture*, among other journals. They have received a Fulbright Fellowship and a Katharine Bakeless Nason scholarship for the Bread Loaf Environmental Writers Conference
.

DIPIKA MUKHERJEE is an internationally touring writer and sociolinguist. She is the author of the novels *Shambala Junction* and *Ode to Broken Things*, and the story collection, *Rules of Desire*. Her work is included in *The Best Small Fictions 2019* and appears in *World Literature Today, Asia Literary Review, Del Sol Review,* and *Chicago Quarterly Review, Newsweek, Los Angeles Review of Books, Hemispheres, Orion, Scroll, The Edge* and more. Her poetry collection, *Dialect of Distant Harbors*, is forthcoming from CavanKerry Press in October 2022 and a collection of travel essays, titled *Writers Postcards*, will be published by Penguin Random House (SEA) in 2023. She is a Contributing Editor for *Jaggery* and teaches at StoryStudio Chicago and at the Graham School at University of Chicago. In 2021, she was awarded *Instructor of the Year* by Stories Matter Foundation. Mukherjee has received grants and fellowships from the Illinois Arts Council Agency (USA), Ragdale Foundation (USA), Faber Foundation (Catalonia), Sacatar

Foundation (Brazil), Rimbun Dahan (Malaysia), Gladstone Library (Wales), and Centrum (USA). She is on the curating team and featured writer in *My America: Immigrant and Refugee Writers Today* at the American Writers Museum in Chicago. She holds a doctorate from Texas A&M University.

JAN NAKAO is a Japanese-American painter and artist living in Evanston, Illinois. As a Jungian analyst, her essay published in *My Postwar Life* focused upon the bombings of Hiroshima and Nagaski. Her art uses bold abstract forms, imaginary landscapes and figurative art. She works in oil and pastel. jnakao8@gmail.com

YORAM NASLAVSKY is the author of two collections of short stories published in Hebrew: *In the Sight of This Sun* (2009) and *A Man on a Bench* (2019). His stories have been published in various literary journals in English and Hebrew. He lives in Tel Aviv.

E. NOLAN has an MFA from the University of Florida and his fiction has been published in *McSweeney's Internet Tendency*, *Passages North*, *X-R-A-Y*, and other magazines. He has just finished writing a novel about the difficulties faced by a first year teacher in a New York City public school entitled *Never Hold Back*, based on his experience teaching English as a New Language in the Bronx. His essays on education, specifically about the process of language learning during remote schooling, have appeared in *The Hechinger Report* and *McSweeney's Internet Tendency*. In his free time he composes music for TV & Film. His music can be heard on, among others, Showtime's *The Circus*, the feature documentary film *It Started as a Joke*, and A&E's *David Cassidy: The Last Session*. Connect with him on twitter @normanuniform and learn more at enolanstories.com.

JACK NORMAN was born and raised in North Queensland, Australia. He is thankful to a modest family of five whose essence will feature heavily here. The North Queensland region is stereotyped and misunderstood...although, sometimes the rumours are true. With any luck, Jack and his contemporaries will help to give it a proper voice. There is something significant about the agonising heat year round that they are all trying to uncover. This is his first piece of published work, and things will only get more rural and esoteric from here on out.

ANN PEDONE is the author of *The Medea Notebooks* (spring, 2023 Etruscan Press), and *The Italian Professor's Wife* (spring, 2022 Press 53), as well as the chapbooks *The Bird Happened, perhaps there is a sky we don't know: a re-imagining of sappho, Everywhere You Put Your Mouth, DREAM/WORK,* and *Sea [Breaks]*. Her work has recently appeared in *The American Journal of Poetry, Narrative, Carve Magazine, Juked,* and *JuxtaProse*.

MATT POLZIN writes fiction and sometimes poetry and screenplays. Originally from Michigan, they hold an MFA in Creative Writing from California Institute of the Arts and are currently a PhD student in Literature at University of California, Santa Cruz, where they work at the intersection of contemporary fiction, critical race and queer studies, and utopia. They have taught creative writing in college classrooms, a prison, and a middle school. Their fiction has appeared in *Bathhouse Journal* and was a finalist for the Arkansas International Emerging Writer's Prize. They are currently finishing a first novel about a group of animal rights activists who live in a house together.

JOHN ROBINSON is a novelist, playwright, essayist, memoirist, and short story writer who lives in Portsmouth, New Hampshire. His work has appeared in *Ploughshares*, the *Sewanee Review*, the *Chicago Quarterly Review*, the *Green Mountains Review*, the *Cimarron Review*, the *North Dakota Quarterly*, the *Tampa Review*, the *South Dakota Review, epiphany, The Bitter Oleander, The Writer, Oyez Review, Concho River Review, 2 Bridges Review*, the *Midwest Review, Mount Hope Magazine*, the *Wisconsin Review*, the *Hawai'i Pacific Review*, the *Tishman Review*, the *Tulane Review*, the *Rhode Island Review*, the *Delmarva Review, redivider, theNewerYork, Meat for Tea: The Valley Review, The Meadow, Zymbol,* and has been translated into thirty-two languages. He has contributed political commentary, created award-winning drama, appeared in various anthologies, and written and lived in three countries: Scotland, Spain, and the United States.

WILLIAM ROEBUCK is the Executive Vice President of the Arab Gulf States Institute in Washington. Roebuck completed his diplomatic career in late 2020, after twenty-eight years of service in postings across the Middle East, including Baghdad, Jerusalem, and Tripoli. He served as U.S. ambassador to Bahrain from 2015-17. As Deputy Special Envoy for the Global Coalition Against ISIS,

Roebuck was embedded with U.S. Special Forces, serving as the senior (and often only) U.S. diplomat on the ground in northeastern Syria from 2018-20. He was born and raised in North Carolina and began his career as a Peace Corps volunteer in Côte d'Ivoire. Roebuck was a finalist for the *Missouri Review*'s 2020 Jeffrey E. Smith Editors' Prize for Nonfiction and has previously been published in the *Chicago Quarterly Review*.

MALCOLM ROTHMAN has been a regular on the Chicago theatrical scene since 1978, performing on stage, TV, film, voice-over, narration and, for the past twenty years, portraying Harry Caray at corporate and private events. Stage credits include performances with the Guthrie Theater, National Jewish Theater, Candlelight/Forum Theaters, Marriott's Lincolnshire Theater, New American Theater, Court Theater, Steppenwolf Theater Co. and many others throughout the Midwest and nationally. His memoir, "Family Photos," appeared in *Chicago Quarterly Review* #28 and was cited as a Notable Essay in *Best American Essays 2020*. Malcolm served as a Navy Hospital Corpsman in the Republic of Vietnam from 1969 to 1970.

ANDREW SCHOFIELD is a writer from Kansas City, Missouri. He earned an MFA at Georgia College & State University. His work has previously appeared in *New South*.

SUSAN SHEPHERD's work has aired on NPR's *Living on Earth*, PRI's *Marketplace*, and on multiple daily NPR shows. Her writing has been published in the *Boston Globe* and *Ploughshares*. Her short fiction podcast *11 Central Ave* aired on *Morning Edition* on NPR affiliated stations around the country and was funded by NPR and Chicago Public Radio. The show won a Gold Medal for Best Comedy from the New York Festivals, and a National Gracie Allen Award for Best Producer, Comedy. "Snakes" is part of an in-progress linked collection of short stories called *Animalia*. "Goats" from the collection was published in the 2020 Summer Issue of *Ploughshares* and was listed as a Distinguished Story in *Best American Short Stories 2021* guest edited by Jesmyn Ward. This past summer she was a Bread Loaf participant in fiction. Susan lives with her husband, her six chickens, and her dog Chivo near Boston and is currently finishing her book and producing a fiction podcast.

A recipient of an NEA fellowship in poetry and an Edgar in fiction, **D. JAMES SMITH**'s work has appeared widely in magazines such as *Blackbird, The Malahat Review, Notre Dame Review, Poetry International,* and *Stand.* His books include two collections of poems, *Sounds The Living Make* (S. F. Austin State Univ.) and *Prayers for the Dead Ventriloquist,* with an introduction by Dorianne Laux (Ahsahta) and the novel *My Brother's Passion* (Permanent Press, New York) as well as four novels in YA lit (Atheneum).

WALLY SWIST's *Huang Po and the Dimensions of Love* (Southern Illinois University Press, 2012) was selected by Yusef Komunyakaa as co-winner in the 2011 Crab Orchard Series Open Poetry Contest. Recent books include *A Bird Who Seems to Know Me: Poems Regarding Birds & Nature* (Ex Ophidia Press, 2019), winner of the 2018 Ex Ophidia Press Poetry Prize and *Taking Residence* (Shanti Arts, 2021). His translations have been published in *Chiron Review, Ezra: An Online Journal of Translation, The Montreal Review,* and *Transference: A Literary Journal Featuring the Art & Process of Translation,* (Western Michigan Department of Languages). Forthcoming books include *A Writer's Statements on Beauty: New & Selected Essays & Reviews,* a translation of Giuseppe Ungaretti's *L'Allegria/Cheerfulness,* and *Taking Care of the Horses,* original poetry and translations, all with Shanti Arts. The translation of "Six Strings" by Federico Garcia Lorca is included in a collection of forthcoming translations from the Spanish, *Fruit of my Flower.*

KRISTINE THATCHER is City Lit Theater Company's resident playwright. Her most recent play, *The Safe House,* was Jeff-nominated for Best New Play. Her other plays include *Waiting for Tina Meyer* (a collaboration with Larry Shue), *Among Friends* (winner of the 2000 Scott McPherson Memorial Award), *Voice of Good Hope* (Jeff-nominated for Best New Play), and *Emma's Child* (winner of the Susan Smith Blackburn Prize; an Illinois Arts Council Fellowship, the RESOLVE Award for Excellence in the Arts; the Cunningham Prize for Playwriting from DePaul University; and the After Dark Award for Outstanding New Work). A revival *of Emma's Child* runs at City Lit in Chicago through May 29, 2022.

MICHAEL TROCCHIA's work has appeared in *Arion, Bitter Oleander, Black Sun Lit, The Chattahoochee Review, Colorado Review, New Orleans Review,* and elsewhere. Work is forthcoming in *The Midwest Quarterly.* He lives in the Shenandoah Valley, where he teaches philosophy and works in the library at James Madison University.

FRANCIS WALSH is a writer from coastal Maine. A graduate of the University of Southern Maine with a BA in English, they currently hold a non-clinical position at a hospital and share an apartment with one human and two rabbits. Their work appears or is forthcoming in the *Masters Review Anthology Volume X,* the *North American Review,* the *South Carolina Review, Yemassee,* and elsewhere.

WHITNEY WATSON holds an MFA in Creative Writing from Hollins University, where she was awarded the Julia Randall Sawyer Fellowship and the Andrew James Purdy Prize in Short Fiction. She has attended the Sewanee, Community of Writers, and Bread Loaf Writers' Conferences. She lives in Charlottesville, Virginia, where she is at work on her first novel.

 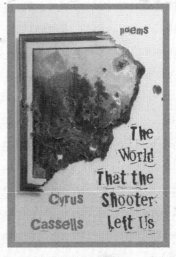

CRDT
CERQUA RIVERA DANCE THEATRE

"These are historic times that call for bravery and leadership. Being quiet is not an option for this company."
– Cofounder and Artistic Director Wilfredo Rivera

Cerqua Rivera Dance Theatre uses dance and music to nourish the mind and the soul. The company unites artists and audiences to explore themes that shape our community.
more on Facebook, Instagram, and www.cerquarivera.org

CATAMARAN

9TH ANNUAL **WRITING**

CONFERENCE

in pebble beach

JUL 31st- AUG 4th, 2022

-*daily workshops in poetry and fiction*
-*evening readings*
-*community meals*
-*on campus lodging*

REGISTER AT CATAMARANLITERARYREADER.COM/CONFERENCE-2022

Keep joyful music playing!

With stages across the world dark, the musical projects of Chicago's Klezmer Music Foundation are on hold. For 37 years, we've brought klezmer and Yiddish music to all generations, from senior citizens to youthful musicians.

Your donation will keep these alive until we can all gather again!
- The Maxwell Street Klezmer Band
- The Junior Klezmer Orchestra
- The Salaam-Shalom Music Project
- Grassroots Community Klezmer Bands
- Performances for Seniors and Schools

Donations will sustain our musicians and keep our office open until we all reach the other side of this health crisis.

Please donate here: klezmermusicfoundation.org or send a check to: Klezmer Music Foundation, 4025 Harvard Terrace, Skokie, IL 60076 For info, email klezmermusicfoundation@gmail.com The Klezmer Music Foundation is an illinois not-for-profit 501(c)(3) organization.

HARMONY
ART GLASS COMPANY

ARCHITECTURAL   STAINED   GLASS
DESIGN AND RESTORATION

ROBERT T. SEITZ

6321 N. CLARK ST.
CHICAGO, IL 60660
HarmonyArtGlass.net

773/743-2004
FAX 773/743-4890
HarmonyArtGlass@sbcglobal.net

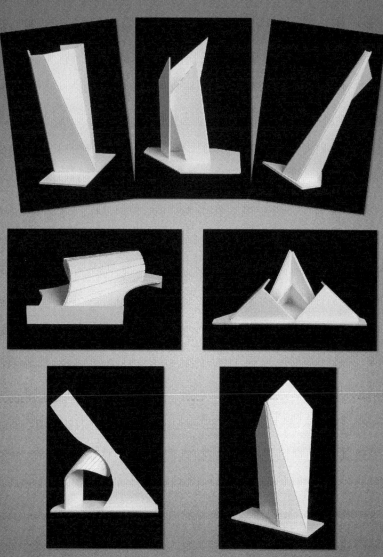

Beautiful "Art Post Cards" for mailing or framing. $10.00 Per Package.

Concept Sculptural Prototypes made of Foamboard
(Architects, Landscape Architects and Developers)

Contact: Alicia Loy Griffin 323. 293.1858 (studio) alicialoy@icloud.com alicialoy.griffin.com

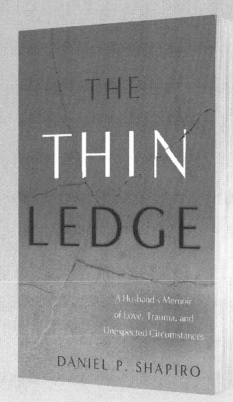

Now Available to Order!

First major publication from the Chicago Literary Hall of Fame in partnership with After Hours Press and Third World Press. https://chicagoliteraryhof.org/

Wherever I'm At
An Anthology of Chicago Poetry

Edited by Donald G. Evans and Robin Metz
with a Foreword by Carlo Rotella

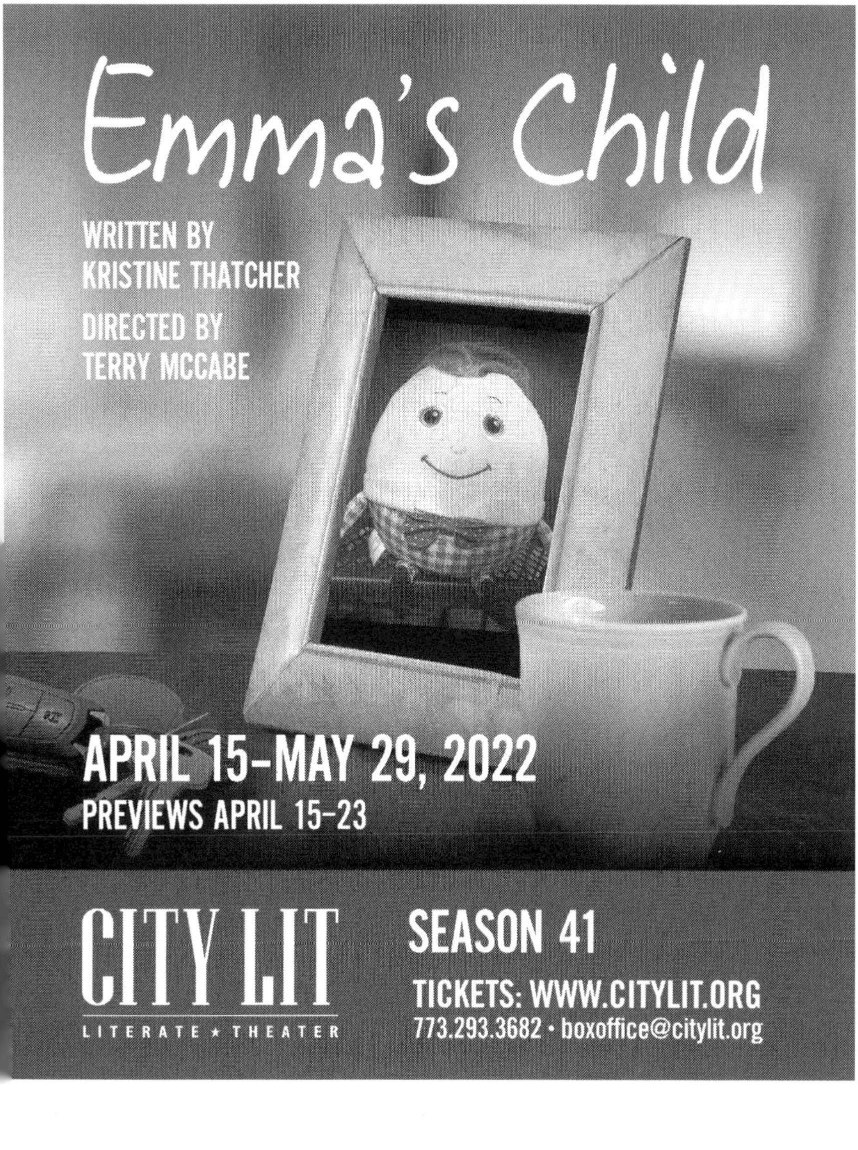
Emma's Child
WRITTEN BY
KRISTINE THATCHER
DIRECTED BY
TERRY MCCABE
APRIL 15-MAY 29, 2022
PREVIEWS APRIL 15-23
CITY LIT
LITERATE ★ THEATER
SEASON 41
TICKETS: WWW.CITYLIT.ORG
773.293.3682 • boxoffice@citylit.org

chicago writers association

MEMBERSHIP BENEFITS AND OPPORTUNITIES

- A personal user-friendly webpage on CWA's official website to promote your writings and happenings
- Participate in CWA author reading and book signing events and industry expo booths, including the Chicago Tribune Printers Row Book Fair
- Chicago Tribune Printers Row Book Fair
- Our own Let's Just Write! An Uncommon Writers Conference
- Participate in our Speakers Bureau
- Participate in our book review service, Windy City Reviews
- Enter your book in our Books of the Year Contest
- Enter our members-only writing contests
- Opportunity to be published in our Write City e-zine and Windy City Writers blog
- Interaction with other writers
Leadership and networking opportunities

ONLY $25/YEAR
www.chicagowrites.org

THE BOOK STALL

811 Elm Street Winnetka, IL/847-446-8880/www.thebookstall.com

The Book Stall is an independent bookstore located in the northern suburbs of Chicago. With over 60,000 titles, our selection has something for all readers. We also carry a variety of stationary, puzzles, games, and other gift items.

The Book Stall is known for its many events, which have continued virtually during the COVID-19 pandemic.

MUNRO CAMPAGNA
ARTIST REPRESENTATIVES

410 S. Michigan Ave. Suite 439
Chicago, IL 60605
+1 312 335 8925

steve@munrocampagna.com
www.munrocampagna.com

Illustrator
Clint Hansen

Portrait of
Amanda Gorman

WRITERS ALOUD

A monthly first read by and for writers who
don't necessarily think of themselves as writers

First Sunday of the month, via Zoom

**Want the Zoom link? Want to read your writing?
Contact Karen.o.fort@gmail.com**

BLACK ENSEMBLE THEATER

The **Season** of
HEALING
& JOY

The Season of Healing and
Joy features productions to
rejuvenate and revive the spirit.
The season continues with...

GRANDMA'S JUKEBOX
Written and Directed by
Michelle Bester
Opens: May 29th

🔲 SCAN 4 TIX

MY BROTHER LANGSTON
Written and Directed by
Rueben Echoles
Opens: August 21st
Sponsorship by Abbott/Abbott Fund

BLUE HEAVEN
Written and Directed by
Daryl Brooks
Opens: October 30th

FOR MORE INFO CALL 773.769.4451 OR VISIT BLACKENSEMBLE.ORG

"A superb display of sharp observations from a man who's been everywhere you'd ever want to go, known everyone you'd ever want to meet, and brought it all alive in a voice you wish you had."

Adam Hochschild, author, *King Leopold's Ghost*

Where Was I?
A Travel Writer's Memoir
Tom Miller

"One of our best nonfiction writers."
– *San Francisco Chronicle*

Tom Miller has been writing about conflict and culture in the Americas for close to 50 years. ***Where Was I? A Travel Writer's Memoir*** zigs and zags through the riotous 1968 Democratic National Convention, smokes marijuana on the rooftop of a comfortable South American hotel, and spends the better part of a year traipsing around Cuba. Miller, a veteran of the anti- (Vietnam) war movement and the underground press of the 1960s, spent months with migrants, musicians, and muckrakers. In Spain he located an original 1605 first printing of *Don Quijxote*, and in Cuba held in his hands Ernest Hemingway's 1954 Nobel Prize in Literature.

www.tommillerbooks.com

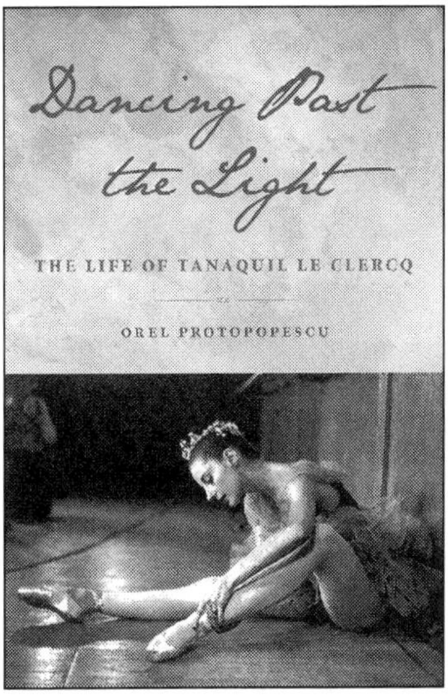

Dancing Past the Light

The Life of Tanaquil Le Clercq

OREL PROTOPOPESCU

Hardcover $35.00

"[A] rich, compelling biography. . . . This thoughtful and elegant narrative is full of wonderful stories about the world of ballet. A fitting tribute to the life and legacy of a beloved dancer that will enthrall balletomanes everywhere."

—*Library Journal, Starred Review*

"Protopopescu has told the story of Le Clercq with grace, weaving in the background of some of the most influential people in her life, all of whom are worthy to have their own stories told. Protopopescu allows the reader to peer through a keyhole into Le Clercq's world, a place that few of us were privileged to be."

—Jacques d'Amboise, New York City Ballet principal dancer and author of *I Was a Dancer*

Dancing Past the Light cinematically illuminates the glamorous and moving life story of Tanaquil "Tanny" Le Clercq (1929–2000), one of the most celebrated ballerinas of the twentieth century, describing her brilliant stage career, her struggle with polio, and her important work as a dance teacher, coach, photographer, and writer.

Enhanced with a wealth of previously unpublished photos, and with insights from interviews with her friends, students, and colleagues, *Dancing Past the Light* depicts the joys and the dark moments of Le Clercq's dramatic life, celebrating her mighty legacy.

UNIVERSITY PRESS OF FLORIDA

@floridapress

upress.ufl.edu • 800.226.3822

The
Nelson Algren
Committee

On the Make
Since 1989

nelsonalgren.org

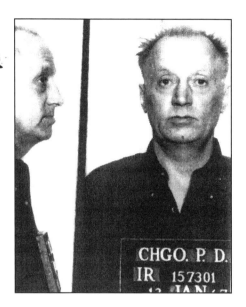

CHICAGO QUARTERLY REVIEW

Issue: 34
Fall 2021

SUNDAY SALON CHICAGO

Is a reading series that takes place every other month

Named one of Chicago's best literary organizations by Newcity

The salon series has brought word power to New York City, Nairobi, Miami and Chicago making our best local and national writers available to a larger community for over 10 years.

We meet at
The Reveler*
3403 N. Damen Ave. in Chicago
From 7 pm to 8 pm on the last Sunday
of every other month

Eat, drink your favorite drinks, make new friends and enjoy excellent readings with us!

Our events are always free

Find us here: Web: SundaySalon-Chicago.com
Facebook: Sunday.Salon.Chicago/

*Because of changing rules for restaurants and bars in Chicago due to Coronavirus, please check our website or Facebook for updated information and be sure to register!

Made in the USA
Middletown, DE
07 May 2022